Programs That Work

Papers and Sessions Material Presented at the Twenty-Fourth
National LOEX Library Instruction Conference

held in Ypsilanti, Michigan
16 to 18 May 1996

edited by
Linda Shirato, Director
LOEX Clearinghouse
University Library
Eastern Michigan University

Published for Learning Resources and Technologies
Eastern Michigan University
by
Pierian Press
Ann Arbor, Michigan
1997

ISBN 0-87650-348-2
Copyright © 1997, The Pierian Press
All Rights Reserved

The Pierian Press
Box 1808
Ann Arbor, Michigan 48106

LIBRARY ORIENTATION SERIES
(Emphasizing Information Literacy and Bibliographic Instruction)

* Pierian Press's ISBN identifier is 0-87650. This identifier should precede the number given for a book (e.g., 0-87650-327-X).

Table of Contents

Articles

Panel Presentation

Instructive Sessions

Poster Sessions

Bibliography

Roster of Participants

PREFACE

In the past, LOEX conferences have addressed many instructional issues, from marketing library instruction to cooperation with faculty and teaching critical evaluation. In 1996 the topic was more basic: What kinds of programs really work?

To address this issue we chose keynoter Lizabeth A. Wilson, associate director of libraries for public services at the University of Washington Libraries and a long-time and successful library instruction practitioner. Her address, "The Way Things Work: Teaching and Learning in Libraries," drew on her past experiences and on current programs at the University of Washington. She provides us with a set of principles for good instructional programs.

At a more specific level, our second speaker, Debra Gilchrist, library director at Pierce College, introduced us to the program for which she and her colleagues have high hopes, the use of the abilities model and outcomes assessment in library instruction. This process is underway at their community college and others in Washington State.

A third group, the PREMIER Program (a program sponsored by the Michigan Library Association's Information Literacy Roundtable), was represented by librarians Linnea Dudley, Michael Kruzich, and Catherine Neis. These librarians explained the PREMIER program, which aims to help Michigan libraries develop instructional programs and make existing programs "work."

A final major element of the conference was a panel discussion led by five librarians from libraries with programs that work: Tom Kirk of Earlham College, Corrine Laverty of Queen's University, Patricia Iannuzzi of Florida International University, Carla List of SUNY-Plattsburgh, and Margaret Fain of Coastal Carolina University. Although the institutions and the methods differed, all were enthusiastic about their past successes and looked forward to continuing successful programs. This lively discussion highlighted some major problem areas for instruction librarians.

A large contingent of practicing librarians also contributed to shorter sessions and poster sessions, making this conference of great practical use. LOEX wishes to thank all these librarians for the contributions they always make.

Linda Shirato

ARTICLES

THE WAY THINGS WORK:
TEACHING AND LEARNING IN LIBRARIES

Lizabeth A. Wilson

A few months back, I told my engineer husband that I was going to give a talk about instruction programs that work. "That should be easy," he said. "All you have to do is take a program apart, examine each component, figure out their relationships, and put it back together."

I took his advice. I tried to mentally take apart instruction programs I have worked with, others I have experienced, and others I have read about. Maybe I *could* systematically dismantle an instruction program just like a machine and figure out how it works. Virtual pieces and parts were strewn all over my office. I tried to mentally draw blueprints for a successful instruction program.

I became a pest of myself. I bothered my colleagues for a month, asking questions over and over. How do programs work? What are the secrets to success? How do you know when a program works? Is there a formula? Does it come down to just dumb luck? What constitutes a successful program? A sustained, visible model? Lots of articles written about it?

After a month of fussing, I still had no schematic. I was beginning to worry. I woke up one night and it was all clear. The critical components required for programs that work had come to me in my dreams. I went back to sleep, smiling and calm. The LOEX keynote was going to be a cinch. I awoke the next morning. And, I *couldn't* remember a thing!

Wilson is associate director of libraries for public services, University of Washington, Seattle, Washington.

Throughout the next few weeks, the pieces began floating back into my consciousness until a picture of the way things work emerged. This morning, I'd like to share that picture with you. What are the components that comprise successful instruction programs? I offer my list. Programs that work

- are learner-centered;

- involve collaboration;

- bring technology into the service of teaching and learning;

- have a solid support framework;

- depend on people and personalities;

- recognize that timing is everything;

- are integrated into the educational lifeblood of the institution;

- provide an instruction lens for the rest of the library;

- create a flexible and agile environment;

- encourage continual learning at all levels; and

- take integrated assessment and evaluation seriously.

Learners Are at the Center of All Efforts

Programs that work keep the learner at the center of all efforts. As Leonardo used his Vitruvian man to demonstrate that architecture should be in proportion to the measure of man, programs that work focus explicitly on the learner. Without the learner, there is no reason for instruction programs to exist. Often this is not apparent in our planning. We tend to plan for our convenience and from our viewpoint and personal experience.

Let me give you an example. Last week, I gave a presentation to a library school class on the results of a user survey. When I reviewed the frequency in which undergraduates said they used the library, a member of the audience said he could not believe it. How could undergraduates possibly use the library that much? When he was an undergraduate, he was in the library only three times. This is a classic example of generalizing from one's personal experience.

Programs that work are based on real, not perceived, learner needs. Several years back, I was involved in a pilot program of subject-based information seminars for undergraduates. We had convinced ourselves that this was the next step in the continuum of learning. We worked hard to coordinate and set up the seminars and persuaded skeptical subject librarians to participate. No students showed up. Well, maybe a few. Had we worked with the students and listened to what they really needed instead of what we thought they needed, we might have avoided a lot of work and a programmatic disaster.

Build it and they will *not necessarily* come. By involving learners in the development of programs, you increase your chances that what you are building makes sense. The University of Michigan's Peer Information Counseling program[1] and University of Colorado's peer reference consultants both engage students in the development as well as the delivery of programs. Both have been highly successful.

To be learner-centered, programs must keep in touch with students. We all know that our students are changing. Of all the transitions, none is more dramatic than the shifts in the population. These shifts are reflected in the decline of the traditional college-age population; an increase in older, part-time, commuter, distance learning, and returning students; an increasing ethnic mix; and the continued influx of international students. Students are coming to us with diverse experiences, motivations, learning styles, and educational demands.

But, we have to be careful not to generalize too quickly and miss the nuances. For instance, demographic shifts have regional variations. Some states are experiencing unprecedented population growth due to the baby boom echo and in-migration, while others are experiencing negative growth.

In addition, some learners are invisible. With global networks and more and more information available electronically, the number of individuals who don't *have* to come through the door to use our libraries is increasing.

Student experience with computers is accelerating. The experience of the students entering our colleges and universities in 1996 is radically different from those of 1992. The University of Washington conducts ongoing surveys on student access to computing. In 1992, 30 percent of students reported they had a campus computer account; three years later, 80 percent did. Take a moment and reflect on how this computer access impacts what learners need. Successful programs adjust quickly and appropriately to changes in their learner base.

The architect Frank Lloyd Wright considered anyone over 5'8" a weed. Consequently, he built his houses with low door jams. In many ways, traditional instruction has ignored the "weeds" and catered to the learning styles of students of a pre-determined norm. In recognizing that students represent a wide variety of weeds as well as flowers, programs that work offer multiple educational options. By putting learners in the center, successful instruction programs have grown from the one-size-fits-all models of the 1970s and 80s to rich and diverse models with a spectrum of choices. These programs have done what Ellen Broidy asked at a 1989 LOEX conference—teach as if people really mattered.[2]

Collaboration

Programs that work depend on collaborative efforts. Collaboration brings together the widest range of talents and resources to solve a problem. The greater the number who come to the table, the higher the probability that we will build coherent programs. The more people involved, the greater the chance of sustaining a program over time. More people take a stake and make an investment, and subsequently will not let a program languish.

Shared visions are fundamental to successful collaborations. Programs that work bring together those who share the same educational goals, although they may be coming from different directions. Librarians and faculty gathered together last spring at the University of Washington (UW) and asked, "What makes a UW graduate information literate?" The answers were strikingly similar among the faculty and librarians. This conversation provides a foundation for shared understanding and educational collaboration.

— LIZABETH A. WILSON —

Jeremy Shapiro and Shelley Hughes in their *Educom Review* article "Information Technology as Liberal Art" ask a question that is very much on our minds:

> What does a person need to know today to be a full-fledged, competent and literate member of the information society?[3]

They suggest that the saturation of our daily lives with information organized and transmitted via information technology and the way in which public issues and social life are increasingly being shaped by issues such as intellectual property and privacy require an information literacy curriculum that is multidimensional. Their proposal encompasses the old concept of computer literacy, the librarian's notion of information literacy, and a broader, critical conception of a more humanistic sort.

If one agrees with their proposal (and it certainly is attractive to me), cross-campus collaboration is required. The broadest range of individuals—faculty, librarians, students, administrators, computer professionals—need to be working together.

What will this successful collaboration look like? Rosabeth Ross Kanter, writing on collaboration, says there are "eight I's that make we:"

- **Individual** excellence of the collaborative partners;

- **Importance** given to the project;

- **Interdependence**, that is, cross-linking of responsibilities, not one unit in charge;

- **Investment** of time and resources;

- **Information** sharing;

- **Integration** of the disparate cultures of the units involved;

- **Institutionalization**, meaning a commitment from the administration; and

- **Integrity** of the project and partners.[4]

What do we need to be able to do to collaborate? Can we be taught to collaborate? Is there a set of skills that one must have? Collaboration requires negotiating skills, being able to make tradeoffs, and being comfortable sharing control (and we all like control). Collaborators learn how to cross boundaries. Collaborators have high tolerances for ambiguity. Or as one of my colleagues says, "Give me ambiguity or give me something else."

Programs that work pay attention to supporting the skills and providing the latitude needed for collaboration. If budget allocation is really about changing behavior, organizations need to explicitly budget for collaboration. Last year at the University of Washington, we instituted an innovation award program. The awards funded proposals that moved the libraries beyond the routine and allowed the "community to really dream." The caveat was that proposals be collaborative—jointly submitted from someone on the libraries staff and someone outside of the libraries. There sure was a flurry of collaboration when money was involved.

Successful collaborators get beyond the subtle barriers created by their professional roles. The persona we librarians present to the world can get in the way. Who we are can create a barrier to what we need to know or do. As my mother says, listen to anybody who knows anything, because you need all the help you can get.

Collaboration is a choice. It can't be mandated. It's hard work. It's fragile. And it is based on trust. Jazz musician Benny Golson describes collaboration:

> First of all, collaboration is a matter of choice. But once the choice is made, it is made because those two or three or more people who are collaborating believe in one another. But then once you do, it is very much like iron sharpening iron. When you rub two pieces together they refine each other. You tend to fill in the gaps that the other didn't consider. One person becomes a barometer for the other. And one person encourages the other. Mutual trust is what lets a jazz ensemble take off. You are going into another zone now, and you are not going alone. You are going with other people, and the purpose is to create. And that can be exciting—as long as you believe in one another.[5]

Technology

Programs that work bring technology into the service of teaching and learning. This is a challenge because we work in an era of technology lusting. This lust is fanned by the media's discovery of the Internet and the World Wide Web. In libraries, we struggle with the phenomena of technology as an end in itself. A colleague of mine speaks about the "I" word (the Internet) when she disparages mindless attention to technology without educational benefit. We are experiencing a proliferation of Internet training at institutions that never before had any type of library instruction.

There is a lot of talk of how information technology will allow us to educate more students faster and cheaper through distance education. Expectations about technology have grown to almost mythic proportions.

Programs that work have been able to maintain balance and a sense of reality as the hype about the "I" word has grown. Programs that work know what they want to accomplish educationally before employing technology. They have brought technology into the service of teaching and learning.

Steve Ehrmann of the Annenberg/CPB Project asks many of the right questions in *Change* magazine:

> [I]f we rush out and buy new technologies without first asking hard questions about appropriate educational goals, the results are likely to be disappointing and wasteful.[6]

If you are headed in the wrong direction, technology will only get you there faster.

In November 1995, ten teams attended the 2d Coalition for Networked Information New Learning Communities Conference. These teams had successfully used networked information to transform curriculums and represented "best practices" across the country. When the teams broke into the "birds of a feather" sessions something interesting occurred. The computing folks met in the bar because they did not have issues to talk about. They had solved all the technology problems or they wouldn't have had successful programs. If technology is truly brought into the service of teaching and learning, it becomes a non-issue.

Support Framework

Programs that work enjoy a framework of solid support. They are in sync with institutional goals. The educational role of the library is prominent in mission and vision statements and strategic plans. And if it is not there, librarians ask why not.

Successful programs have an organizational home in the library, which is visible and easily identifiable. Instruction is explicitly defined as a responsibility in position descriptions.

Programs that work have adequate and stable resources. If programs are embraced and integrated into the support framework, resources will flow in their direction. But, there is never enough staff or enough money for all of our ideas and energies. Hustling for additional resources, creatively scavenging, and seeking grants give programs that work the margin of excellence.

While we all recognize that developing a program requires managing up and over and around and down, there is one person who is more important than everyone else in the support framework. That person is the library director. Programs that work, *really work*, have the full support of the director. Conviction is good. Leadership is even better. As one instruction coordinator said, "The director has access to channels of influence that line librarians do not. The director can seize opportunities to advocate, lobby, plant seeds, and make things happen. When the director makes instruction his or hers, it becomes a priority. It is important that the director is respected on campus. This creates a halo effect around the library. It makes people want to be connected and involved and identified with the library."

People and Personalities

Programs that work are the result of people and personalities. Many I talked to while preparing this paper felt, when all is said and done, that successful programs come down to people. Who are these people and what are they like?

People who make programs work are confident and articulate in their expertise. They demonstrate that confidence through action. They understand what special skills they have and communicate them. They have created and cultivated a voice for themselves. They are people who follow-up and produce. They are creative, passionate, committed, dedicated, and driven people who find joy in teaching and learning.

Some of these people are visionaries. Others are gurus. Still others are charismatic. This is not surprising given research on personality type and vocations. Educators and trainers are EIFs (extrovert, intuitive, feeling). These folks find collaboration and boundary-crossing second-nature. From years of working with programs, I have observed a special skill these individuals have—they can move groups forward.

People who make programs work are always on the lookout. They strike up conversations on the bus, at the grocery store, during college receptions in hopes of finding educational connections. As the New York Lotto slogan says, "Hey, you never know."

People who make programs work make great mentors. They share their experiences, having realized long ago that it's not a zero sum game. These mentors share the mantel and pass it on. I still remember my first Association of College and Research Libraries Bibliographic Instruction Section dinner years ago. I was a brand new librarian. Sharon Hogan sat down next to me and asked me what I was doing in the area of instruction. I was flabbergasted. She was famous. She had written one of the most important books on

— LIZABETH A. WILSON —

instruction. Could she actually be interested in what I had to say? By the simple act of listening to me, she let me know I was in the right place. I encourage you all to do the same throughout this conference. Listen and encourage each other.

Timing Is Everything

Programs that work recognize that timing is everything. The more years I am in the field, the more I am convinced that you've got to time it just right with the right combination of people and ideas. But, I do believe there are strategies for influencing timing.

First, look for connections in all the right places—at receptions, at sporting events, over e-mail. These connections will pay off later. Second, get out there and be ahead of the curve. When a change or innovation (such as graphical Web browsers) presents itself, ask what it means for teaching and learning. Finally, keep your network of enterprises working overtime. By keeping many things going at once, you will create more opportunities.

No matter how heroic your efforts, the moment can't be forced. It comes when circumstances are right. When energies won't or can't flow on one front, it helps to have another to turn to. The most productive people and programs have lots of different things going on. If they run into obstacles in one area, they put it aside for a while, and move on to something else. By having multiple projects, you are more likely to have a breakthrough somewhere. Don't forget that the greatest idea at the wrong time is a loser. Is the timing right? What if you waited six months or a year? What will you miss if you don't do it now?

Poet Doug King says, "Learn to pause...or nothing worthwhile will catch up to you."[7] Lori Arp, in her article "Reflecting on Reflecting," tells us that focusing inward is not all bad.[8] Research on metacognition shows that there are benefits from being more introspective during a time of rapid change. Arp advises us that a little introspection is worth its weight in gold. Don't get impatient. Successful programs emerge in the fullness of time.

Lifeblood of the Educational Enterprise

Programs that work are part of the educational lifeblood of the institution. They are integrated into the curriculum, not adjunct services. However, the degree of cooperation will determine what you can do. With increased institutional integration, programs move from stand-alone orientations to instruction that is part of the curriculum.[9]

Being part of the lifeblood requires that librarians communicate on a variety of levels and through many

methods. When I hear librarians lament, "Why doesn't the faculty consult with us?" I think, why aren't we talking to them?" Successful programs are based on continual, deliberate, and targeted communication. And when we communicate, we need to know what we can deliver so we don't build programs we can't support.

While our goal is to be part of the educational lifeblood, we must realize that curricular innovation and change in higher education is a long process. Recently, I heard a state senator remark, "The hallmark of higher education is the ability to resist change." And he meant it as a compliment. Larry Hardesty reminds us that curricular change is very slow.[10] Kindergarten is an example. After its initial introduction in the U.S., more than 50 years elapsed before schools widely adopted the kindergarten concept in the 1930s and 1940s.

Instruction Is the Lens

Programs that work provide a lens for the rest of the library. Cerise Oberman first suggested that "Instruction is the lens through which every function in the library needs to look."[11]

If education is really embraced as part of the library's mission, then the notion of "programs" begins to diversify and extend itself in new and creative ways. One insightful colleague says, "It isn't just classes or tours. Everything the library does can be examined and evaluated in how it contributes to this mission."

The instruction lens can help us create the environment needed for user self-reliance.[12] If we use the instruction lens to view our libraries, learner-centered questions quickly emerge. How have we organized our space? Can users find their way? Are we providing opportunities for self-orientation? How do our systems and interfaces fare under the instruction lens? By looking through the instruction lens, we may be able to create what Michael Gorman calls the "BI-less" library so we can get on with the business of education.[13]

Flexible and Agile Environment

Programs that work are flexible and agile. They thrive in environments that reward and support experimentation. They pilot, experiment, discard, renew, and adjust. This dynamic agility promotes continual improvement. You must be willing to tweak, experiment, and keep on tinkering.

Programs that work take risks. Some meet with success, others failure, but all keep moving forward. Go on an occasional wild goose chase. That's what wild geese are for. All you ball players out there know that you can't hit a home run unless you step up to the plate. And when you do, as Seattle Mariner play-by-play announcer Dave Niehaus says, "My, oh my! Get out the rye bread and mustard, Grandma. It's a grand salami!"

Continual Learning at All Levels

Programs that work provide continual learning at all levels. An environment that supports, rewards, and encourages librarians to keep learning is critical. Ongoing staff development is directly related to the way things work.

Because we are in a period of unprecedented change, the skills and expertise we need are also changing. It should come as no surprise that model staff development programs for instruction librarians are at institutions with model instruction programs for students.

By keeping up and incorporating new ideas and approaches, programs that work keep on working. You don't need an expensive staff development program to do this. There are many things you can do yourself with few resources.

First, take it all in and build your theoretical base:

- Read and devour; talk and interact.

- Create a critical mass of ideas and people.

- Build a reprint file; mark those Web sites; make hotlinks.

- Route key journals; use SDI services; subscribe to listservs.

- Contact LOEX.

- Pay attention to the Coalition for Networked Information (CNI), the American Association of Higher Education, and the National Learning Infrastructure Initiative.

- Attend lectures; better yet organize lectures.

Second, watch experts:

- Sit-in, visit classes, watch videos.

- Find a master teacher (at your institution or beyond).

- Travel in packs (or pairs) to conferences and workshops; it helps with application of new ideas back home.

But most critical, get support:

- Find like minds (inside and outside of the library).

- Brown bag it with people who share your interests; everyone has to eat lunch.

- Find a mentor, be a mentor (on your campus or off; in person or e-mail).

- Get out of your library box and find other experts.

- Exploit your professional organizations.

Later today you will be hearing about an innovative staff development program called Premier. It provides an excellent model for continual learning on a statewide basis.

Integrated Assessment and Evaluation

Programs that work take assessment and evaluation seriously. Assessment and evaluation tends to be one of the last things we do. We say we don't have time. We can't afford it. I suggest to you that programs that work realize that they can't afford *not* to do this. They put assessment first and foremost. Programs that work ask the right assessment questions; systematically listen; gather routine information; and use it to improve and enhance.

Why should you take assessment seriously? First, we are motivated by accountability, credibility, and results. Second, what we teach is changing. It is no longer enough to teach how to read a periodical citation (it never was). The notion that we can produce informed citizens capable of critical thinking and life-long learning has been embraced in higher education. This shift toward process in instruction creates a re-examination of how to measure learning. Finally, we are seeing the influence of cognitive science on our field. We now know much more about how people learn. We have learned that individuals vary in the way they learn. If people learn in different ways, and we are evaluating only one type of learning, how valid are our results? The relative merits of qualitative versus quantitative evaluation as well as control versus relevance issues become more critical than before. We must be even more versatile in our ability to deal with different evaluation techniques. We must acknowledge that different techniques are valid in different circumstances. We must be knowledgeable about the strengths and weaknesses of each. And we must be willing to mix and match methods so that evaluation results in the greatest amount of usable information. As one assessment guru said, "You can't fatten a pig by merely

— LIZABETH A. WILSON —

weighing it every week." Isn't that a typical quantitative approach? Successful programs rely on assessment and evaluation to keep them in touch with learners and understand their needs.

Case Study: UWired

I would like to shift a little and use a case study on the way things work. I will present the case of a program with you that has many of the components on my list. The program is called UWired and is underway at the University of Washington.[14] UWired seeks to

- integrate electronic communication and information literacy skills into teaching and learning;

- create learning communities not bound by place or time;

- encourage intellectual engagement among faculty, librarians, and students;

- integrate appropriate technology into curriculum content and delivery; and

- explore models for institutional collaboration.

UWired was developed to respond to real needs and challenges: bringing technology into the service of teaching and learning, the new information literacy, and the creation of community at a large research university. We all know that new technologies have the potential to change profoundly the ways students learn and we teach. We are all struggling to discern which technologies will provide pedagogical advantages and cost-benefits in student learning. Technology has driven equally significant changes in our libraries and scholarly communication. As research and teaching increasingly rely on global networks for the creation, storage, and dissemination of knowledge, a new information literacy has emerged. Students often lack the skills necessary to succeed in this multidimensional information environment. The quality of the student experience is both heightened and harmed by the size and complexity of a large research university such as the UW. While students have a great breadth of opportunities for learning, they often feel isolated from both the faculty and one another.

During the UWired pilot year (1994-1995), 65 freshmen enrolled in three freshmen interest groups and selected faculty were targeted for intensive technology and information literacy instruction, and were loaned laptop computers for the year. Librarians taught

an information and technology seminar focused on hardware and software skills, sophisticated and responsible use of the Internet and the Web, and critical use and evaluation of information. A new kind of classroom, called a collaboratory, was built in the undergraduate library using a podular format, not rows of computers. Teaching and technology seminars and workshops were attended by over 1,000 faculty.

Based on the lessons learned from the pilot year, UWired launched several new pilots and expanded successful components in its second year (1995-1996). Highlights of the year include the following:

- Technology and information instruction was integrated into all 60 freshmen interest groups reaching 1,500 students.

- Two more collaboratories have been built in the undergraduate library.

- Intercollegiate athletics became involved through the participation of the men's and women's basketball teams. We were interested in how laptops could extend the academic day and reach of students while they are on the road.

- Thirteen upper-division classes in a wide variety of disciplines have been revised to incorporate technology and networked information into course delivery and content.

- Two large introductory lecture classes were prototyped as distributed learning courses.

- Campuswide faculty development and training has been expanded. The Center for Teaching, Learning, and Technology will be dedicated 21 May 1996.

- Plans are underway for a Community College Symposia this summer. Teams made up of faculty, administrators, librarians, and computing experts from the 32 community colleges in Washington state have been invited to participate. The symposium is designed to exchange strategies for improving teaching and learning through integration of information technology and to improve policy making and planning through campus collaboration.

- A technology and teaching in-service day for 700 Seattle public school teachers is planned for October. It is tentatively entitled "Educating the Citizen for the 21st Century: Information Literacy and Civic Education."

• UWired continues to serve as a testbed for Mary Gates Hall, a technology-intensive undergraduate facility, opening in 1998. The hall is named for Mary Gates, long-time UW regent, advocate for undergraduate education, and the late mother of Bill Gates III.

UWired uses a number of tools to evaluate the effectiveness of its efforts, including pre-testing and post-testing for computer and information literacy, e-mail monitoring and polling, evaluation surveys, focus groups, and instructor evaluations. UWired student performance is being tracked longitudinally and will be measured against comparable students. We are maintaining contact with all UWired faculty to assess their experiences incorporating information technology into their courses.

What have we learned? UWired has improved student learning and faculty teaching, created electronic learning communities, and provided a coordinated institutional approach to teaching and technology. UWired "jump-started" freshmen by enabling them to develop information and technology skills. UWired students used electronic mail to a much more significant degree than other students. Students were taught how to use the Web knowledgeably. When compared to non-UWired students, they were five times more likely to know how to evaluate Web information, used the Web twice as frequently, and were better able to describe specific ways in which this information would help them.

Fred Johnson, professor in fisheries and UWired faculty, compares the UWired freshmen to "rocket ships: once they left the earth, they kept going faster and faster. In one quarter, these students had gone past what juniors and seniors in our department had mastered in terms of transferable skills. Teaching is never going to be the same again. It brings in a whole new suite of possibilities and allows me to think about teaching more broadly."[15]

The UWired student-athletes became adept at communicating through e-mail with professors, coaches, librarians, and classmates; using information from databases, the Web, and the Internet; creating electronic publications; and connecting while on the road. The student-athletes wonder how they ever got along without their laptops. The laptops have expanded their academic day, addressing severe time constraints. The women's basketball team has a cumulative GPA over 3.0 for the first time ever. The coach credits UWired.

Student-athlete Patrick Femerling used his computer skills while on a road trip to Arizona to send his portion of a geography project back to classmates in Seattle. And while doing a search for his English paper, Patrick joked, "I go to all the best parties and I go to all the best databases."[16]

According to faculty and librarians, UWired opened new teaching possibilities including distributed learning over time and place; more interaction with students; student-directed learning; nonlinear, more spontaneous learning; and the use of the Web as a central site for course information and communication.

Few efforts have brought together the diverse expertise needed to enhance campuswide learning and teaching. UWired represents an innovative approach to involving the widest range of personnel in the educational process. Faculty teach students. Upperclassmen serve as peer instructors. Computing staff provide technology training. Librarians teach access, retrieval, and evaluation of information. UWired instructional teams focused on learning, not technology. By capitalizing on the existing campus information network, UWired allowed faculty and librarians to directly engage students in learning through the use of electronic communication.

We searched for a model that took advantage of networked information and facilitated collaboration when we were designing the collaboratories. We borrowed ideas from other institutions and the concept of the collaboratory from the sciences. The collaboratories have proven to be exciting models and have generated national interest. Students give the collaboratories high marks for increasing their sense of belonging. With increased virtual communication, coming together physically takes on new meaning. We think there are some important lessons here for distance education.

UWired has provided an institutional structure for prototyping and testing technology and teaching. UWired has allowed for coordinated and wise use of scarce resources. UWired allowed the UW to move from what was once a piecemeal, fitful, and slow approach to one that is comprehensive, innovative, and hopefully sustainable.

Why has UWired worked? What pieces and parts does it have? How does UWired fit my blueprint for the "way things work?"

Learners Are at the Center of All Efforts

Students are integral to development and implementation and participate in all planning groups. UWired uses peer instructors (a longstanding tradition at the University of Washington) to teach in the freshmen interest group program. At the November 1995 CNI New Learning Communities conference, the UW was the only team to include a student on its team.

— LIZABETH A. WILSON —

The student reported he loved all the attention *and* the free food.

Collaboration

Hundreds of faculty, librarians, computing experts, students, and administrators have been involved in UWired. Collaboration has been *the* key to success. It is an initiative that has pieced together funding and support at the margins. By collaborating together, those involved in UWired have achieved much more than they could have dreamed alone. In UWired, collaboration takes place on many different levels (among students; between faculty and students; among UWired instructional teams; and among administrative units). UWired recognizes that diverse expertise is needed and that no one unit or department can go this alone. UWired has created new ways of budgeting, credit giving and taking, and organizing. UWired provides one model for campus collaborations.

Technology

From the beginning, UWired was not about technology. UWired is about community and learning. Technology has been the lubricant. In UWired, we learned that

- appropriate technology used *effectively* enables more than it constrains;

- appropriate technology used *efficiently* disappears more than it interferes; and

- appropriate technology used *effectively and efficiently* is neither cheap nor easy.[17]

Support Framework

UWired has an exceptional support framework. Some of us call it the holy trinity. It is comprised of the director of libraries (Betty Bengtson), the vice provost for undergraduate education (Fred Campbell), and the vice president for computing and communications (Ron Johnson). They have access to the legislature, the UW president, professional organizations, and resources. They can "talk" UWired without a script. They epitomize that the best administrative commitment is manifested as a trusting hands-off. Because of these three individuals, UWired has developed a halo effect. Many across campus are excited about becoming involved.

Loose and fluid organizational structure is necessary for innovation. We have resisted bureaucratizing and over-organizing the program. Planning groups are fluid and inclusive with heavy use of e-mail collaboration.

People and Personalities

UWired has its share of visionaries, gurus, and charismatic folks. They are excited and energized producers and collaborators with enormous self-awareness of what each brings to the table.

Timing Is Everything

The story of UWired begins in 1994. Legend has it that then-Provost Wayne Clough (now president of Georgia Tech) said, "Let's give laptops to students." He turned to Louis Fox in the Office of Undergraduate Education and assigned him the responsibility. Louis thought to himself, "Is this a bad idea whose time had come?"

Louis, the creative and resourceful soul that he is, sent e-mail SOSs to a few of his colleagues. He had heard me wax about the role of libraries in the educational process a year earlier on a special presidential task force. "Remember all your talk? Here's your chance to put words into action." With the hard work of a lot of people, UWired was born and turned a potentially bad idea into a good idea whose time had come.

Educational Lifeblood

UWired has rapidly become integrated into the lifeblood of the university. Our new president, Richard McCormick, has said that information literacy will be the hallmark of a UW graduate. UWired has become a visible symbol for the university, parents, legislators, and students.

Instruction Is the Lens

The educational role of the libraries has been prominent in the UW Libraries' vision and mission since its 1991 strategic plan. There has been a concerted effort to involve librarians and staff from throughout the libraries—from technical services, systems, administration, public services—in UWired.

Flexible and Agile

UWired pilots and tests, discards and readjusts. We haven't fallen in love with elements that we can't scale (such as the laptops) or ideas that don't work. We have learned that most broad-based change is incremental and slow.

Continual Learning

Learning at all levels has been supported with ongoing workshops, classes, and lectures for faculty and librarians on teaching and technology. We have found that staff development has paid off with a critical mass of expert librarians and faculty. We are excited to see how the new Center for Teaching, Learning, and Technology will impact curricular transformation in the coming year.

Integrated Assessment and Evaluation

Assessment has been integrated throughout UWired from the beginning. We have worked hard to ask the right questions and measure meaningful things, but we have missed the mark at times. We continue to track projects such as the Annenberg Flashlight Initiative (<http://www.wiche.edu/flshlght/flash. htm>) and the American Association of Higher Education assessment project for guidance on assessment issues involved in education and technology.

The most important lesson we have learned from UWired (and we have learned it so many times that we adopted it as our motto): *Nil Facile*. Nothing is Simple.

UWired is barely two years old. It is a baby as far as programs go. But it appears that UWired has many of the components that make programs work. Can UWired be sustained and expanded? Given the high levels of collaboration, the melding of cultures, integration into the educational lifeblood, and attention to learners, our hopes and expectations are high. I guess we will know in the fullness of time.

Conclusion

I would like to remind us all that there is no one blueprint to follow for successful instruction programs. Each environment is different with its own history and culture, people and personalities, resources and requirements. Although each institution presents unique circumstances, there do seem to be components that are common to programs that work. I have shared my "bill of materials" with you this morning. You can substitute parts and be inventive, but the greater the number of critical pieces you have, the easier it is to build and sustain successful programs.

During the next two days you will hear about many programs that work. Take advantage of the opportunity to share your blueprints with each other. I encourage you to gather all the pieces and parts you can and take them back home where they can be recycled and reassembled. Maybe my engineer husband was right. Maybe you can take something apart to figure out the way things work.

NOTES

1.   Barbara MacAdam and Darlene P. Nichols, "Peer Information Counseling: An Academic Library Program for Minority Students," *Journal of Academic Librarianship* 15:4 (1 September 1989): 204.

2.   Ellen Broidy, "Celebrating Diversity: Teaching Library Skills as if People Mattered," in *Library Orientation Series 19: Reaching and Teaching Diverse Library User Groups*, ed. by Teresa B. Mensching, 1-9 (Ann Arbor, MI: Pierian Press, 1989).

3.   Jeremy J. Shapiro and Shelley K. Hughes, "Information Technology as a Liberal Art," *Educom Review* (March/April 1996): 31-35.

4.   Rosabeth Ross Kanter, "Collaborative Advantages: the Art of Alliances," *Harvard Business Review* 72:4 (July/August 1994): 100.

5.   Daniel Coleman, *The Creative Spirit* (New York and London: Dutton, 1992): 121.

6.   Stephen C. Ehrmann, "Asking the Right Questions: What Does Research Tell Us about Technology and Higher Learning?," *Change* 27 (March/April 1995): 24.

7.   Roger van Oech, *A Whack on the Side of the Head: How You Can Be More Creative* (Stamford, CT: U.S. Games Systems, 1990): 189.

8.   Lori Arp, "Reflecting on Reflecting: Views on Teaching and the Internet," *RQ* 34:4 (Summer 1995): 453-457.

9.   Lori Arp and Lizabeth Wilson, "Structures of Bibliographic Instruction Programs: A Continuum for Planning," *Reference Librarian* 24 (1989): 25-34.

10.   Larry Hardesty, "Faculty Culture and Bibliographic Instruction," *Library Trends* 44:2 (Fall 1995): 339-367.

11.   Cerise Oberman, "Avoiding the Cereal Syndrome: or, Critical Thinking in the Electronic Environment," *Library Trends* 39 (Winter 1991): 189-202.

12.   Harold W. Tuckett and Carla J. Stoffle, "Learning Theory and the Self-Reliant Library User," *RQ* 24 (Fall 1984): 58.

13.   Michael Gorman, "Send for a Child of Four! or Creating the BI-Less Library," *Library Trends* 39 (Winter 1991): 354-362.

14.   A fuller description of UWired may be found at <http:www.washington.edu/uwired/>.

15.   Fred Johnson, "Plugging into UWired," *Paideia: Undergraduate Education at the University of Washington* 3:2 (Winter 1995): 1-3.

16.   Jill McKinstry, "Husky Athletes in UWired: Taking Care of Business." <http://weber.u.washington.edu/~new media/husky/husky.html.> (26 April 1996).

17.   Quote from Mark McNair, consultant/software engineer, computing and communications, University of Washington.

PREMIER: SHARING AND ENCOURAGING PROGRAMS THAT WORK

Linnea M. Dudley, Catherine Neis, and **Michael J. Kruzich**

ALTERNATIVE PROFESSIONAL DEVELOPMENT

PREMIER is the consulting and training component of the Michigan Library Association's (MLA) Information Literacy Roundtable. PREMIER stands for "Promoting Research Education in Michigan: Inservice Educational Resources." "Research education" is its integrated, collaborative approach to information literacy, and "in-service resources" are an extended and indepth process of consultations and workshops made possible through professional volunteerism.

Project History

PREMIER began in 1993 with the newly elected officers and board members of what was then the MLA Bibliographic Instruction Roundtable. With data in hand from the Southeast Michigan League of Libraries Committee on Research Education's recent survey of bibliographic instruction in Michigan, the board met for the first time in a spirit of hope and frustration: frustration, because they were extremely aware that far too many instruction librarians were trying to teach without classrooms or instructional technology; without

Dudley is PREMIER project manager and coordinator of reference services, Marygrove College Library, Detroit, Michigan; *Neis* is head of reference and instruction, Woodhouse Library, Aquinas College, Grand Rapids, Michigan; and *Kruzich* is coordinator of research education, Mardigian Library, University of Michigan-Dearborn, Dearborn, Michigan.

adequate time for preparation or assessment; without sufficient administrative support; without even recognition of the role of librarians as educators. There was a sense, also, that at a critical time in the history of academic libraries, the traditional activities and relationships of the professional library associations were not empowering instruction librarians. Hope came from the fact that at least some Michigan programs were seen to be thriving, and from the opportunity to try something new, something that would draw on the pool of local talent and experience identified in the survey.

From Programs to Practice

One issue that came up repeatedly in the survey was the lack of funding for professional development in the area of library instruction. Another, perhaps more significant, involved the difficulties inherent in translating ideas and information from conferences and workshops into the reality of a specific institution, with a distinct set of resources and challenges and a unique organizational culture and history. PREMIER, accordingly, was designed to address both problems: by taking the program, custom-made, to the institution, and by being affordable in terms of time as well as money.

Professional Volunteerism and Community Building

The key to both affordability and genuine relevance was the concept of professional volunteerism (i.e., the belief that interested librarians would be willing to share their expertise and experience as part

— PREMIER: SHARING AND ENCOURAGING —

LOEX-96 13

of a grassroots effort to further information literacy, and that academic library directors would enable them to do so). PREMIER was also explicitly intended to enhance the community of academic librarianship in Michigan, by creating new opportunities for interaction, by exploring new forums for discussion and by fostering ongoing relationships that would alleviate the special professional loneliness of the instruction librarian.

The PREMIER Process

With permission from the executive board of the state association, the BI board began a period of study and planning. A series of monthly meetings were held with roundtable members and other interested volunteers to elicit a vision of effective in-service education for academic libraries. The working model involved a cycle of self-study and facilitated meetings culminating in a workshop, the content of which would be determined by the needs and interests of the client library. The self-study eventually took the form of a program portfolio, drawing as much as possible on existing documents, but providing opportunities for reflection and dialogue among the site librarians. As the PREMIER concept expanded to include non-librarians with an interest in information literacy, especially classroom faculty, workshops on bibliographic instruction were renamed research education colloquia. As originally envisioned, the colloquia would provide models of successful programs; then, in guided breakout sessions, the site librarians and their non-library colleagues could creatively explore applications appropriate to their students, programs, and facilities.

Funding

It was the intention of the project that colloquium presenters—who volunteered their time and expertise—be reimbursed for travel and other expenses. The roundtable board, therefore, began to investigate grant possibilities to fund a development period and pilot year, originally to include two libraries. In July of 1994, PREMIER was invited to submit a proposal to the H.W. Wilson Foundation. In August, Madonna University indicated its willingness to become the first PREMIER site, and in September, the project received $5,000.

Madonna University Library

Meeting twice over a six-month period with teams of PREMIER volunteers, the Madonna librarians prepared a program portfolio, which was then made available to the planners and presenters of the first colloquium, held in May of 1995. The day-long program was attended by Madonna University administrators and faculty representatives from the departments of communication arts, education, history, nursing, and psychology. PREMIER provided four presenters and six additional facilitators. The Madonna colloquium covered three topics, which have since become almost ongoing PREMIER themes: first, the integration of library instruction into the curriculum as a whole; second, the development of closer collaboration between classroom and library faculty, and, finally, practical aspects of administering a strong research education program.

Since the PREMIER colloquium, library instruction at Madonna has continued to increase, and the library has acted in partnership with the university writing center to further the concept of information literacy among both faculty and students. Recently, the Madonna librarians wrote a successful grant proposal to help fund expanding instructional activities.

Aquinas College Woodhouse Library

The second PREMIER site was Aquinas College, where Catherine Neis had been a PREMIER volunteer from the project's earliest days. This is her lively account of that experience:

PREMIER as a 12-Step Program

The first step is to admit you have a problem—that was easy. The bibliographic instruction program at Aquinas had not changed since its inception, almost 15 years ago. We updated pathfinders annually when instructors called to book sessions. The actual booking of sessions was fairly informal—sometimes faculty didn't call in advance and often scheduled sessions for when they were going to be away. I basically refused to continue to update our pathfinders—where was the learning, the active learning, if we led our students to every source? As we expanded electronic resources, that old Search Strategy form from LS 616 came back to haunt me: give them a search or teach them to search?

About the same time, the college began a three-year project of general education renewal. This had also been languishing for about 20 years with the exception of a first-year humanities course instituted five or six years ago. The library was to be an integral component, but after the first year, the course became so content-driven, faculty began putting all materials on reserve (again leading students to the sources) and the library component fell by the wayside.

The second step is to believe in a power/force greater than ourselves—anyone remember getting that hot pink flyer about the first PREMIER meeting and what you were doing when you got it? Step three is to turn our lives over to that force—I began attending the meetings with fervor and volunteering Aquinas as a pilot site every chance I got. Meanwhile, at Aquinas, the library staff attended most of the Gen Ed discussions and acted as if integrated library instruction was a given. We had been to a presentation at, and had discussions with, Hope College about their program and had some ideas for the renewal process at Aquinas.

The next two steps deal with a searching and fearless moral inventory and admitting our "wrongs"—both addressed by tackling our portfolio. The Woodhouse Library began our portfolio before we were actually accepted as a pilot site; whether you participate in PREMIER or not, the portfolio can give you an excuse/opportunity to talk about bibliographic instruction—it did for us. The portfolio not only pointed out our "wrongs" or shortcomings, but also allowed us to recognize what we were doing right. It gave us a handle on our commonly held beliefs and ideas regarding BI and, as a result, we renamed our BI program Research Education, and have asked the Academic Assembly (faculty governing body) to re-recognize us as the library instead of the Learning Resource Center (LRC).

Steps six through nine are all about getting ready to change, asking for help changing, and making amends. This is what the colloquium is all about: change and collaboration. The library staff bought into the idea of a change happening from within the library, not dictated by the institution or specific programs. We met with PREMIER representatives to focus on what we wanted and how best to accomplish it. PREMIER recruited presenters to address our needs while we went about getting others to buy into the process. Luckily, the academic dean was a willing enlistee. She helped select departments and specific faculty for inclusion; drafted an invitation that endorsed not only the colloquium but also faculty participation; underwrote the cost with faculty development money; and baked cookies for the potluck!

I am firmly convinced that faculty perceptions of librarians have been challenged and improved by the PREMIER Colloquium and our exploration of faculty status for librarians—so much so that we have been asked by numerous faculty to accept the responsibility for instructional technology as part of our mission, something we will have to negotiate with the Academic Assembly.

Into the home stretch now, the final three steps have to do with an ongoing commitment to the "new" us. Step ten is a continuing inventory—a portfolio is never done! We have added a lot to our portfolio, not just more papers to bulk it up but documentation of substantial changes in our program. I would say the most dramatic change is in the area of collaboration as this year, we have done a tremendous amount of research education (RE) for faculty and staff. Attendance has been sporadic, but the interest is high and we are intending to keep it a part of our program.

Seeking knowledge and the will to use that knowledge are the gist of step 11. I hope I have indicated in some small degree the level of growth—personal, programmatic, and departmental—that we have experienced this past year. Our RE program struggled this first year, right along with the new first-year course. Despite this struggle, the library is welcome and expected to participate in ongoing discussions on how to make the course better and, more importantly, how to make the library component more meaningful. The humanities class is now required of all second-year students and the faculty teaching it have information literacy and skills expectations for their students who participated in Inquiry and Expression this year.

The final step is to spread the word—having had a "spiritual awakening" as the result of the first 11 steps, we are urged to carry our message to others *and* practice what we preach. This is the third time I have spoken about our experience, the Woodhouse Library's experience, of PREMIER, and it is true: each time I have been more emphatic! I welcome the opportunity to be a participant, in any capacity, for future colloquiums.

In closing, I would like to point out a few other similarities to multi-step groups. Oftentimes, new members have sponsors or mentors. Looking around this room, I see many people who have been involved in PREMIER from its inception and I know my life, both personally and professionally, has been improved by meeting and working with them, my friends. There is also a support group component to many programs, and that too is a benefit of PREMIER. The meetings have always been a part of the BI roundtable and the roundtable discussions have been enlightening, entertaining, and educational over the years. In fact, when we had a vacancy occur at Aquinas, it seemed logical to think of people I had met through the roundtable. We did, in fact, hire someone who not only came to the meetings but had been carpooling to them with me! Finally, let me say that while this has been an intense year, a year of dependence and relying on others, it has ultimately led to a greater sense of independence for the entire Woodhouse Library staff at Aquinas College.

Demand for PREMIER's services exceeded expectations, and in the third of the "two" pilot experiences, the Monroe County Community College (MCCC) LRC's research education colloquium became part of a collegewide contractual in-service day. The PREMIER sessions covered collaboration, assessment, and administration, and the presenters included non-librarians, modelling team-teaching with librarian counterparts.

PREMIER's open meetings, attended by librarians from many types of colleges and universities throughout Michigan, have devoted a great deal of time to the question, What makes a successful library instruction program? One early realization was that providing instructional services upon request was not the same as having a program. The PREMIER portfolio concept developed as a means of analyzing and focusing instructional practices and resources, and the portfolio guidelines highlight the essential elements of a strong program. For example:

- **Institutional information**—The educational role of the academic librarian is demonstrated by knowledge of institutional mission and programs, and by familiarity with important issues in higher education today, such as critical thinking, retention and assessment.

- **Library instruction policies and philosophy**—A strong instructional program must be founded on shared concepts, such as process-based research, or resource-based learning, which can be readily and consistently articulated to the non-librarians with whom we hope to work.

- **Overview (including budget)**—Unfortunately, few library budgets include a line item for instruction, which means that even strong programs may be seen as marginal and vulnerable.

- **Specific examples**—Is there evidence for a developmental sequence of student library experiences? Writing Across the Curriculum provides an excellent model for information literacy instruction.

- **Assessment**—By measuring students' attainment of information literacy skills, librarians can participate in an important task of the greater educational community as well as work to evolve more effective instructional strategies and methods.

In the original proposal to its parent organization, the Information Literacy Roundtable identified a number of advantages beyond the primary consulting and educational activities of the project. PREMIER promised to

- enhance the communication function of the association;

- offer additional avenues for participation;

- facilitate cooperation among libraries;

- promote shared standards for bibliographic instruction.

As an officer of the roundtable, volunteer consultant and colloquium facilitator, Michael Kruzich was especially qualified to help evaluate the community building aspects of the project. These are his observations:

Inclusive Leadership

PREMIER entered into its pilot phase at the same time that I became chair of the (then-called) Bibliographic Instruction Roundtable. I offer the following observations and reflections on the experience of the formation of the project from this perspective.

In a sense this is a story. Stories embody values be they cultural, moral, or spiritual. The story of PREMIER illustrates to me the power of three values inherent in our vocation as educators: the challenge to create and nurture community; the courage to "profess" and practice what we believe about teaching and learning with integrity; and the commitment to graciously learn from one another through volunteering our time, knowledge, and experience. These three values—community, professional development and volunteerism—are the heart of PREMIER.

Teaching can often be a lonely experience, especially if one feels "marginal." We librarians have a long oral and written tradition of how we feel marginalized by our institutions. There are some stories that do not liberate us, but keep us feeling isolated and discouraged on the one hand; and on the other hand may drive us to overcompensate through the slavish attachment to the idea that "If I work harder, someone will certainly notice that the work I'm doing is important," or that "The students need me; if I don't do it, no one else will." The stories we tell to each other and ourselves are most revealing. If we decide to wait for our institutions, or for that matter "fill-in-the blank" (eg., ALA, ACRL, or whatever organization you think needs to change), we will wait a long time. The well-known author and lecturer on higher education, Parker Palmer, proposes an alternative. The "movement approach" he writes about sees change flowing from the development of community.[1]

The Information Literacy Roundtable board, comprised of seven officers, meets monthly. PREMIER has energized the roundtable and increased attendance at our monthly meetings, becoming a model of inclusive leadership within the Michigan Library Association. As chair of the roundtable, I witnessed the transformation of librarians who had "lost their spark" or had nagging self-doubts about their effectiveness as teachers.

We listened to each other and our stories connected us by the values we individually and collectively cherish as well as our willingness to take risks to create a climate for personal and professional support. Veteran librarians became excited as we began to chart new directions and take responsibility for our own professional development. Novice librarians, eager to learn, became self-confident as their voices were acknowledged and valued in the conversation. From Houghton in the upper peninsula to Holland on the shores of Lake Michigan; from Metro Detroit, Grand Rapids, Monroe, and Lansing, PREMIER has brought us together as a teaching and learning community.

Professional development is often equated with workshops and seminars, taking a class or attending a conference. Certainly these activities are worthwhile and necessary to keep pace with the changing nature of libraries and the trends in higher education. However the words "professional," "profession," and "professor" harken to a more profound reality, which is important to reflect upon from time to time. What do we "profess"? What is it that we believe and give witness to when we engage students in the learning process?

Again, as chair of the roundtable, I heard the stories of genuine concern for students, for their success in their studies and their lives. I witnessed something that we too seldom acknowledge: our fondness for those we call "my students" and our hopes for them.

In becoming a community of teachers we became a community of learners as well. Peer mentoring has brought home to us the meaning of "lifelong learning." Volunteering comes in many forms but is essentially an act of hope. It is unthinkable that one should volunteer without hope that the effort will make a difference. And so it was as I observed my colleagues, volunteering their ideas, enthusiasm, and time; serving as consultants, observers, and presenters. What I learned from them was that we are a hopeful presence and that our efforts are making a significant difference in the transformation of academic librarianship in the state of Michigan. It was a rich and rewarding experience to chair this roundtable during a time of such extraordinary innovation and growth!

PREMIER's Future: Promoting Programs That Work

In February of 1996 the roundtable board met again with PREMIER volunteers to evaluate all aspects of the project to date: planners, presenters, facilitators, and others compared experiences and considered verbal and written feedback from the three pilot libraries. The consensus was that PREMIER had in good measure met its stated goals; the result was that PREMIER is no longer a pilot project, but continues to meet with interested libraries and is currently involved in planning its next research education colloquium, to be held early in 1997.

PREMIER's goals for instruction librarians and academic libraries—based on more than two years of open meetings and on the self-studies and subsequent experiences of its client libraries—continue to be

- the identification of instructional librarians as educators;

- articulation of the theoretical bases of information instruction;

- allocation of appropriate resources to support instructional services;

- the integration of information literacy into specific courses and curricula overall;

- the ongoing assessment of learning outcomes in libraries; and, finally;

- the key to all of the above, the development of close and continuing collaborations with classroom faculty and other academic professionals who contribute to the success of student researchers.

NOTE

1. Parker J. Palmer. "Divided No More: A Movement Approach to Educational Reform," *Change* 24 (March/April 1992): 10-17.

TO ENABLE INFORMATION COMPETENCY:
THE ABILITIES MODEL IN LIBRARY INSTRUCTION

Debra Gilchrist

INTRODUCTION

I'd like to talk today about outcomes assessment as revolutionizing learning, about outcomes assessment as one way to make programs work.

I must admit to feeling somewhat like an imposter addressing a conference with a theme of "Programs That Work" because we at Pierce College are just beginning our venture into this area. So I've taken the liberty of temporarily altering the conference theme to

"Programs That *Will* Work—We Hope."

I am not an expert in assessment, so my presentation will not be about how we "did it right," but instead about how we are attempting to have our program grow and develop within this assessment framework. I'd like to share our thoughts and philosophies as we worked through several scenarios and hopefully inspire you to think about your program in this light.

Our program was inspired by the program developed at Alverno College in Milwaukee, Wisconsin. They have 20 years of experience with assessment and have been a model for us as we forge ahead.

Gilchrist is director, library/media services, Pierce College, Lakewood, Washington.

Acknowledgment: This model was collaboratively developed with Kyzyl Fenno-Smith, instruction librarian, Pierce College.

I need to begin with recognition of my colleague Kyzyl Fenno-Smith, instruction librarian at Pierce College; this is not my work, but our work. This presentation is built upon sessions she and I have collaboratively developed.

My plan for the next hour is to look at three areas:

1) abilities as theory—the thinking Alverno did on assessment;

2) what we did with that thinking at our library; and

3) what this looks like in our library instruction curriculum.

To begin, please take a few moments to write down the goals for your interactions at reference. When a student approaches you at the reference desk, what do you most want from that interaction?

Abilities as Theory

Most outcomes assessment has been rooted in accountability or justification to administrators or funding sources. Indeed that was the case for us since our beginning was a legislative mandate. In 1990, the Washington state legislature directed all institutions of higher education to begin developing an outcomes assessment program. We were fortunate, however, since our legislature gave with that mandate several supportive elements.

The first was autonomy—they gave each college in the state complete freedom to develop a system that worked for that curriculum and for that campus. They wanted accountability but said we could each do it our own way.

Second, they gave each of the community colleges $60,000 per year for the last six years. From these funds we could all give release time to faculty members to coordinate assessment activities, fund mini-grants and travel, and offer workshops.

The third was the leadership provided by the hiring of an outcomes assessment coordinator for the state who could help us communicate with each other, plan statewide events, publish a newsletter, and keep us motivated.

Pierce College Process

We refer to 1991-1994 as our "dinking around" years. The college offered mini-grants to individual faculty or groups of faculty to test different assessment methods. In the library, we chose to examine quantitative and qualitative assessment.

We started out being very focused on skills, probably because quantitative evaluation was what we were most familiar with. We were looking to measure student success with individual tools and resources: for instance, whether students could find books on subjects they were looking for. We knew soon after we started that this was not the way to proceed since what we were measuring had little to do with our real teaching goals. We quickly moved on to qualitative assessment. As a progression, we examined the impact of library instruction with a few individual courses that utilized qualitative evaluation tools. At this phase, we administered pre-tests and post-tests with English classes that did and did not use library instruction, and we devised questions we wanted our faculty to think about and give us feedback on as they graded research papers.

We started this entire outcomes assessment process by asking, how can we determine what our students are learning and that we are teaching what we say we are teaching? But after our experimentation, it once again became clear to us, for at least the third time, that this wasn't the direction we wanted to go. We consequently ended up with a different and more substantive question, which was, how can we change our teaching to help students learn better? What we discovered is that we wanted an assessment program that helped our students become better learners. As we looked around the country for models, we were drawn to the work of Alverno College.

The central question at Pierce College had always been, "What do we want our students to *know* when they finish this course, this degree, this program?" Consequently, our course outlines, course goals, standard testing, et cetera always focused on knowledge. The Alverno model encouraged us to make a slight shift in that question and asks, "What do we want our students *to be able to do* after completion of this course, this degree, this program?"

As I mentioned, Alverno began this process 20 years ago. There, traditional outcomes assessment became what they call "student assessment-as-learning."

As you have on your handout, they define assessment-as-learning as "a process, integral to learning, that involves observation and judgment of each student's performance on the basis of explicit criteria, with resulting feedback to the student" (see sidebar 1).

Assessment-as-learning is multidimensional and performance-based and based on criteria that is explicit and "public." The learner participates in the assessment and the individual learner receives feedback.

At the heart of this theory is the belief that educators need to be concerned with what students achieve, not what teachers provide. To carry this out, they have identified eight abilities that they believe result in a successful liberal education—abilities such as communication, analysis, and social interaction. They have said that in order to be effective, these abilities must be integrated, developmental, and transferable.[2]

I put their definitions of those terms in sidebar 1, but I would like to tell you what they mean to me in terms of library instruction.

- **Integrated**—a combination of skills, behaviors, knowledge, values, attitudes, motives, and self-perceptions. Within library instruction, to be able to research effectively, students must be able to understand your perspective or the perspective of others, evaluate what they already know and need to know, to capture and relate key ideas or concepts, manipulate sources, value the process or their own questions enough to do good jobs, and perceive themselves as being able to be researchers.

- **Developmental**—progressive, implementing increasingly complex elements or processes for learning and assessing performance. Within library instruction, it is not just the research skills or research problem that progresses, but the student's thinking. For example: from writing basic citation

SIDEBAR 1:

Alverno College's Influence

Student Assessment-as-Learning:

A process, integral to learning, that involves observation and judgment of each student's performance on the basis of explicit criteria, with resulting feedback to the student.

Foundational Assumptions for Education at Alverno

1. Education goes beyond knowing to begin able to do what one knows.

2. Educators are responsible for making learning more available to the learner by articulating outcomes and making them public.

3. Abilities must be carefully identified in relation to what contemporary life requires.

4. Assessment is integral to learning.

Defining Abilities

● **Integrated:**
Combination of multiple components including skills, behaviors, knowledge, values, attitudes, motives or dispositions, and self perceptions.

● **Developmental:**
Increasingly complex elements or processes for learning and assessing performance.

● **Transferable:**
Prepare students for the many roles and settings in which they perform in life.

From: Student Assessment-as-Learning at Alverno College, Alverno College, 1994.

formats, students can see relationships between works; from those relationships, they can build mental connections between ideas and time and point of view; and from those connections they can understand development of ideas and influence of ideas.

- **Transferable**—prepare students for the many roles and settings in which they perform in life. Within library instruction, can students make meaning from their research questions and apply it to different circumstances? When faced with new inquiries, can they understand that information will assist them in their inquiries/decisions, use effective but modified search strategies from the time before, manipulate information found to correspond with these specific inquiries, and apply the information to satisfy the inquiries?

With each ability, students at Alverno are given specific criteria upon which they will be evaluated, the assessment is performance-based, and each student has an opportunity to play a role in the assessment. With an abilities approach, faculty are providing an opportunity for a student to respond to and demonstrate specific instructional goals or components, to tell you why they feel they met those goals.

The attraction here for us was that mystery grading is gone—students know how an instructor will be evaluating them. They can shift their efforts from guessing what the instructor wants to understanding what is actually important in the learning. They have measurable criteria upon which to act and it is no longer a secret, invisible process.

PIERCE'S PROGRAM

Pierce College is one of 32 state-funded community and technical colleges in Washington. We have a student population of 6,500 fte, 11,000 head count, and 4.75 library faculty. Our library contains 60,000 volumes, which is soon to be 90,000 due to the opening of a new branch in the fall of 1996. This places us on the large side of small and the small side of medium. The library has a teaching mission and all library faculty participate in reference and instruction.

Our Beginnings

The library started serious work with abilities in November 1994, and pilot-tested two courses in the 1994-95 academic year. This year we are refining our curriculum and expanding that scale, as well as placing

the information competency ability in the context of the faculty at large.

As a college, our faculty have identified five collegewide abilities:

- multiculturalism,

- citizenship/responsibility,

- information competency,

- communication, and

- critical thinking/problem solving.

These abilities will extend across the curriculum. As you can see, information competency is one of those collegewide abilities. What this means to us is that all faculty will be responsible for placing information competency into their curricula at appropriate points, and that we as library faculty will be teaching to the other four abilities as well.

When we looked at how to begin to implement the information competency ability, we started with the following questions (see sidebar 2).

1) What are abilities—what process do we need to understand?

2) What do we as a library faculty want to be able to do? use an abilities model in curriculum design, pedagogy, student-evaluation, self-evaluation.

3) What activities will demonstrate that we are able to use an abilities model for teaching and learning?

When we are able to

- define information competency—what is the student able to do?

- design abilities-based curricula—how will the student do this in a particular course?

- design abilities-based assignments—how will the student demonstrate the ability in the course?

- design abilities-based assessments—how will the performance be evaluated?

- use abilities-based pedagogy—how do we teach to the objectives, performances, and criteria we've defined? How do we teach our colleagues?

SIDEBAR 2:
The Library's Process:

1. What are the abilities - what processes do we need to understand?

2. What do we as a library faculty want to be able to do?
   Use an abilities model in:
   - curriculum design
   - pedagogy
   - student-evaluation
   - self-evaluation

3. What activities will demonstrate that we are able to use an abilities model for teaching and learning?
   We are able to:

   Define information competency   What is the student able to do?   Definition

   Design abilities-based:

   Curricula   How will the student do this in a particular course?   Objectives

   Assignments   How will the student demonstrate the ability in the course?   Performance

   Assessments   How will the performance be evaluated?   Criteria

   Use abilities-based:

   Pedagogy   How do we teach to the objectives, performances and criteria we've defined? How do we teach our colleagues?

   Assessment   How will we evaluate students, teach students to evaluate themselves and how will we evaluate our own teaching?

Handout conception by Kyzyl Fenno-Smith and Linda Strever, Pierce College, Lakewood WA

- use abilities-based assessment—how will we evaluate students, teach students to evaluate themselves, and evaluate our own teaching?

What we came up with is reflected in appendix 1: our definition, ability components, and generic criteria.

We developed generic criteria appropriate to the entire curriculum, but felt it was important to put specific criteria within the course, just as we do with our current course-integrated instruction. These criteria are not linear, and do not represent steps in a research process. Most of our criteria focused on the critical thinking aspects of research.

What struck me throughout this whole process was not what a tiny shift this was, but what a large product we got for such a small shift. It's common to develop goals for our teaching and to put those on a syllabus. But what Alverno taught us to do was to center those goals on the student and structure them in terms of ability and performance....it is subtle, but powerful and multi-dimensional in terms of impact.

We are now working with individual faculty to implement these criteria into specific courses. Using a current assignment, we discuss not only what they expect of the students, what they teach within the course, and what specifically they assess via this assignment, but also how to improve the assignment to effectively incorporate any of the information competency criteria we both agree are appropriate. This process is portrayed in appendix 2. The diagram is intended only to illustrate the process we use and questions we ask—it is not a form we complete. It depicts the progression the assignment might take if it were improved to incorporate one of our criteria. Faculty are often surprised at how much knowledge they have assumed their students have when they make a research assignment.

The collaboratively developed criteria are relayed to the student as part of the course assignment. Appendix 2 includes two examples, one for an English course and the second for a business course. Knowing that the research process is part of the final product and part of the evaluation process creates a new dynamic in the library instruction classroom, as more students directly inquire about the process and clearly understand why the session is part of the course.

Student self-assessment is a piece we are just beginning to develop. To give you an idea of how this might operate, sidebar 3 includes four examples of possible self-assessment techniques that could be used with assignments. Through these questions, students will evaluate their own work in light of the given criteria.

What Makes This Work?

I would like to propose several ideas for why I believe abilities are such a powerful tool for teaching information competency.

1) It revolutionizes learning, not just teaching. The fact that it is student-centered focuses our attention on their growth and their ability.

2) It is coordinated, integrated instruction, and very cross-disciplinary. We're very good at the departmental stuff but we often get stuck in the narrow chasms between our disciplines.

3) The research process gets evaluated—not just the end product of a student's work.

4) It gives students a way to grow beyond what they conceive of as research and what the faculty conceive of as research, as well as set the library's curriculum.

5) The interface between classroom instruction and reference is seamless.

6) Students learn to self-assess; they have a way to measure their quality after they leave the college. We talked a lot about lifelong learning in relationship to all education at Pierce College and how that was especially appropriate with library curriculum, and this piece that involves student self-assessment struck us as a particularly strong piece of that continued learning. Because they do self-assessment, students are aware of what comprises quality—they have a way to measure their own quality after they leave our institution. Their learning transitions them to new levels of thinking and independence.

7) The program is a multi-tiered approach that includes faculty and students, and is building on the current program.

8) The approach is consistent and has shape, but it is structured so as to be relevant to individual curricula. We work collaboratively with other faculty to both achieve goals for students in the context of their course, or, in the case of the vocational programs, their career training.

SIDEBAR 3:

INFORMATION COMPETENCY SELF ASSESSMENT

1. What are the important parts of this assignment?

2. How well have I done this? How do I know?

****

Describe the 3-5 most important things you learned about the research process while doing this assignment.

Describe the 3-5 most important things you learned about yourself as a researcher while doing this assignment

****

1. Briefly describe the assignment. What was it about?

2. Give 1 or 2 examples of your most successful research techniques or "finds." Explain what made them successful or good.

3. Give 1 or 2 examples, if relevant, of less successful research techniques or sources. What makes you say they are less successful?

4. The next time you confront a similar situation, what if anything could you do differently to increase your learning, research methods and productivity?

****

Looking at the criteria for information competency, which of these would you say you have accomplished through this assignment? Briefly explain why and how.

The Abilities Model in Library Instruction
Debra Gilchrist, Pierce College, Lakewood Washington

9) Students ask questions about the criteria, which makes library instruction a real two-way street. We have a way to make them aware of the components in library research. They ask what all of the criteria mean, which extends their own learning. We envision this will make reference even more of a key part of our instruction program.

10) This leads into the solution that our traditional 50-minute "problem" is resolved. No longer will we be looking at a "classroom time allowance" to fulfill an instructor's conscience about learning how to use the library.

Application to All Environments

Our entire college is adopting an abilities model, but what can you do with abilities on an individual level?

1) Let it inform your teaching and reference work. Prepare reference interactions around the outcome for the student, not your presentation of the answer.

2) Work with individual faculty with whom you do course-integrated instruction to set abilities/criteria into their assignments. In individual courses, you can teach to these abilities and students are aware of your goals.

We still have many questions. Do we show them *all* the criteria at once and overwhelm them? How do we do this with part-timers? What will this look like in the full curriculum?

EXERCISE:

At the beginning of the hour, I asked you to write down goals for your interactions at reference. If you would now, instead, write what you want your students to be able to do when you finish with them at the reference desk. Are these any different? Why? How can you articulate advantages to either or both? Our goal at Pierce College Library is to make these as much the same as we possibly can.

As I started to prepare this talk, I initially noted what I wanted you to be able to do after this hour:

1) explain/define abilities on a basic level;

2) understand the context in which our library operates with abilities and what we are doing with them to achieve information competency;

3) become interested enough in abilities so as to inquire about them by 1) asking a question; 2) conversing with someone during the conference; 3) reading an article;

4) understand the benefits/challenges of abilities in library instruction;

5) identify one way to begin to move toward this model yourself, if interested;

6) express/realize your own reactions and attitudes about abilities.

Looking Ahead

At Pierce College Library, we are anxious for the day when our students expect to be taught this way, when we reach critical mass with students who expect abilities in all their classes.

I can't think about outcomes assessment now as anything but educational reform. That's a long way from our initial beginnings that were focused on accountability. The real reason I want to assess is not because our legislature or accrediting body says that I should—but because I want to know more about what I am doing and what my students are learning. Using public, explicit criteria, students can engineer their own learning and assume key responsibility for their own education.

Abilities are a way to move beyond traditional ways of evaluating. It is an instructional endeavor that is not merely student-centered but student-active. Abilities are an effective way of instituting an information literacy/competency program that works for all.

NOTES

1. *Student Assessment-As-Learning at Alverno College* (Milwaukee, WI: Alverno College, 1979), 6.

2. *Student*, 9.

— DEBRA GILCHRIST —

APPENDIX 1:

Pierce College Library
Information Competency
Ability Components and Generic Criteria

Information competency is the ability to recognize a need for information, to persist in acquiring it, and to understand the value of information in personal, work, and academic life. An information competent individual can access, evaluate, organize, and apply information from a variety of sources and in a variety of contexts. An information competent student can:

1. **Recognize the value of information.**

   A. Student can recognize and value her need for information.

   B. Student can recognize herself as a questioner and inquiry as central to learning.

   C. Student persists in obtaining information that will meet her needs.

2. **Develop or formulate vocabulary based on the information needed.**

   A. Student can identify and use appropriate search language for the topic in question.

   B. Student can identify and use appropriate search language for the source being used.

   C. Student can identify and use language which describes broader, narrower, and related terms (synonyms).

   D. Students can identify and use thesauri and other tools to gather vocabulary.

3. **Understand information structures in different sources and contexts.**

   A. Student can identify and use macro structures, e.g. entire library, database or multi-volume work.

   B. Student can identify and use micro structures, e.g. search interfaces, indices, finding aids.

   C. Student can recognize and use conventions within micro structures, e.g. searchable fields, logical operators, alphabetical (browse) or keyword indexing and searching.

   D. Student can examine the whole, identify its parts, select and use appropriate micro structures or conventions in order to retrieve information.

4. **Identify potential sources.**

   A. Student recognizes libraries as providers of information and that different types of libraries serve different information needs.

B. Student can identify interested disciplines/groups/individuals who might produce information on a topic.

C. Student can analyze the presentation of information in various formats and select the most appropriate.

5. **Formulate Questions; develop and apply appropriate search strategies.**

A. Student recognizes the importance of formulating and asking questions.

B. Student can concisely articulate a specific problem/question.

C. Student can progressively state questions and identify subtopics while researching

D. Student can prioritize sources in order to organize her search effectively and efficiently.

E. Student is able to retrieve information, using a variety of methods and technologies.

F. Student can locate the pertinent sections of each information source.

G. Student is able to ascertain if there are gaps in the information found, and whether additional sources might be required.

H. Student can recognize when she has sufficient information to resolve her initial question.

6. **Analyze information sources.**

A. Student can recognize the bias or point of view of an information source and identify differing or opposing viewpoints.

B. Student can state several reasons why the chosen information source is valuable to the question.

C. Student can evaluate the authority or validity of an information source by considering:

   1. The qualifications of the author

   2. The date that the information was published or produced

   3. The relevance of the information: is it related directly or indirectly to the topic being researched?

   4. The completeness of the information

   5. The depth of the author's analysis

   6. The medium in which the information is published.

7. **Use information in critical thinking and problem-solving.**

A. Student can critically evaluate new information and, if warranted, integrate it into her existing body of knowledge.

B. Student can recognize the context and implications of information and determine the extent to which the information can be applied to other contexts.

C. Student can recognize the cultural context within which beliefs and knowledge exist.

D. Student can recognize her prior knowledge and critically evaluate its impact on her question.

E. Student can evaluate previously held assumptions or beliefs in the light of new information and modify those assumptions or beliefs accordingly.

F. Student can accept new information that is contrary to, as well as consistent with, previously held beliefs.

G. Student can recognize and tolerate the ambiguity of multiple points of view.

H. Student can explain how and why information applies to a specific problem.

8. **Organize, store, and manipulate the information gathered, ready for practical application.**

A. Student is able to document sources of all types and formats appropriately.

B. Student can identify the most widely-used styles of documentation, and use the appropriate style as determined by discipline.

C. Student can organize and reorganize the information found in ways that will ease future access to it, and that will enhance its usefulness, both to her and to others.

D. Student can recognize patterns, and categorize her information accordingly.

E. Student can construct a broad outline of the information found.

F. Student can write an abstract of each source, utilizing paraphrasing skills.

G. Student is able to re-retrieve information gathered earlier.

9. **Identify public policy issues relating to the access to and uses of information.**

A. Student can explain the concept of intellectual property rights, as it relates to patents, trademarks, and copyrighted materials.

B. Student can discuss the cultural contexts of intellectual property concepts.

C. Student is able to distinguish between "fair use" and plagiarism in various media and formats.

D. Student can discuss concepts and issues relating to freedom of expression.

E. Student can discuss the concepts of classified information and proprietary information.

10. **Identify the influence of market forces on information access.**

   A. Student can distinguish between mass market and specialty publishing, e.g. academic, small press, government.

   B. Student can describe the impact of advertising revenue and/or circulation (number of subscribers) on access to information, e.g. subscription prices, editorial influence of advertisers.

   C. Student can identify several factors that might influence their own access to information, e.g. cost, availability through libraries or bookstores, in/out of print.

APPENDIX 2:
"INCORPORATING CORE INTO ASSIGNMENTS" COMPETENCIES

Assignment: Research a company you might consider employment with, including size, structure, earnings, philosophy, history, and competition

Core Competency #6
Analyze information sources

	Expect	Teach	Assess
1. Student can recognize the bias or point of view of of an information source and identify differing or opposing viewpoints.			
2. Student can state several reasons why the chosen information source is valuable to the question.			

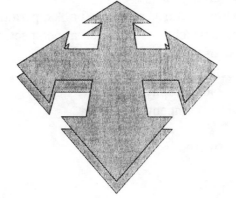

Assignment: Include information that indicates how the company sees itself, and how others (on the outside) perceive the company

Core Competency #6
Analyze information sources

	Expect	Teach	Assess	Learning Activity	Assessment Meas.
1. Student can recognize the bias or point of view of of an information source and identify differing or opposing viewpoints.					
2. Student can state several reasons why the chosen information source is valuable to the question.					

Assignment: Career and Employment Outlook Information Analysis

Goals: To locate information about specific companies; To utilize the information in preparing for an interview and/or determining if the company is one you would be interested in working for. To build understanding of the types of business information available and how to think about and access that information.

Select and investigate a company you would like to be employed with. Prepare a typewritten report including the following information: size of the company; organizational structure; holding company (if applicable); location(s); earnings; company philosophy; company history, competition. Include information that indicates how the company sees itself, and how others (outside of the company) perceive the company and how you used the information to determine you wanted to work there. Compare and contrast the types of sources you used, including criteria you employed to select these sources as authoritative information.
A bibliography with a minimum of 4 sources is required.

The project is due on Wednesday May 29

You will be evaluated on your ability to:
Identify and use a variety of sources, such as reference books, periodical articles...
Identify , describe and use sources which provide different perspectives or point of view, and to
       identify the point of view of the source
Evaluate why the source was useful
Properly format citations for the bibliography
Use the information to illustrate the company
Write clearly
...Additional criteria from the instructor.....

English 221, British Literature

Assignment: A research paper on a topic of the student's choice. The purposes of the assignment are to learn how to begin to conduct research and to integrate the resulting information with the reading of an assigned literary text to further illuminate the interpretation of that text....

You will be evaluated on your ability to:

Choose a research topic appropriate for enabling a more indepth interpretation of the literature
Formulate the central question to narrow and focus the search
Study the new information and synthesize it with the previous interpretation of the literature
Start the composition process; produce a topic outline
Explain in writing exactly what the new information reveals about the literature and how this
       expands the interpretation of the text.
Document with parenthetical citations and a Works Cited page according to Modern Language
       Association guidelines.

In a research journal format:
Identify key concepts, words and names
Develop and describe an effective search strategy
Analyze the information for usefullness and return insignificant data

****

"The Abilities Model in Library Instruction," Debra Gilchrist, Pierce College, Lakewood, WA

PANEL
PRESENTATION

PROGRAMS THAT WORK: PANEL DISCUSSION

Thomas G. Kirk, Jr., Patricia Iannuzzi, Corinne Laverty, Carla List, and Margaret Fain

Through e-mail communications and a telephone conference call the panel developed the following factors considered characteristic of a successful library/information research instruction program. The program

√ is linked to the goals and educational philosophy of the institution;

√ receives library (and college) administrative support;

√ is supported by the teaching faculty;

√ has stated objectives/outcomes/mission/goals (perhaps not the entire program but for individual sessions);

√ is designed to meet the needs of the students;

√ evolves continually to incorporate changing technology and curricula;

√ is assessed/evaluated regularly;

√ incorporates active learning techniques whenever possible; and

√ includes an infrastructure to provide clerical support, instructional materials, facilities, and so on.

Based on this list of characteristics each panel member provided a written description of her or his institution's program and how the program exemplified the characteristics of success. What follows is a brief summary of the program descriptions and the panel presentations of each panel member. Each panel member can be reached at his or her appropriate e-mail address above.

Kirk is college librarian, Lilly Library, Earlham College (kirkto@earlham.edu); *Iannuzzi* is head, reference department, Florida International University Libraries, University Park, Miami, Florida (Iannuzzi@servms.fiu.edu), < http://www.fiu. edu/~library/assistance/index.html >; *Laverty* is instructional services librarian, Queen's University at Kingston, Ontario, Canada (lavertyc@QUCDN. QueensU.CA); *List* is librarian, instruction services group, State University of New York (SUNY) at Plattsburgh, Benjamin F. Feinberg Library (listck@splava.cc.plattsburgh.edu); and *Fain* is assistant head of public services, Kimbel Library, Coastal Carolina University, Conway, South Carolina (margaret@coastal.edu).

EARLHAM COLLEGE

Thomas G. Kirk, Jr.

The Institution

Earlham College is a four-year liberal arts college of about 1,100 students located in Richmond, Indiana. In addition to the liberal arts college, the libraries serve two seminaries: Earlham School of Religion (Society of Friends, i.e., Quaker) and Bethany Seminary (Church of the Brethren). The college is well known for its emphasis on teaching and learning and the quality of its programs. It has been cited in a number of guides and studies as a program of high quality.[1]

The college's curriculum is highly interdisciplinary, with a global focus, and emphasizes active learning through student research, laboratory, and field work and other experiential learning.

The Libraries

The Earlham libraries consist of the main Lilly Library and the Wildman Science Library, which is located within the science classroom/lab/office complex. Lilly Library was built in 1963 and renovated and expanded in 1990-1993. It houses the campus Computer and Media Services, but they are administratively separate units. Both libraries have 24-hour accessible computer labs. The Earlham libraries

√ contain approximately 360,000 volumes and subscribe to 1,250 periodicals and newspapers. Earlham is a selective depository for U.S. government documents;

√ are members of PALNI (Private Academic Library Network of Indiana), a consortium that provides the library catalog and an integrated online system. The library has a number of non-networked CD-ROMs and uses FirstSearch and DIALOG for expanded access to databases. In the case of DIALOG, we are a Classroom Instruction Program (CIP) user and have four simultaneous subscription accounts and 12 hourly rate accounts;

√ have an information technology and reference/instruction librarian who, among other things, is developing the library's World Wide Web pages. These pages provide highly selective links to resources that we are teaching in our instruction program (<http://www.earlham.edu/htmldocs/library/pages/li binfos.htm>).

The Instruction Program

Earlham's program of bibliographic instruction has been widely presented in the literature.[2] However, the description is not completely up-to-date. Because of the earlier descriptions, what follows will highlight very recent developments and projected changes for 1996-97. The changes are partially in response to the college's move from a three-courses-per-term/three-terms-a-year calendar to a semester calendar.

The first contact the library has with new students is through the administration of a short library test during New Student Week. This test has long been used at Earlham for two purposes: 1) It emphasizes the importance of library use and gives us some introductory contact with students; and 2) The results were used to select about 20 to 25 students who appear to have had little experience in using the library. They were asked to come to the library to do a few exercises that provided a basic introduction to the catalog and a general periodical index. We now believe, because of

the variety of online catalogs and electronic indexes, that we cannot accurately detect the students who have little experience. Furthermore, we had declining success in getting students to come in and do the exercises. We continue to use a test that has been dramatically redesigned to examine for search skills and decoding of citation types. The test results are used by the instruction librarians as a guide to what problems we might need to address in first-year classes. Of course, the giving of the test continues to serve the larger purpose of giving us contact with new students and demonstrating the central role of the library and the importance of information research techniques.

In the new semester system, the introduction to the library will continue to be "housed" in the first-year humanities courses (Humanities A and B). During the first semester, students will meet in the library in small groups to be introduced to librarians and to carry out an exercise that focuses on use of the online catalog. At some time during the rest of the year, faculty will make a mini-research assignment that involves finding information related to the books being read in the course. These will most likely fall in one of four categories: 1) biographical information about an author, 2) book reviews, 3) background study of the time period treated in the book or the time period when the book was published, or 4) word decoding. During Humanities C (which is a course in history or literature), best taken during the sophomore year, students will write full-fledged research papers and students will have class sessions on the use of library resources provided by the librarians.

Ecological biology, which introduces the use of the scientific literature, will continue largely unchanged. This course is taken by about 55 percent of all graduates as part of their science general education electives and therefore makes a major contribution to the bibliographic instruction program. The course-related program of instruction in support of library assignments in departmental offerings also continues. We are making changes in the content and the style of our teaching. Because of the extensive use of DIALOG's CIP program, a major effort is being made to teach it wherever appropriate. This activity is done as a lab with one or two students to a microcomputer. After a brief introduction to the basics of searching, students log on and practice. Students receive a short handout of instructions and the bluesheets for the relevant databases. We are also introducing the World Wide Web, as appropriate, to courses. We have not emphasized search engines and have instead pointed to sites which have the information that is useful for specific assignments. To support these activities, we plan to install a microcomputer lab in the reference area this summer.

The key element of our course-related program is the interaction between librarians and classroom faculty. Each term librarians are assigned to faculty, usually by department. The librarians make contact with the faculty to gather information on assignments and to plan how the library will support the students' work on library-related assignments. This leads to classroom presentations, bibliographies, and other instructional material.

Definitions of Success

Elements of success (or effectiveness) are never absolute nor a universal perception. Rather success or effectiveness is a perception that is articulated by library constituencies: college administration, faculty, students, college alumni and friends, and others. Because of differences in the relationship of the constituencies to the library, their expectations and the sense of how well the library has met those expectations will be different from that of other constituencies. A second important concept on which this definition of success is based is that the library's success cannot be independent of the success of the college generally. Therefore, definitions of success or effectiveness must be more inclusive than narrowly defined library skills and use.

Evidence of Success

1) Students demonstrate competence in locating, reading, evaluating, and summarizing information resources in upper-level project papers and presentations.

   Repeatedly students give testimony as to the importance of the research skills that they learned at Earlham. Most recently a group of students returning from internships off campus were asked to write about their experiences. Two of the questions asked were, "What did I bring to the internship?" and "How did Earlham prepare you for the internship?" The most consistently articulated idea in the interns' responses was their research skills that they had confidently learned at Earlham.

   Other evidence of students' competence in information and library research comes from the many letters from alumni that talk about their undergraduate experiences and the importance of the library and research skills in their endeavors after college.

2) Faculty are proactive in involving library use in course planning and in contacting librarians when assignments are to be made.

It is not uncommon for faculty early in their course planning to call librarians and get them involved in the design of course assignments. Recently a professor in politics who wanted teams of students to develop a set of World Wide Web pages on a global problem called upon the library for help. Since the assignment had a different purpose and research product, she was interested in how the library might assist students who would be using both print resources and Web resources. While the library did not teach hypertext markup language, it did provide instruction in using traditional print reference works, CD-ROM periodical indexes, DIALOG, and Web search engines.

A second example involves the restructuring of the humanities sequence described above. The faculty recognized a responsibility to support the library's efforts and the questions focused around how to best integrate the library into the course so that the goals of the course and the library meshed.

3) The extensiveness of the program's contact with students.

   In the last few months, the library has completed a study of the extensiveness of the instruction program. A survey of the courses taken by the class of 1993 reveals some interesting characteristics of the distribution of the instruction program and students' exposure to it. Of the some 2,500 courses that the class of 1993 took over the years they were enrolled at Earlham, only 598, or 24 percent, used bibliographic instruction. However, 94 percent of the graduating seniors of 1993 (235) had six or more sessions of bibliographic instruction during their time at Earlham. Furthermore, those sessions were dispersed across the curriculum and included courses in humanities, the social sciences, and the sciences. The six percent who did not have at least six sessions were not concentrated in one discipline or program. Rather they appear to be isolated cases with unusual programs or were transfer students who had beginning courses waived.

4) Members of the administration and the faculty give high priority to the library and have demonstrated an awareness of the library's role.

   Perhaps the best example was the faculty's strong support of the library during a period of severe pressure on budgets. Despite cuts in other areas of the college's budget, the faculty expressed strong support for an increase in the library's budget. The support was often expressed in terms of the importance of the library to their teaching and student learning. While such statements might be perceived as hollow "library as heart of the college" rhetoric, in this case that is untrue. Given the level of library use and instruction and the strong emphasis on helping students become self-learners, it is clear that the faculty see the quality of the library's collection as directly related to their ability to make course assignments that engage students in library research.

Another example is a faculty-student collaborative research program funded by grants from the Ford and Knight foundations. The endowed fund allows faculty to be released from teaching one regular course in a year to work on research projects with usually four to six students. The projects are areas of faculty interest that are outside their specialties and therefore engage the faculty and students in collaborative efforts to learn the subjects. The program is a competitive one to which faculty must submit proposals. In developing the program, administrators and faculty recognized the need to include library purchases in the project proposals so that adequate support from the library would be available. The faculty recognized that since the areas of research were going to be subjects that had not been taught, the library's collection would presumably not be sufficient to support the intense work of five to seven researchers and therefore the library needed extra support.

5) The library program has a central place in the nature of the college and the quality of its program. This central role is prominent in the publicity about the college and its program.

The college's admissions and development offices give special attention to the library's program in their publications and in recognizing the quality of the college's academic program and resources. Typical of this attention is the section of the admissions/public relations' "Curriculum Guide" used to describe Earlham and its program. Here are several examples.

In the section describing the nature of Earlham's general education program it states:

Second, the general education requirements force (and there is an element of compulsion it this) to acquire a variety of skills. Students must learn to write clearly (humanities), to conduct laboratory experiments (sciences),...to use the library (all departments)....

In the section describing the libraries of the college, the importance to the academic program is stressed:

The primary purpose of a college library is to supply students with appropriate study and research material. This seems a straightforward and simple task, and yet it has implications for the library program at Earlham College. First it means providing an environment....Second, it means building a collection....Third, it means making these materials available....Fourth, it means making connections with other libraries. Finally, it means ensuring that the library is used effectively. This final implication for library service—ensuring that students make effective use of a library's resources—...is taken seriously at Earlham College, and in many courses the means of finding and evaluating information is stressed.

The library system, consisting of Lilly Library and Wildman Science Library, is widely recognized as one of the best teaching libraries in the nation.

6) Students have an appreciation for the role of the library, have basic skills in research, and act upon that appreciation and use those skills.

Perhaps the best, although insufficient, evidence of the students' appreciation is the change in the frequency with which the library is used between entering students and graduating seniors. Regularly the college administers a survey to determine the values and orientation of students. The survey results indicate that aside from increased use of computers the largest change in behaviors is the increased use of the library. The survey in 1993, for example, indicated a 35 percent increase in agreement with the statement "Studied in the library."

7) Students have a sense of confidence in using libraries and therefore can exercise their skills in a variety of settings and for a variety of purposes.

8) The quality of the program is recognized by outsiders who visit and study the program.

The Earlham program has been widely studied by visiting librarians, library school students, and researchers of higher education. Sidebar 1 is a list of some of the publications that describe it.

While the Earlham program has been and is successful it also faces significant challenges in maintaining that success. Some of those challenges are enumerated below:

1) The most obvious is complacency. The program could continue to exist and operate for a number of years on the basis of past successes. However, unless the challenges listed below are addressed the momentum will be lost and the program will atrophy.

2) The program is in a period of significant uncertainty created by changes in library staffing and faculty. The library staff now looks very different than it did a few years ago. The new staff must develop an ownership of the program and must create the program to meet their goals and those of a new curriculum and new faculty.

    For the past few years and into the early part of the next millennium there will be significant turnover among the faculty. The support for the program that was developed over the first ten or so years of the program may disappear. A new generation of faculty, as they enter the college, will need to be cultivated and the value of the program demonstrated all over again.

3) The college is changing from a term calendar (i.e., a quarter system without the summer quarter) to a semester calendar. It is important that the library staff be in close touch with faculty as they restructure their courses. In arguing for a semester system the proponents of the change pointed to the longer period available for students to develop a research project. The library staff needs to be attentive to making the projects work.

4) The content of the program needs to be revised as the nature of the library's resources evolves. The increased use of electronic resources such as DIALOG, FirstSearch, and the World Wide Web needs to be integrated with continued attention to print resources. The program must give increased attention to basic electronic searching skills (e.g., distinctions between heading searches and keyword searches, Boolean operations, adjacency and truncation; the nature of databases and the special challenges of full-text searching) and to evaluation of electronic resources since so much of the Web's sources are inadequate from a scholarly point of view.

SIDEBAR 1: PUBLICATIONS THAT DESCRIBE EARLHAM COLLEGE'S LIBRARY INSTRUCTION PROGRAM

Breivik, Patricia Senn. "Making the Most of Libraries in the Search for Academic Excellence." *Change* 19 (July-August 1987): 44-52.

Cline, Hugh F., and Loraine T. Sinnott. *Building Library Collections: Policies and Practices in Academic Libraries*. Lexington, MA: Lexington Books, 1980.

Eberhart, George M. "Earlham College Still a Model for Course-Integrated BI." *College & Research Libraries News* 46 (June 1985): 295.

Feinman, Valerie Jackson. "Library Instruction: What Is Our Classroom?" *Computers in Libraries* 14 (February 1994): 33-36.

Hardesty, Larry, Jamie Hastreiter, and David Henderson. "Earlham's BI Enhances Teaching and Learning." *College & Research Libraries News* 53 (June 1992): 402-403.

Johnson, Pyke. "A Day with a College Librarian: Quaker School Library Takes an Activist Role." *Publishers Weekly* 213 (9 January 1978): 41-44.

Rader, Hannelore B. "Bibliographic Instruction Programs in Academic Libraries." In *Increasing the Teaching Role of Academic Libraries, New Directions for Teaching and Learning* no. 18. Ed. by Tom Kirk, 63-78. San Francisco: Jossey Bass, 1984.

Rader, Hannelore B. "Information Literacy and the Undergraduate Curriculum." *Library Trends* 44 (Fall 1995): 270-278.

Taylor, Susan Krehbiel. "Successful Bibliographic Instruction Programs at Three Small Liberal Arts Colleges." (Earlham, Berea, and Sterling Colleges) *Research Strategies* 11 (Fall 1993): 242-247.

Wilkinson, Billy R. *Reference Services for Undergraduate Students; Four Case Studies*. Metuchen, NJ: Scarecrow Press, 1972.

5) The methods of delivery need to be revised to respond to new ideas about active learning and changes in the way courses are taught.

6) Because higher education is increasingly being challenged to demonstrate the effectiveness of its programs the library must do a better job of

demonstrating its effectiveness. This requires thoughtfully constructed mechanisms for getting feedback from both current students and alumni. This most likely means integrating the library into surveys conducted by academic departments and programs of their graduates, and surveys conducted by the college at large.

NOTES

1. Loren Pope, *Colleges That Change Lives: 40 Schools You Should Know about Even if You're Not a Straight A Student* (New York: Penguin Books, 1996).

2. The most recent description is contained in *Library Orientation Series 24: Bibliographic Instruction in Practice: A Tribute to the Legacy of Evan Ira Farber*, ed. by Larry Hardesty, Jamie Hastreiter, and David Henderson (Ann Arbor: Pierian Press, 1993).

FLORIDA INTERNATIONAL UNIVERSITY

Patricia Iannuzzi

About Florida International University

Florida International University (FIU), the public university serving South Florida, is one of ten universities in Florida's State University System (SUS). Only 24-years old, we are one of the fastest growing public universities in the country, with 28,000 students, 860 faculty, and over 200 degree programs, including 100 at the graduate level. The main campus, including University Park, is located in Miami, in southwest Dade County, and the North Miami campus is located approximately 60 miles northeast in North Miami. FIU serves the dynamic, intensely multicultural, urban community of South Florida. Pertinent demographics about our students include the following:

- 54 percent are part-time students,

- six percent are international students,

- 66 percent are minority, and

- the average age of an FIU student is 27-years old.

Miami Dade Community College, the largest community college in the United States, is our major feeder institution, providing several thousand transfer students each year. All first-year students are required to take at least one, and usually two semesters of freshman composition. All first semester students are also required to take a freshmen experience seminar.

About the FIU Libraries

The FIU Libraries are comprised of two physical buildings, one centralized facility at the University Park campus and one at North Miami, as well as a wide array of electronic library services offered to remote users. Holdings include one million volumes and 9,800 serial subscriptions. The Florida Center for Library Automation (FCLA) provides programming and other systems support for the statewide Library User Information System (LUIS). LUIS is the Notis-based integrated library system containing the OPACs of the SUS libraries, dozens of mounted databases, and gateways to subscription and other services accessed via the Internet (RLIN, RLIN-Citadel, Uncover, library catalogs worldwide, and more). In addition to LUIS, the Libraries have a two-campuswide area network for CD-ROM databases available from within the library as well as from remote locations. We are currently migrating LUIS access from dumb terminals to networked PCs capable of providing access to multiple services including the CD Network and the WWW using Netscape, in addition to LUIS.

The library at University Park is halfway through a three-year, $23 million construction project. The reference department at University Park has a staff of ten librarians and three library assistants. Point-of-use instruction is provided at a reference desk, a LUIS help and general information desk, and from LUIS "rovers." Staff from other library departments volunteer as teachers or trainers in the library instruction program.

The Library Instruction Program

The library instruction program is comprised of several smaller programs designed to complement each other. One of the major objectives of our library instruction program is to insure the participation of every student at FIU. Since over 100 sections would be necessary for a required credit course, the size of the student body prohibits that strategy. In order to meet our objective of reaching every student, we designed the first key component of our library instruction program: the Library Certification Program. Partnered with the freshman composition program and required for all sections, first-year composition classes are scheduled by their instructors to come to the library for a sequence of two classes. The first class, "Critical Thinking in the Information Age," introduces students to LUIS as a "gateway to the world of information."

A LUIS competency test is part of this class. The second class, "Research Strategies," is scheduled when students have topics and uses an active learning "research strategy worksheet" for students to complete as part of the class session. A third class previously included in the sequence has recently been restructured as a multimedia-based tutorial.

Building upon our success with the Library Certification Program, we have expanded the program into the core curriculum, working with specific departments and programs to build in required sequences of classes linked to core classes for upper-division students. Each program is designed together with faculty from that program, coordinating course objectives and outcomes to library classes and designing assignments together. We are working our way across the curriculum, and examples of our established programs include engineering, biology, history, public speaking, and psychology. Programs vary from as little as one required class for psychology majors, to an eight-class sequence for engineering majors.

For many departments we provide tailored workshops of varying length from three to eight hours in length for graduate students and faculty incorporating a wide range of resources spanning print and electronic formats. These popular "Research Strategies" workshops are generally coordinated with the department chairperson or library representative.

A continuing component of our library instruction program is the traditional "course-related" instruction. Increasingly, however, students in these classes now have a foundation of skills acquired through the Library Certification Program in their freshman year. Furthermore, a request for course-related instruction is a beginning of a negotiation process with the department to develop a more formal sequence of instruction for that discipline. This coordination must take place at the department chair/program director level in order to involve all faculty and to build in the "required" component. Faculty are often helpful in initiating the process, helping to design the library classes, and collaborating with librarians to design assignments.

Other components of our program include a term paper advisory service; open sign-up for training on specific electronic products and services; a self-paced audio tour; assignment troubleshooting service; and a wide variety of course-related instruction.

We Know We've Been Successful When...

• Faculty submit more requests for library instruction than we can meet.

• Student evaluations show increased knowledge of library collections and services.

• FIU students demonstrate greater skills using LUIS and LUIS databases in our public areas, and ask more sophisticated questions.

• Faculty evaluations note an improvement in the quality of sources cited in papers.

• We still see students using print abstracts and indexes because they know about them and understand when they still need to use them.

• Statewide database use for the mounted and gateway files shows FIU use proportionately and consistently higher—a fact we attribute to increased awareness from aggressive instruction and assignments requiring a wide range of services.

• There was that day in September when we taught 14 classes in one day.

• The faculty senate voted to include librarians as eligible for "Excellence in Teaching" awards.

• The provost funded two new lines to the reference department, including one for a new position of library instruction coordinator.

• We got our second classroom, and our first one is being wired to accommodate 16 networked workstations for hands-on instruction.

• We received our first grant from the Academy for the Art of Teaching.

• We taught 139 classes to 3,839 students in 1991/92 as compared to 516 classes to 10,489 students in 1994/95 with the same level of staffing.

We Will Be More Successful When...

• We hire a coordinator of library instruction.

• We have articulated goals and objectives modeled on the ACRL model.

• We develop a strategy to reach all the transfer students.

• Every department chair and dean knows what information literacy means for his or her discipline, and works with the library to build in a requirement for his or her students.

QUEEN'S UNIVERSITY AT KINGSTON, ONTARIO

Corinne Laverty

INTRODUCTION

The Institution

Queen's University is the earliest degree-granting institution of higher learning in central Canada and comprises 15 faculties, colleges, and professional schools: Arts and Science, Applied Science, Business, Education, Graduate Studies and Research, Industrial Relations, Law, Medicine, Music, Nursing, Physical and Health Education, Policy Studies, Rehabilitation Therapy, Theology, and Urban and Regional Planning. The university currently enrolls 16,000 degree candidates (including 2,500 graduate and 4,000 continuing education students) from every Canadian province and territory and from more than 80 nations around the world. Queen's employs 4,000 people (40 librarians) on either a full-time or a part-time basis, including 1,000 full-time faculty.

Queen's University Library System

The Queen's University library system is decentralized and includes 16 libraries. Stauffer Library houses the humanities and social sciences collections, government documents, maps and air photos, reserve service, special collections, library administration, and special readers' services.

There are three major faculty libraries in education, law, and health sciences, and 12 branch libraries are spread across the campus. A new engineering and science library will open in 1997 to amalgamate the corresponding branch libraries.

The library system holds over four million items including 1.7 million volumes as well as microforms, maps, air photos, recordings, videos, and subscriptions to 12,000 periodicals and newspapers. There are 17 networked journal indexes available across campus and from home, and another 25 databases are used at stand-alone CD-ROM workstations. Queen's libraries have a strong presence on the Web (<http://130.15.161.74>) with various pages on information-related tools and sites as well as a variety of subject pathfinders which present a complete research strategy with recommended indexes and Internet resources. A section of "how-to" guides and library tutorials is under development as the library system moves to a Web interface as its default access point from the public terminals. Web access is available from all 100 workstations at Stauffer Library and selected machines at other campus libraries. Stauffer is also equipped with a 24-machine electronic training room.

STAUFFER LIBRARY INSTRUCTION PROGRAM

Orientation Programs

The Stauffer instruction program responds to information skills training in a number of ways. At the beginning of the school year, eight orientation programs are used to create awareness of the library as a dynamic learning resource. New arts and sciences undergraduates (about 1,500) are divided into five-person teams to participate in a library quiz. Each team is led by an upper-year student who sets the tone for the need to learn to use the library. The quiz itself focuses on useful information such as the whereabouts of the calendar advertising instruction programs, the location of the reserve collection, and the library directory showing call numbers and collections on each floor. New faculty, graduates, dons-in-residence, international and part-time studies students, and teaching assistants (TAs) attend other introductory events. Physical tours of the Stauffer Library are offered for two weeks at the start of each term. A self-guided walking tour and special tours by appointment are also provided.

All new graduates (about 800) receive flyers in their registration packages inviting them to attend a one-hour hands-on introduction to the library relating to either the humanities/social sciences or the general sciences. These sessions are timed to initiate new users at the beginning of the fall term by providing an overview of electronic resources and special graduate-student concerns such as interlibrary loan service, borrowing privileges, and Internet access. Many classes of graduate students return later in the year with their instructors for a specialized workshop on research tools associated with particular courses.

Seventy dons-in-residence (upper-year students) are trained to give basic library direction to any of the 3,100 students who live in residence. In late August they attend a three-hour jigsaw workshop that presents key study skill and information-finding concepts. This includes working through a sample research strategy including how to formulate a topic, brainstorm for keywords, identify appropriate types of information tools, recognize the principles of keyword searching in electronic databases, and evaluate information. This experience will reinforce the basic problem-solving skills needed to undertake research, the methods by which they can help students, and the people to whom they should turn for comprehensive assistance. This September, all residence rooms will be wired to access the library system so dons will provide increasing assistance to students in terms of offering basic library instruction and directing them to pertinent help sources.

Teaching Assistants Workshops

Workshops for TAs focus on their roles as research strategy mentors in bi-weekly meetings with 25 to 30 students who are enrolled in classes of up to 1,000. Although Stauffer has offered walk-in sessions on using the catalog, various indexes, and the Internet throughout the term in the past, TAs are better able to work with students one-on-one and in small groups on an ongoing basis. A session to train the trainers who in turn make arrangements for subsequent TA learning sessions is given in the summer and outlines how the library can help prepare them to demonstrate appropriate research strategies for their students.

Library Initiatives for Faculty

Several learning initiatives for faculty are offered throughout the year to stimulate interest in the library and to forge new faculty/librarian partnerships in the teaching process. These include a Technology and Education Day, a Spring Institute where innovative approaches to teaching are discussed and practiced, and faculty awareness sessions during the term concerning new library products and programs of instruction. The first awareness session provides an overview of electronic information tools in the library system, describes common student problems in navigating these resources, and offers support to train students in the use of materials that faculty expect them to consult for their assignments. Teaching librarians give instruction in the electronic training room but also travel to lecture halls to give presentations to large classes. Workshops for faculty provided later in the year address new tools of common interest such as *Current Contents* or comparisons of search engines on the Internet.

Course-Integrated Instruction

Course-integrated instruction offered at Stauffer Library involves tailor-made workshops for individual course assignments. Students attend hands-on classes in the 24-computer electronic training room. Handouts describing research strategy, applicable indexes, examples of search techniques, and student tasks are designed for each assignment. Stauffer currently provides this type of instruction for 50 courses in the humanities and social sciences. The library also offers a research strategy assignment, which can be adapted to any course. It outlines a series of research steps and requires students to record their information-gathering

process and the resulting list of resources on their topics.

Research Strategy Assignment

Last year, the curriculum-integrated library assignment for a first-year sociology class of 1,000 students was formally evaluated. For the past three years, each class of students completed a four-page research strategy library assignment as part of his or her first research essay in the second term of classes. The strategy is introduced by the instruction librarian during class time and then followed up by teaching assistants within weekly tutorial hours. The assignment is marked by TAs as part of an essay in classes for geography, sociology, physical education, and political science and student evaluations indicate that it is a valuable tool for library users. This year, women's studies has agreed to incorporate the strategy assignment into all four years of its degree program, increasing the complexity of search tools over the course of the degree.

General Instructional Sessions

During the 1995-1996 term, three different hands-on sessions were offered to the Queen's community. From September to May, sessions on "Navigating the Electronic Library and Searching Indexes on CD-ROM" were offered at the start of each term. At peak times, such as the month of September, these sessions were offered three times a week. An "Internet Primer" class continued to be popular throughout the year, and in January 1996 an advanced class on search engines was launched; it continues to be offered twice a week throughout the term and twice a month during the summer.

All instruction sessions are designed with clearly defined knowledge, skills, and attitudinal objectives. An example of these objectives for the introductory Internet class is shown in sidebar 2.

Definitions of Success

The effectiveness of a library instruction program may be measured in different ways depending on the nature of library involvement within an organization and the perception of that involvement by members of the institution. While noteworthy characteristics of a successful program have already been outlined, the key component in the success of the program at Stauffer Library is its continual evolution to meet changing user needs, adapt to new information technologies, and focus campus attention on the role of libraries in the learning process.

SIDEBAR 2: EXAMPLE OF OBJECTIVES OF INTRODUCTORY INTERNET CLASS

Internet Primer: Part 1

Knowledge Objectives
Students will understand

- that finding information on the Internet requires a multi-step research strategy;

- that resources on the Internet should be viewed as part of a continuum of information resources rather than as a replacement for traditional materials such as books and articles;

- that the Internet provides access to a wide range of resources including software, files, statistics, electronic journals, selected books, and complete databases;

- that Internet resources are not evaluated or standardized and that Internet contributors include commercial enterprises, academic and other educational institutions, and private individuals;

- that the basic uses of the Internet are to communicate and to find information using a variety of navigational tools;

- that the World Wide Web is the largest information system on the Internet, includes graphics and sound, and is a focal point for searching the Internet because all Internet resources can potentially be accessed from it;

- that addresses for useful sites can be recorded within a bookmark file which can be copied to disk;

- that part or all of specific files can be printed, copied to disk, or pasted into existing documents;

- that Netscape is the preferred browsing software for the Web at Queen's and that it is available free-of-charge to members of the Queen's community for use at home and in the office, given the required supporting hardware and software. Students are referred to the Computing Information Centre to obtain copies of software and accompanying information sheets;

- that information on the Internet is not standardized or evaluated and must be reviewed carefully with reference to the evaluation checklist provided; and

- that information quoted, cited, or copied from the Internet must be referenced accurately in footnotes and bibliographies according to standard procedures for the citing of electronic information.

Skills Objectives
Students will be able to

- identify and execute a series of information-gathering steps that comprise a research strategy as they use the browser Netscape to search the Web;

- recognize hypertext links and their corresponding URLs;

- accurately type addresses into the Location Box recognizing the importance of spacing and case sensitivity;

- create a bookmark file of selected Web sites and identify how the file can be exported and imported;

- identify how text files, HTML files, and graphics can be saved to disk;

- distinguish between Web pages created by commercial enterprises, educational institutions, and private individuals;

- distinguish between Internet subject collections that provide access by subject and Internet search engines that provide access by keyword;

- manipulate the button and scroll bars, and use the mouse to move to hypertext links, in order to control Netscape effectively;

- identify the signs that a file is loading, has stopped loading, or has loaded imperfectly;

- identify signs that Netscape is no longer operational and close the application; and

- search the reserve collection on the Queen's Library home page as well as Internet resources by subject and by academic department.

Attitude Objectives
Students will have confidence

- that they can use Netscape to perform basic Internet information searches; and

- that they can inquire at the reference desk for assistance with future Internet searches.

Measures of Success

The Stauffer Library instruction program can be considered successful from the following points of view:

1) Librarians continue to witness a growing appreciation by students, staff, and faculty of the role of the library and librarian in the learning process. This is reflected in the number of students attending instruction sessions (see figure 1); the number of faculty interested in working with librarians to provide instruction; increased student interest spurred by Internet instruction (see figure 2); and more advanced questions asked at the reference desk for discernible groups that have received instruction.

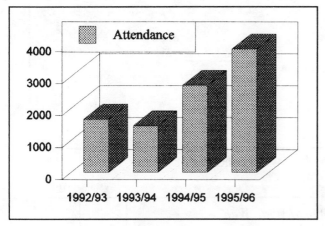

Figure 1: Stauffer Library Instruction

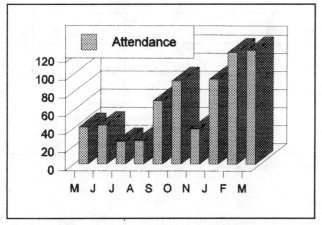

Figure 2: Internet Primer 1995/96

2) More students receive contact with the library each year as a result of new liaisons with faculty, and the training of teaching assistants and dons-in-residence to serve as library mentors at the introductory level. Figures 1 and 2 document this trend.

3) The instruction librarian is proactive in communicating and collaborating with faculty, advertising the program, and inventing new ways of providing instruction. Library instruction is responsive to new learning technologies and has been acknowledged on campus for its leading role in Internet training for faculty, staff, and students. This year a special class on Internet search engines was added to the series of workshops offered each week throughout the term.

4) Faculty contact librarians when classes new to the research process begin an assignment. Stauffer Library currently provides curriculum-integrated instruction for over 50 courses in the humanities and social sciences. All new faculty are invited to reserve two-hour slots in their course timetables to schedule in-class library instruction.

5) Apart from in-class instruction, the library provides ongoing training at the reference desk, and through quality handouts, newly created Web tutorials, follow-up by teaching assistants, and advising by dons-in-residence.

6) Library instruction incorporates current educational thinking such as use of active learning techniques, conceptual frameworks, and metacognition, and is based on stated objectives (see the Internet example in sidebar 2) and continually evaluated. Handouts describing an overall research strategy, appropriate indexes, examples of search techniques, and student tasks are designed for each assignment. All classes are evaluated on the basis of learned skills and basic knowledge acquired during those classes. Evaluations are reviewed after each class and those gathered from the same series of classes are later analyzed for discernible strengths and weaknesses. A sample evaluation is shown in figure 3.

7) Library instruction meets student needs in that it addresses tools that relate to particular assignments at the time they are being worked on. Faculty are invited to use a "Research Strategy" library assignment to accompany any investigation involving a search for information resources. This strategy will be used with sociology, political studies, geography, sociology of sport, and women's studies classes. Returns from 653 student evaluations demonstrate that it is an extremely

A. Please rate each category using the following scale.

1	2	3	4	5
Not Satisfied	Somewhat Satisfied	Satisfied	Very Satisfied	Excellent

_____ **Overall Presentation** _____ **Computer Demonstration** _____ **Pace**

_____ **Subject Content** _____ **Handouts** _____ **Length**

B. Please complete these sentences:

The instructor's presentation was ...

To improve this session ...

I learned how to..

I still don't know how to...

The handouts were...

I really enjoyed ...

C. Please indicate whether or not you understand the following concepts or terms:

	yes	no		yes	no
internet			*World Wide Web*		
Netscape			home page		
search strategy			Net Search		
news group			bookmark file		
URL (address)			hypertext link		
keyword search			downloading internet files		

Other Comments:

Figure 3: Your Opinion Counts!

valuable tool for new library users, as shown in figure 4.

Future Challenges

The Stauffer Library instruction program will see significant changes in the coming year as a result of reduced library staffing and time available for teaching activities. We have already planned to drop the daily workshops on searching the book catalog and periodical indexes. The two Internet workshops will be condensed into a single two-hour class. Because fewer hours are available for dedicated class time, Web tutorials will be tested as a means for independent library learning.

Figure 4: Research Strategy Evaluation

	Percentage out of 653 Returns	
	yes	no
1. The research strategy helped me find information for my essay.	93	6
2. I will use the research strategy for my next essay.	90	8
3. The research strategy helped me create a mental map of the steps needed to find information.	79	19
4. I understand the idea of keyword searching.	98	2
5. I understand the difference between subject headings and keywords.	84	14
6. I learned to find articles.	95	4
7. I understand the relationship between journal indexes and Queen's holdings.	85	14
8. Using the research strategy made collecting information easier than usual.	71	26
9. The research strategy taught me something.	92	7
10. The steps in the research strategy are clear and easy to understand.	92	5

Many of our initiatives involve trying to "train trainers" who will help us teach novices how to use the library. To this end, we are trying to develop strong working partnerships with groups on campus who also play a teaching role with the student population. For example, the Instructional Development Centre provides support for faculty in the development of teaching strategies and assignments. They offer faculty seminars on topics such as cooperative learning, active learning techniques, and alternate assignments. The library has been invited to contribute sessions on teaching the Internet and designing successful Web assignments. Other training groups involve teaching assistants and dons-in-residence. Establishing these links from the bottom up is one way to reach new audiences as well as to gain support and assistance for the teaching mission of the library.

The future will also see special sessions for public service librarians on topics that address current teaching methodologies and new information tools. Although the library staff complement is decreasing, competency requirements are increasing. More of our teaching time needs to be spent with our trainers in order to maximize effectiveness during reference transactions and in the classroom. In support of this effort, workshops on a methodology for teaching the Internet, active learning techniques, search engines, and designing Web pages were offered in the past and more are in preparation for the future.

SUNY-PLATTSBURGH

Carla List

The College

SUNY at Plattsburgh is a four-year liberal arts college that also offers some graduate degrees. The largest programs include business, education, environmental science, and nursing. There are approximately 5,500 full-time students. The college follows a semester calendar and offers two summer sessions of five weeks each.

The Library

Feinberg Library, centrally located on campus, opened in 1977. Its collections now include over 300,000 monographs and more than 1,400 periodical subscriptions. The library is a selective U.S. depository. Librarians in SUNY hold faculty status with 12-month appointments. Feinberg currently has nine full-time library faculty and two less-than-full-time faculty; there are more than 20 support staff. The library's director is also the dean of library and information services, a position created in 1995 that combines management of the library and the college's computing faculty and staff. In mid-1995, the library implemented a team-based management approach with six programmatic "groups" of librarians; some groups also include other library staff. The computing staff is in the process of adopting this management style and it is expected that some of the groups formed there will interact and possibly merge with groups in the library.

Each librarian has four "core responsibilities" in this management approach: teaching LIB 101 (see below), liaison responsibilities for one or more academic departments, reference desk duty, and programmatic group participation.

The Instruction Program

Feinberg Library's instruction program is managed by the Instructional Services Group. It has three components: "electronic" workshops, course-related instruction and tours, and a one-credit course, "Introduction to Library and Information Research" (LIB 101).

The electronic workshops began when librarians perceived a need, primarily among teaching faculty, for instruction in the use of then-new CD-ROM databases. Workshops are added as interest from teaching librarians and interest from users dictate: in 1994-95, 20 workshops were offered while the 1995-96 early count indicates 20 workshops in spring semester alone. Titles of the workshops range from "Feinberg Library Catalog" to "HyperResearch: Searching on the Internet."

Course-related instruction has been popular among teaching faculty: 1994-95 statistics report 46 sessions presented to 650 students; this year 91 sessions were presented to approximately 1,300 students. The most difficult issue for course-related instruction is staffing because of the decrease in library faculty over the last two years and the uncertainty of filling vacant positions in the near future.

The Course

The most visible component of Feinberg's instruction program is its one-credit course in information research. The course was included as a part of the college's general education program in 1979 and has remained a requirement for graduation since then. It began as "Library Skills" and has retained that name colloquially (among students it's "Library Thrills") even though the title and the approach of the course have changed. The most recent title is "Introduction to Library and Information Research," an effort to tie it to the new Division of Library and Information Services.

The course is required of all students who graduate from SUNY Plattsburgh and the library accepts few substitutions from incoming transfer students to satisfy the requirement. It is taught by librarians only. Each librarian teaches two sections per semester with a

rotation allowing several librarians every third semester "off." The library has hired adjunct librarians every semester; the usual complement of adjuncts has been four, but it has reached seven at times.

A proficiency exam for LIB 101 has been offered to students since the mid-1980s. It is optional, offered once per semester. Students may take the exam only once. The exam is not specific to Feinberg Library; rather, it is a multiple-choice, 50-question test that attempts to measure a student's ability to deal with many information tools and systems. It is not the ideal implement for such a measurement but it is the only method that will handle large numbers of students.

LIB 101 sections meet once per week for eight weeks. Each students is required to complete a final project and a final exam. Focused sections are offered each semester, taught by Feinberg librarians, two each of "Introduction to Library and Information Research" in business, education, sciences/mathematics; and one in nursing each spring semester for telenursing students.[1] Several sections are offered as part of "cluster courses" for incoming freshmen in fall semesters.

LIB 101 schedules 20 to 23 sections of 35 students each semester. The classroom is currently equipped with 18 PCs and an instructor's workstation with a Power Macintosh that can be used with an LCD projector plate for overhead projection. A proposal has been submitted recently to create a classroom LAN that would enable all students to access databases simultaneously for in-class exercises without competing with campus network users for databases available on the network.

Each librarian is responsible for her or his in-class approach to the stated objectives for the course. General education course instructors are strongly encouraged to use active learning techniques in the classroom and most LIB 101 instructors devise in-class exercises as well as take-home assignments. The course objectives were drawn by a task force of four Feinberg librarians from the 1989 ACRL "Model Statement of Objectives for Academic Bibliographic Instruction." Their work was submitted to the library faculty and adjunct librarians; the final document was approved in 1992. A textbook, *Introduction to Library Research*, second edition, was written by Carla List to flesh out the objectives for students.[2]

The course is evaluated by students every semester using a questionnaire that was devised by librarians with input from the campus assessment administrator. It uses some questions from the student instructional report that is used by most courses on campus; it also includes a number that are unique to LIB 101. Information from these evaluations is used by individual librarians to fine-tune their teaching. It has not been used in a critique of the entire course in the past, but the Instructional Services Group is beginning to examine its value in such a review.

Courses in the general education program are reviewed regularly by the campuswide general education committee. LIB 101's most recent review was in 1992; it was approved to continue as a part of the general education program at that time. It is scheduled for another review in 1996-97 but the entire general education program is under close scrutiny currently and may be revised *in toto*. A librarian is presently a member of the general education committee—at this time the librarian is the coordinator of LIB 101 serving a three-year term—and is involved in the program's review. The librarian is in a good position to ensure the course's continuing presence in the general education program, especially in light of the inclusion of information literacy in the accreditation standards of the Middle States Association of Colleges and Schools.

How Is an Instruction Program Successful?

The success of an instruction program could be assessed by the number of students it reaches, by the measured effect it has on those students, or by the support received from teaching faculty and library/college administrators. Less measurable effects might include the contributions the program makes to the students' success in college and to their lives after graduation.

Feinberg Library's program is often seen entirely in terms of its primary component, LIB 101. The status of the course as a requirement in the college's general education program demonstrates the position it holds in the eyes of teaching faculty...and of students: When students are asked on their course-evaluation forms if the course should remain in the general education program, they answer strongly "yes" (a steady 65 percent for years). As a required course, it reaches every student, 1,200 to 1,300 per year, a measure of success in some eyes. One indication of the value of the course to faculty is the recent proposal to make it a requirement for majors in business, management, and marketing. Faculty in those departments want their students to become knowledgeable about the computerized retrieval of information and its evaluation, and LIB 101 does this. In this proposal, the course would be included in the majors as a partial replacement for a three-credit course in computer science—two one-credit courses in computer applications and in information management systems comprising the remainder of the replacement.

The additional components of the library's complete instruction program, electronic workshops and course-related instruction, are solidly supported by the teaching faculty. Demand for these services has increased (see above) with the realization that students and faculty need to understand and become skilled at using the latest information technology and that the library can help them move toward proficiency.

Contributors to Program (Course) Success

LIB 101 is a concept-based course that has stated coursewide objectives. The course clearly benefits from the fact that the objectives are explicit, shared by all librarians who teach it. The concept approach enables students to do information research more competently using more than just Feinberg Library's information research tools and collections. Efforts continue to keep the course from becoming tool-based, an approach that is tempting when using one database as an example in exercises or assignments. The course's emphases are on the way *all* databases work; the fact that information on *any* tool's screen will be similar, even if arranged differently; the need to evaluate *all* information that is found, especially that which may have a falsely elevated status because it is "on the computer."

The librarians who teach are committed to helping students in their research, another component of success. Active learning approaches are used in virtually all the sections of LIB 101. Students get some hands-on activity in class (and not all are hands-on the computer!), work in groups to teach each other, try research steps with the librarian available during class for help. The course also offers librarians the opportunity to present a "face" to students so that they have someone they recognize when they use the library. The commitment of dedicated librarians is an absolute requirement for the success of a program.

The longevity of SUNY Plattsburgh's required course both is a beneficiary of and contributes to the support received from the library and college administrations. Such support makes funds available for hiring adjunct librarians; provides a budget for instructional materials purchase and production; allows dedication of support staff to LIB 101 during the weeks that the course is in session; and furnishes support to librarians for professional development in bibliographic instruction. The fact that the course generates many ftes (full-time equivalents) for the college is almost certainly an important factor in college-level administrative support. The fact that Cerise Oberman is the dean of library and information services is definitely a factor in library administrative support for instruction!

Teaching librarians have had several retreats devoted only to instruction where ideas were floated and (sometimes) pursued. Retreats are a necessary component of the continuing success of the program because they offer instructors the opportunity to explore new and perhaps radical ideas in a setting designed to encourage open and freewheeling discussion. Pre-semester meetings are held each semester to communicate the latest room/equipment developments. Post-semester meetings are held to elicit librarians' reactions to technological changes, to share successful assignments or classroom strategies, and even to whine a bit—a *most* necessary component of interaction among instructors! Communication among the teaching librarians is open and continuous, an indispensable feature of the program. Management of the course and its communication channels is handled primarily by one librarian.

A successful instruction program succeeds only because it continues to evolve. Renewed concern about the applicability of course content for students is driving the search for new connections for the course; recent directions include binding some sections of the course to cluster courses for incoming freshmen and the possibility of having it required as part of a major rather than only as a general education requirement. One result of such connections is more collaboration between librarians and teaching faculty, an outcome also derived from the discipline/program sections. The librarians at Feinberg Library are old hands at evolution and are committed to it. They know it will enable them to continue their success indefinitely.

Should librarians offer "just in time" or "just in case" instruction in information research? Course-related instruction may be a better approach than a course that students often see as disconnected from other academic pursuits. The Instructional Services Group in Feinberg is examining this question, as well as new instructional approaches offered by advances in technology, in its current review of the entire library instruction program. While somewhat apprehensive about tampering with success, the group is willing to take some risks if they become necessary to improve the outcomes for students.

Technology is making more obvious the need for effective information research skills. Any program that keeps its focus on enhancing those skills for its patrons will be assured of success.

Copies of materials related to Feinberg Library's instruction program that are mentioned in this report may be requested from Carla List, (518) 564-5307, listck@splava.cc.plattsburgh.edu.

NOTES

1. Carla List, "Branching Out: A Required Library Course Targets Disciplines and Programs," The *Reference Librarian* 51-52 (1995): 385-398.

2. An examination copy of the book, ISBN 0-07-037977-7, can be obtained by requesting one from Jean C. Laughlin,

associate editor, College Custom Series, McGraw Hill, Inc., 6512 Six Forks Road, Suite 602, Raleigh, NC 27615.

COASTAL CAROLINA UNIVERSITY

Margaret Fain

INTRODUCTION

In preparing for the LOEX presentation, I spent much time thinking about and distilling the essentials of our library instruction program at Coastal. Defining what constitutes "success" at Coastal made the librarians here sit down and really think about what it was that we were doing right. Working with the other panelists to define overall characteristics of success was a very rewarding experience. At the end of the process, I had two distinct products: one was a handout package designed for the LOEX conference and the second was the comments made during the panel presentation at the conference. The handout package for LOEX included an institution and library instruction program description and the definition of success at Coastal, as well as copies of the library instruction policies and procedures, the training program, and the librarian evaluation form. The information from the two primary handouts is reproduced below. Due to space considerations, the other sections can not be reproduced here, but copies can be obtained from Margaret Fain via e-mail. The first section contains a description of the institution and the library instruction program. The second section defines program success for the program at Coastal Carolina University. A summary of the remarks I made during Coastal's portion of the panel presentation follows these sections.

DESCRIPTION OF INSTITUTION AND LIBRARY INSTRUCTION PROGRAM

The Institution

- Coastal Carolina University is primarily an undergraduate, state-supported, liberal arts institution, located in Conway, South Carolina (SC), with approximately 4,000 students

- Masters degrees are offered in education.

- Kimbel Library, built in the mid-seventies, is the sole library on campus and serves not only the campus community, but the local community as well. Current staffing is eight librarians and 8.5 paraprofessionals.

- Kimbel Library has a collection of over 150,000 items and subscribes to 1,000 periodicals. The library is a selective federal depository and a full SC state depository.

- The current online system is NOTIS. Periodical indexes are available on individual CD-ROM stations. DIALOG is available through the Classroom Instruction Program (CIP) and by appointment.

- The library is in the process of selecting a new online system to include an online catalog, Internet access, and access to periodical indexes.

Library Instruction Program

- Course-integrated, covering freshman to graduate-level classes.

- Sessions typically last for one 50- or 85-minute class period.

- The majority of the instruction takes place in the students' classroom.

- 195 sessions were taught by five librarians to 3,000 students in 1994-95.

Staffing

- Program is run by the library instruction (LI) coordinator, whose other duties include reference, collection development, and overseeing the nonprint collection,

- Coordinator schedules and assigns sessions, develops bibliographies and session materials, provides training and evaluation to participating librarians, collects statistics, runs the assessment program, and acts as liaison to the faculty regarding LI opportunities and problems.

- Sessions are taught by the LI coordinator (50 percent), two reference librarians (20 percent each), the assistant technical services librarian (five percent), and the head of public services (five percent).

- Training program is in place for librarians new to instruction.

- In-house workshops on effective teaching skills are offered during semester breaks.

- Formal evaluation, consisting of classroom observation based on written guidelines, is conducted for librarians teaching LI sessions.

- Peer observation of sessions is encouraged as an aid for developing teaching expertise.

Policies and Procedures

- "Library Instruction Policies" states the basic goals and objectives of the LI program. The document is used to guide the program and to provide a benchmark for assessment.

- "Library Instruction Procedures" covers the basics of running the program.

- "Library Instruction Training Program" covers methods for training librarians new to teaching.

Sessions

- Freshman library instruction is taught as a segment of English 101-102 sequence. The English 101 session is a basic introduction to resources in Kimbel Library and research methods. Students complete a "walking tour" of the library before the session. After the LI session, students are required to complete a worksheet, which ensures hands-on experience with all resources discussed in class. The sessions are geared to the research requirements of the class section.

- The English 102 session focuses on subject-specific (literary) resources and includes a post-session worksheet.

- Upper-level LI research sessions are taught as part of the research and writing intensive courses in the various disciplines. Sessions are cooperatively designed with faculty and are individually tailored to meet the research needs of the students in the class. Typically, research strategies in the discipline and in-house and external resources are covered. Instruction in searching DIALOG through the CIP program is given when appropriate.

- The research sessions currently reach the following disciplines: art, psychology, sociology, business policy, marketing, history, interdisciplinary studies, computer science, marine science, biology, health, education, and English.

- Workshops are offered on an as-needed basis to faculty, staff, and students. Past sessions have covered new online systems, CD-ROM indexes, and the Internet. Internet workshops are team-taught with staff from information technology services.

Methodology

- All sessions rely heavily on class participation and active learning techniques, such as buzz groups, questioning, individual seatwork, and small groups.

- Emphasis is on cognitive skills coupled with recognition of resources.

- 90 percent of the sessions are conducted in the classroom. Physical limitations of the library building make in-house sessions infeasible.

Assessment

- The English 101 section of the freshman sequence is assessed each fall using a multiple choice pre/post test. Tests are administered during the first two weeks of the semester and again during the final two weeks of the semester.

- Additional assessment tools include worksheet evaluations, in-class writing, student and faculty survey questions, and informal feedback.

Definition of Program Success

Why is Coastal's library instruction program a success?

- 195 sessions were taught last year, as opposed to 77 sessions ten years ago.

- The annual student survey shows LI reaching a higher percentage of students each year. The number and variety of classes taught increases each year.

- 90 percent of all freshmen receive library instruction through the English 101-102 sequence.

- Freshman assessment results show statistically significant improvement on the post-test.

- Assessment results demonstrate achievement of the programs' goals and objectives.

What Contributes to This "Success"?

- Willingness to experiment with the program, with new teaching styles and strategies.

- Enthusiasm of librarians involved in LI coupled with support of the library administration.

- Increasing use of active and collaborative learning techniques to replace lectures.

- Emphasis on student responsibility for learning.

- Ongoing communication between librarians and faculty and librarians and students.

- Collegial atmosphere among instructional librarians.

- Willingness to ask why. Why is it working? Why isn't it working? How can we fix it?

- Assertive approach to increasing faculty involvement in LI.

- Polices and procedures are constantly revised as the needs of the students, the institution, and the library evolve.

How Does This Translate into "Success?"

- Over the past five years, programs were set up for assessment, evaluation, and training. Policies, procedures, and objectives were formulated, written, and implemented.

- Freshmen English sequence was overhauled from straight lectures to a more participatory format.

- Library's assessment program has been held up as model for other departments.

- Developing library skills is a main tenet of the university's core curriculum.

- Library research sessions are appearing on more and more syllabi.

- Feedback from students and faculty indicate overall satisfaction with the process and the end result.

- Enthusiasm and creativity overcome physical limitations of the library facility and its resources.

CONFERENCE PRESENTATION

After listening to the four previous panelists, I feel kind of like the red-headed stepchild. At Coastal, we don't have a library instruction classroom we have no room in the library to conduct sessions, and no traveling laptop presentations, and I hate overheads. But we are creative. I find it liberating; without the facilities to teach hands-on techniques, we can focus more on critical thinking skills. When I initially responded to Linda Shirato's request for successful programs, I said we were a success because, despite our physical limitations, Coastal has an active, course-integrated program, covering freshmen to seniors, that reaches its objectives.

I addressed all the categories from the "Successful Library/Information Research Instruction Program" in my handouts, so what I would like to do now is focus on the highlights of our program and mention some issues not covered in the handouts. I receive support from the library administration in terms of release time from the reference desk to handle library instruction responsibilities. More importantly, I operate in an atmosphere of trust and am given free rein to experiment with course content, strategies, and so on as long as it doesn't require expensive equipment.

The librarians receive support from the faculty by working closely with them in developing sessions. We say we are a success because we can see a change in student attitudes over the years. When we walk into a freshman class, the common response is "Oh god, it's the librarian," whereas juniors and seniors are more likely to respond with "Thank god, it's the librarian." All instructional sessions are based on student research needs, with follow-up by individual appointment or consultation at the reference desk.

The new library instruction program is six-years old and continually evolving. The librarians who do instruction sessions are enthusiastic and not shy about offering suggestions and comments. At the end of each semester, we meet to talk about what went wrong, what was right, what we need to fix and how, where we lost the students' interest. From these sessions, new ideas are developed and implemented.

On the evaluation front, the librarian evaluation program is only three-years old and a good example of evolution. The program was developed because there was no way to demonstrate that individuals were becoming better instructors. They might teach more sessions each year, but no other information was available regarding their effectiveness or capabilities as teachers. I researched the literature and developed a program. Being over-organized, I created a lot of paper. We started out with a peer evaluation that had

three sheets to fill out and an LI coordinator evaluation that had three sheets to fill out. The first year, only half the evaluations were done, few sheets were filled out, and the results were not what we wanted. The second year we dropped peer evaluation in favor of peer observation. Peer observation was designed to benefit both parties, the observer learning new skills and the observed getting some non-threatening constructive feedback. The LI coordinator went to two sheets to fill out. This year, the LI coordinator has one sheet to fill out and is actually attending the stated number of sessions, while peer observation is still ongoing. We keep trying until we get it right.

The last characteristic I want to mention is one that didn't make it to the main list, but is one I had on my original list and Betsy Wilson mentioned in her speech, and that is having enthusiastic librarian/teachers. I am fortunate to work with enthusiastic reference librarians. They have helped create a collaborative atmosphere in which new ideas can be suggested, examined, and tried in our quest to create a library instruction program that is responsive to the needs of Coastal's students and faculty.

SUMMARY

In pulling this piece together, I happened on an early note from the panels' initial discussions about characteristics. It reads "attributes: collaboration, communication, and flexibility." I think these sum up all programs that are successful. You have to collaborate with each other, with faculty, and with students in order to make a program work. Without communication, you will be at cross-purposes and without flexibility; you will never change or adapt. What it all comes down to is this: does our program help our students learn to use the library and its resources? Are they better searchers, better researchers, better questioners? If so, then we are successful.

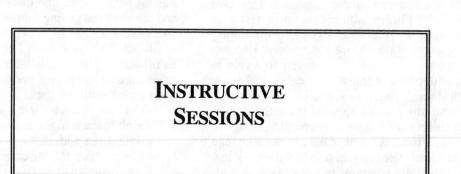

INSTRUCTIVE
SESSIONS

For Faculty and Graduate Students Only: An Instruction Program on Electronic Research Resources

Patti Schifter Caravello

Introduction: What Makes Faculty and Graduate Students Different?

This instructive session describes a program recently developed at the UCLA University Research Library for faculty and graduate students in the social sciences and humanities.

Assumptions, Similarities, Differences

The assumptions regarding the level and type of knowledge graduate students possess about the library and its electronic resources go something like this:

- Graduate students already know how to get around in a major research library.

- What they don't know they can simply figure out on their own.

- Despite computers, learning to do research is pretty much the same as always.

The literature and our experience supply many examples of how false these assumptions are.[1] Many professors assume that graduate students acquired information skills in their undergraduate years. Many faculty who teach undergraduates have made the same assumption—that their students already know how to use libraries, having "picked it up" in high school or

by osmosis. This "widening skills gap," as one author put it, leads to a situation where, as he said, "the further up the educational ladder students progress, the greater the gap between their exposure to library skills instruction and the level of library work which is expected of them."[2] At the very least, it is clear that, due to many factors, "undergraduates do not leave school with uniform library skills," as another author put it.[3]

The background to library instruction for faculty is similar in some respects to that for grads, and brings out the differences between these groups and other library users. (Some of this is outlined in figure 1.) These are sophisticated researchers with a strong grounding in the subject area, they have highly specialized or evolved needs for information, they probably want to break new ground with their research, their information needs often extend beyond the institution in which they are located, and they may well not have had any prior systematic library instruction despite the assumption that they have the requisite skills.

But there are also differences between faculty and graduate students. The expectations may be even greater that faculty possess honed library skills, and they therefore may find it more difficult to expose the holes in their knowledge. Second, faculty have conducted publishable research for years without this kind of training.[4] They also have less time to give over to it, and there is still some resistance to the computer, especially among older faculty. Another key difference is the librarian's perspective: we want to sell faculty on the technology and information literacy idea so that

---

Caravello is instructional services coordinator, UCLA University Research Library, Los Angeles, California.

— Instructive Session 1 —

Loex-96   55

**Differences in the Contexts for Instruction
Between Faculty, Graduate Students, and Undergraduates**

Faculty	Graduate Students	Undergraduates
Assumption they possess good library/info skills		Assumption they lack skills
Researchers with long-term topical focus		Research for a paper this term
Strong grounding in subject area		Usually little subject grounding
Information needs extend beyond institution		Need info available here and now
Need to find primary and secondary materials, be original		More likely to need only secondary sources
Have least time & inclination to attend library classes	Have opportunities for course-related instruction	
Some resistance to computers (esp. in Humanities, or older faculty)	Are likely using computers already for many things	
Adult learners	Adult/Student	Student
Have done publishable research without it	Seem to understand importance of instruction	
Find it hardest to expose lack of library/info skills		

<=   Would like to get the most of resources with minimal effort & training   =>

Patti S. Caravello, UCLA University Research Library 5/95

Figure 1: Differences in the Contexts for Instruction

they (or we) will incorporate these things into the courses they teach.

Programmatic Approaches

Among the approaches to graduate student library instruction documented in the literature are course-integrated and course-related instruction,[5] discipline-based research clinics or workshops,[6] individual instruction,[7] a whole course,[8] a multi-faceted approach including document delivery,[9] and some combination of orientations plus seminars or a one-shot coupled with consultation services.[10] Although a few authors suggest that the most effective route is that of individual instruction[11] (and few graduate students would probably disagree), in a large university with a pared-down professional staff, individual instruction can be only a part of the overall instructional service for graduate students, not the only mode of instruction delivery.

At a large university library like UCLA's it is also unrealistic to think that we can reach every graduate student through course-related instruction, however diligently we may work at making inroads to accomplish this. Although at UCLA we have had feedback that it is valuable, some of the literature indicates that course-related instruction is not necessarily the best way to go with graduate students because it is far away on the spectrum from the one-on-one considered so effective.[12]

Faculty prefer individualized instruction, but again, it needs to be a component of instructional service to them, not the only option, if we are to be realistic. Clearly some kind of group training is called for, not only for the numerical efficiencies achieved, but also as a way of offering to show faculty things they did not know to ask about, and to provide them with a well-planned program of classes to choose from and to take in a logical sequence. A newly formed UCLA group of graduate students in the humanities (called graduate technology consultants, or GTCs) who help faculty in their departments to use computers ventured some reasons why faculty seem to resist group training and why group sessions are so hard to arrange. What they decided is "faculty needs are too disparate to justify classes" and "faculty are interested in problem resolution, not abstract training."[13] (GTCs dealt with faculty on connectivity and hardware issues, not research instruction, so the context is somewhat different. Still, their conclusions give one pause.)

Yet, faculty seminars have been offered at UC Berkeley for 20 years to teach faculty about resources and information strategies. Faculty even pay a fee to take them.[14] Other universities have also offered faculty workshops or seminars which graduate students (as in the Berkeley program) are also allowed to attend.[15] I

was aware of the challenges of getting faculty to attend classes, but as I began this adventure I was also encouraged by these examples. Our experience has taught us that if you build your contacts and reputation for knowing about electronic resources and market it right, some faculty *will* come.

UCLA University Research Library

I have given you some background about what makes graduate students and faculty special, and I have mentioned the types of programs libraries have offered to this clientele. Now I will focus on the UCLA setting and the new program developed against this background.

The UCLA University Research Library (or "URL" as it has been known for 30 years before the Web appropriated it) is the largest of the 11 UCLA libraries. Designed as a graduate library (though it is open to all), URL has collections in the social sciences and humanities developed by the URL bibliographers, who are subject specialists, not reference librarians. The URL reference department, and two libraries located in the same building—special collections and Maps and Government Information (MGI)—each provide their own reference services and develop their respective collections. All four of these URL units (bibliographers, reference, special collections, and MGI) serve largely the same UCLA clientele and provide some form of instruction to them. As the instructional services coordinator for the reference department, I also coordinate instruction for the University Research Library.

Prior Efforts

Our prior attempts to offer formal instruction to graduate students and faculty were never systematic, but rather occasional; there was no defined, identifiable program of which they were a part, no unified effort or shared goals to support them. I believe this is why they never took off.

Still, here is what we learned from our prior efforts:

1) Targeting one academic department assures very low turnout.

2) Attractive, effective, well-aimed publicity is important and not simple.

3) It is impossible to cover all the important electronic resources faculty and grad students should know about in one or even two sessions.

4) You cannot offer a library class once; it is imperative to offer it multiple times for people to attend.

5) One or at most two librarians are sufficient to teach a small hands-on session.

6) Conducting the session in the building where faculty are located does not lead to higher turnout.

7) There is a difference between occasional and systematic programs: occasional librarian effort and committed, systematic effort.

Building up to a Program

Building up to our launching the new program were several fortuitous steps or events (If you can make some of this happen in preparation for mounting a new program, all the better):

1) **Creation of an informal "URL BI Group" (of representatives from the four units) to discuss common instructional issues**—This began a process of communication and coordination of instructional efforts that later paid off. (Those of you in libraries where reference librarian and bibliographer are one and the same can still consider which other units serve the same clientele and can join forces with you to mount a program.)

2) **Restructuring the reference department's approach to faculty outreach and instruction, assigning each librarian between four and six academic departments for this purpose**—This enhanced instructional specialties and subject expertise within the reference department, increased librarian-faculty contacts, and led to more teaching collaboration between reference and other URL librarians.

3) **Library administration's identification of instruction as one of the library's top goals**—This opened the door to acceptance and support of new programs.

4) **The opening of a high-tech classroom in the University Research Library building**—This simply made it physically possible for us to proceed.

After reference reorganized its approach to course-related instruction (as noted in number two above), we put most of our efforts there for a few years. While our statistics for course-related instruction skyrocketed, we were getting used to working together with other URL librarians to reach the same clientele to improve the instruction and to lessen duplication of effort. By creating this environment of collaboration, we—not completely unwittingly—set the stage for librarian interest and "buy-in" to the new program.

LAUNCHING A NEW PROGRAM

Initial Process

In many ways the time was right, and I did what is usually not done in a large institution: without benefit of a new committee (although I used ideas from past committees), or a new survey, general discussion, or supervisor's direction, I wrote a proposal for a new URL program. It included goals and objectives of four seminars for faculty and graduate students only, the concept that librarians in various URL units would participate, and ideas about targeting this clientele.

I distributed the proposal to my unit head, the reference librarians, and the URL BI Group as representatives of the other units who would be involved, and they all said "Great!" When it seems that "the time is right," it is usually that people are thinking on the same wavelength, and someone is able to pull it all together in a proposal. Although not everyone in each unit actively participated in the first year's program, no one resisted the idea of this program. I think they were thrilled that someone had done the initial work on it because it eased the early part of the process, and they could just provide ideas to improve on the plan.

Collaboration

With this encouragement and some good suggestions from everyone, I proceeded to write an outline for what each seminar would cover (see figure 2). One or two librarians volunteered to work with me on each seminar script to flesh out the outlines with real demonstrations, good examples, and so on. This critical phase —developing the seminars with a small team of two or three—is time consuming but well worth the effort to make sure that the seminar content can meet the goals and objectives, and that the goals and objectives are realistic in terms of graduate student and faculty needs. It was helpful that as coordinator I was on every committee.

When we had good first drafts, I scheduled practice sessions for librarians to try out the new classes on each other. UCLA librarians had used this valuable method when we first started teaching the Internet. Librarians give feedback to make the session better, the instructor gets to see how well the session goes in a live situation, and everyone learns something.

UCLA UNIVERSITY RESEARCH LIBRARY SEMINARS
ON ELECTRONIC RESEARCH RESOURCES
For Faculty and Graduate Students

The URL Seminar Program is designed to provide faculty and graduate students an arena for learning about a variety of electronic resources in the social sciences and humanities. Classes on the Internet, MELVYL databases, and other electronic research tools are offered with faculty and graduate student needs in mind.

Internet Traveler Seminars

With a focus on subject areas, these seminars introduce tools that enable educated exploration of the Internet and searching for topical information. Participants will experience the World Wide Web through demonstration and hands-on practice. En route to a better understanding of the methods of searching for information using Netscape, participants will become acquainted with specific Internet sites in their fields. Demonstration will be Windows-based. A basic knowledge of Windows is helpful prior to taking this class. *(90 minutes, plus 30 minutes hands-on)*

Internet Traveler:
Subject areas offered in this series in academic year '95-'96 : Social Sciences, Humanities, Latin American Studies, Education, History, Worldwide Government Resources

Spotlight Seminars

Electronic indexes are a boon to research and now abound in CD-ROM format and/or on the ORION and MELVYL Systems. Many CD-ROM titles are available in URL, and some are also accessible through local networks like SSCNet and HUMNet. Each session will spotlight one or more of these sources, detailing their scope and value relative to other tools covering similar topics. Participants will learn searching techniques of each title and special system features such as downloading or mailing. *(90 minutes)*

Spotlights:
Individual databases spotlighted in academic year '95-'96: *MLA Bibliography, LLBA, America: History & Life, SSCI, Patrologia Latina.* Subject areas spotlighted (and databases covered): Public Policy (*Sociofile* and *Mags*), Urban Planning (*PAIS* and *Avery Index*), Ethnic Studies (*Ethnic NewsWatch*), Literature (*MLA* and *English Short Title Catalog*), Education (*ERIC* and *Education Index*).

Beyond MELVYL® Seminar

The MELVYL System is your gateway to an array of resources, including many specialized periodical indexes (some providing the article text), other libraries' catalogs, and databases that represent the holdings of thousands of other libraries. Participants will learn how to make use of these resources and reach beyond the holdings of the UC libraries with WCAT and RCAT. Certain MELVYL features (update and mail) will also be highlighted. Basic knowledge of MELVYL commands is useful prior to this class. *(90 minutes)*

Information Management Seminar

Most online and CD-ROM sources offer ways to manipulate the information found on them by emailing and/or by downloading search results. Once manipulated, the information can be edited and organized using wordprocessing systems or information management software packages. This seminar will explain the principles of moving bibliographic data from one place to another, downloading, and uploading. Participants will see how this is done on ORION, MELVYL®, and a CD-ROM source. Basic knowledge of ORION and MELVYL® is recommended prior to attending. *(90 minutes)*

Managing Your Bibliographic Files with *Pro-Cite*

Pro-Cite software is one of the more powerful, user-friendly systems for retrieving, organizing, managing, and formatting bibliographic citations, and is widely used in the academic community. This session for beginners will demonstrate how to use *Pro-Cite* to: organize and manage files by creating a bibliographic database from scratch; produce bibliographies in several styles; and edit, detect duplicates, and retrieve citations using multiple search approaches. Also included, time permitting, will be a brief presentation on in-text referencing (creating bibliographies from references in a word processing file) and downloading citations to *Pro-Cite* from selected bibliographic databases and online catalogs. *(2 hours)*

Figure 2: UCLA University Research Library Seminars—Part 1

Seminar Enrollment

To enroll in the seminars, either:

- *Send this form to:* **Rose Marie Valdez,**
  University Research Library Reference Department, 157511

  (*from off-campus:* **UCLA, Box 951575, Los Angeles, CA 90095-1575**), *or*

- *Email* ecz5val@mvs.oac.ucla.edu *with all the information requested on this form.*

☞ **Please Note:**

- *No confirmation notice will be sent; you are enrolled by sending in this form or emailing the information.*
- *Mark your calendars; we will have handouts and a place for you if you have enrolled.*

Name _____

Department _____ *Check one:* **FAC**____ **GRAD**____

Campus Address _____

Email Address _____

● **All classes are held in the URL Media Classroom, Room 23167, 2nd floor, URL.** ●

Internet Traveler:

- ❑ Social Sciences: Apr. 15, 1-3 pm
- ❑ Humanities: Apr. 24, 1-3 pm
- ❑ Social Sciences: May 3, 10-12 noon
- ❑ Worldwide Government Resources, May 8, 1-3 pm

Beyond MELVYL®:

- ❑ Apr. 11, 10-11:30 am
- ❑ Apr. 17, 12-1:30 pm
- ❑ Apr. 25, 2:30-4 pm

Spotlight Seminars

- ❑ MLA Bibliography: Apr. 18, 10-11:30 am
- ❑ Social Sciences Citation Index: Apr. 29, 1-2:30 pm
- ❑ Latin American Studies: May 1, 2-3:30 pm
- ❑ Patrologia Latina: May 7, 1-2:30 pm

Managing Your Bibliographic Files with *Pro-Cite*:

- ❑ Apr. 22, 1-3 pm

● *What seminars would you like to see offered in the future?* _____

Questions? Contact Patti Caravello, 825-1544

Figure 2: UCLA University Research Library Seminars—Part 1 (continued)

— PATTI SCHIFTER CARAVELLO —

It becomes a way for librarians to train each other in electronic tools. I plan to continue practice sessions as part of the process of program development.

Publicity and the Coordinator Role

Much effort went into the look and content of the publicity. I wrote it and worked with the library's graphic arts service to make it look professional and appealing to the target groups. I had the publicity printed and mailed to faculty, hand-delivered to graduate student boxes, e-mailed to the distribution lists of the social sciences and humanities local area networks at UCLA, and placed on the library's Web page and in various campus print publications. It was also available to pick up in the library. (The brochure was the most frequently cited means of finding out about the sessions.)

In addition to this, my role as coordinator included

- overseeing the development of each seminar,

- talking to librarians to clarify and re-clarify the goals of the program,

- asking individual librarians to teach particular seminars,

- preparing some handouts,

- scheduling all the sessions in the library's media classroom,

- establishing enrollment procedures,

- analyzing the evaluations and reporting the results to my unit head, and

- gathering ideas for additional seminars from the evaluations and from librarians, which helped in planning.

Mine was the name on the enrollment form in case people had questions. It is paramount in a multi-unit effort to have one person (or perhaps a team of two) take the coordination role seriously and give it time and thought if the program is to succeed and keep up momentum.

The Seminars

I called them "seminars" to signal that these were not meant as basic classes open to all, but rather small-group sessions for which enrollment and faculty or graduate standing were required, where discussion and questions were expected, and where content would be focused on electronic research resources and strategies, typically in defined subject areas. We all thought "seminars" would appeal to the academician in a way that "free classes" or even "library workshops" would not.

Which is not to say that the seminars are "advanced" classes. Our approach has been to be ready with seminar content ranging from sophisticated-basic through advanced, and to gauge from the questions and interactions how much to cover in a given session. You can do this with small groups of graduate students and faculty as they will make their needs and questions known, and they are determined not to waste time.

Since many faculty and graduate students in the social sciences and humanities have been among the slowest in the university to harness the power of the library's electronic research resources, these became the cornerstone of the new program. All the seminars teach electronic sources as part of the solution to research needs and problems.

Overall goals of the program were broad:

- to provide instructional sessions that respond to the needs of faculty and graduate students in the social sciences and humanities;

- to introduce faculty and graduate students to an array of electronic resources; and

- to dovetail with existing instructional programs in order to tailor sessions in content and format to URL's primary clientele.

The seminar descriptions and enrollment form from the publicity brochure are appended. Additional details about goals and format are given below.

1) The "Internet Traveler Seminars" all focus on a group of disciplines (social sciences, humanities) or a single area (e.g., history, education, Latin American studies). The main goals of this class are to show how to find information on a subject using Netscape search engines and what kind of information can be found on the World Wide Web that is useful for research.

We do give basic Internet background and show features of Netscape like download, mail, and bookmark, but this is taught in the context of the search for information in particular subject fields. These have been the most well attended of the seminars, probably because the Web is what everyone hears about and wants to know about. We give a short lecture with

PowerPoint slides, a live demonstration, and a 30-minute hands-on segment.

2) The seminar we call "Beyond MELVYL" I view as the most critical one for UCLA faculty and graduate students because it teaches about the array of databases available to them through the online, intercampus system called MELVYL to which they all have access. MELVYL offers a UC union catalog, full-text databases, WorldCat, FirstSearch, Eureka, many periodical indexes, and connections to other libraries' online catalogs. While the undergraduate needs MELVYL for a periodical index or two, faculty and graduate students need also to use the databases that get beyond these, beyond UC's holdings, to the books and primary resource materials held at libraries beyond their own institutions that may be of value to their research. This session includes a Power-Point introduction and is primarily a live demonstration; interaction with attendees allows us to actually plug in some of their topics to the demo.

3) The "Spotlight Seminars" focus on one or two electronic tools (such as the MLA Bibliography, SSCI, America: History & Life) or a few tools in a particular subject area (for instance urban planning or public policy). The databases shown might be available on CD-ROM and/or on MEL-VYL. We originally called this series the "CD-ROM Spotlights" but soon realized that the format of the tool was unimportant; the idea of using electronic indexes, however they are made available, was. These sessions teach how to use the databases for research and also provide some context by covering the relative value of the tools. This is a live demonstration, and one or two of the sessions have also included a hands-on segment.

4) The "Information Management Seminar" teaches ways to manipulate the information found electronically by downloading, e-mailing, and uploading. We convey the concepts of moving data around and we demonstrate how to do it using the local online catalog, MELVYL, and a CD-ROM index. We even upload what was captured to WP51, so they see the whole process. We taught this the first two quarters of the seminar program, including some discussion of information management software packages. We had so many requests to hold a seminar on one of these packages, that the third quarter the only information management seminar given was a class on ProCite. We had wanted to do this earlier, but none of the URL

librarians knew ProCite. Another librarian on campus agreed to teach the seminar, and he has also agreed to teach ProCite to URL librarians so that we can continue to offer it in the program.

Key Elements for Success

Four elements of the program have been extremely important in making the program work:

1) **Collaboration between librarians from different URL units and their commitment to the program**—This provided a larger group of instructors enabling us to offer more classes; acknowledges that this was not just a reference department program, but a program defined by a wider variety of librarians to serve a particular, common clientele; and enriched the subject-specific content of each seminar which was highly valued by participants;

2) **A program identity**—which was communicated by a carefully conceived publicity plan, simple enrollment procedures, clearly defined goals and target clientele, and a new look to presentations, using PowerPoint at the beginning of most sessions;

3) **Administrative support**—A "Do it!" attitude which encouraged line librarians to take the risk to design, steer, alter, and put on the program without directives from above; and funding for the production and mailing of the brochure in the first two quarters, which ran about $600 to $700 each quarter (the reference department took on the cost in the third quarter); and

4) **Focus on electronic resources and subject disciplines**—electronic tools are the "hook" to create interest; a non-general approach; discipline-specific or social sciences/humanities-based; and research orientation.

STATISTICS AND EVALUATION

The "Statistical Summary" (see figure 3) gives a snapshot of how many enrolled and attended, how many sessions were held, the evaluations, and expenditures.

Enrollment and Attendance

We saw the decent enrollment figures—especially in the fall and winter—as a "Yes!" vote for the pro-

UCLA University Research Library Seminars
on Electronic Research Resources

Statistical Summary

Enrollment and Attendance

For three quarters combined (one academic year), an average of 18 people enrolled per session. An average of 10 people attended each session. Faculty made up about 33% of the enrollments and about 20% of the attendance.

	Internet Traveler			Beyond MELVYL®			Spotlights			Information Management		
	Enrolled	Attend.	# of Sess.	Enrolled	Attend.	# of Sess.	Enrolled	Attend.	# of Sess.	Enrolled	Attend.	# of Sess.
Fall	161	87	8	105	53	6	72	31	3	66	23	4
Winter	131	67	5	79	43	3	63	34	5	45	12	2
Spring	55	36	4	23	21	3	27	18	3	26	26	1
TOTALS:	347	190	17	207	117	12	162	83	11	137	61	7

	TOTALS		
	Enrolled	Attended	# of Sessions
Fall	404	194	21
Winter	318	156	15
Spring	131	101	11
TOTALS:	853	451	47

Evaluation

The return rate on evaluation forms increased with each quarter from 44% to 78%. The first item on the evaluation forms asked for an overall rating on a 3-point scale. "This seminar was...:"

	...Very Useful	...Somewhat Useful	...Not Useful
Fall	71%	29%	0%
Winter	74%	26%	0%
Spring	87%	13%	0%
AVERAGE:	77%	23%	0%

The next 6 or 7 items on the evaluation forms asked for a rating of particular aspects of the seminar content on a 6-point scale (1 = not useful, 6 = very useful).

	Between 1-3	Between 4-6	Score of 5 or 6	Score of 6
Fall	9%	91%	76%	55%
Winter	6%	94%	78%	53%
Spring	4%	96%	84%	51%
AVERAGE:	6%	94%	79%	53%

Expenditures

	Printing of Brochures	Mailing to Faculty in Social Sciences & Humanities
Fall	$550.00	$77.00
Winter	$550.00	$96.00
Spring	$615.00	$90.00
SUBTOTALS:	$1715.00	$182.00
	TOTAL COST: $1897.00	

Patti Caravello/jk 5/96

Figure 3: UCLA University Research Library Seminars—Part 2

gram we floated out. It apparently looked interesting enough to the target groups for them to consider and go to the trouble of enrolling. Several people contacted me to ask if we would offer these classes at other times because they had conflicts for every session of a particular seminar, indicating enrollment might have been higher.

The ratio of "enrolled" to "attended" ran about 50 percent in the first two quarters, and 78 percent in the last quarter (when there were fewer seminars offered and lower enrollments overall). Spring quarter is notorious for how few people will attend library classes: we stopped offering basic demonstrations of our online catalog in spring years ago because *no one* comes, so we were gratified that we did have 131 enrollments for the seminars. At first, the ratio surprised us. We got used to it (there were exceptions to the rule both higher and lower, and even somewhere there was 100 percent in the spring). We sent brochures to about 3,000 people in 30 departments each quarter; we had 853 enrollments for these classes over the first academic year from people in over 40 departments. These numbers are encouraging, especially in a library with no tradition of this type of program.

Now the task is to continue to make the seminars so worthwhile that word of mouth will increase enrollment and attendance. For now, the small class size is one of the pluses of the program from the point of view of faculty, grad, and librarian; questions get answered, individual needs are more likely to be met, hands-on is more manageable, and content and level can be more closely geared to the people in the classroom.

What They Liked

Evaluations were almost uniformly positive, and many good suggestions came from them for additional seminars much like the ones we had offered (only additional topics), which showed us we are on the right track. Many people were effusive in thanking us for putting on a program like this just for them. The most frequently listed "most successful aspect of this seminar" was the specificity of the information (for instance, Web sites in their fields, databases in their subject areas, special database features meant for advanced researchers, and manipulating the information found). Also, our emphasis on research strategies with these systems seems to have come across, as several evaluations mentioned this. Finally, many respondents mentioned they were glad to know about the various databases they hadn't known were available to them. Thus we feel the seminars achieved several of their goals.

Unexpected Results

Beyond the evaluations and statistics, we have been quite interested to see some unexpected results from the program. We are seeing a dovetailing of the course-related programs with the seminar program. For example, when discussing with a professor what his class might need by way of library instruction, the librarian mentioned that his class might benefit by attending an upcoming Seminar; the professor told his class of ten to enroll, and most did. One librarian told graduate students in a course-related session she was giving for social welfare to come to the "Spotlight on Public Policy" for exposure to databases that she had been unable to cover, and several of them came.

When the history department chair first saw our fall brochure, he requested that we schedule additional seminars (Internet and Beyond Melvyl) just for history faculty, and we did. I think it is important to be open to faculty scheduling difficulties and to respect the feeling some faculty have of not wanting to show too publicly the holes in their knowledge of library resources and their discomfort with computers.

When some of the graduate technology consultants I mentioned earlier (in the program to help faculty with computers) found they were being asked to teach the MLA bibliography to faculty, they turned to URL for assistance, specifically to see if one of us could "do one of those seminars" for their faculty members. After we held an MLA session for them, we went to talk to the GTCs as a group to get a sense of what else might be needed in the near future, and to let them know what we can do. Already we have another request for a librarian to do an Internet Traveler session just for linguistics faculty. So, one good program can lead to another.

ISSUES AND CHALLENGES

Issues

As I look to the summer when I will be planning next fall's seminar program, here are some of the issues I see that will need to resolve:

1) Last fall we offered some faculty-only sessions, and we are of mixed opinion whether to try this again. Enrollment and attendance are lower at faculty-only sessions; but faculty have a strong preference for individual or small-group sessions with their own kind. It is a balancing act.

2) In order to teach new systems, librarians have to master them first. How to keep up with librarian

training needs in order to keep the seminar program vital and increase the pool of instructors is a real challenge. (Case in point: Pro-Cite, which was more popular than the other information management class)

3) Whether to offer more sessions to accommodate the demanding schedules of faculty and graduate students, giving them more options to attend. We are not sure if the added librarian commitment (already rather taxing) is worth the chance that more people might attend.

4) Whether to charge fees to faculty (as Berkeley does) to ensure faculty attend has come up, but so far there is certain cringing at this suggestion. We want to see the program more well established (for at least another year) before we seriously consider fees.

Challenges

As coordinator, I also have several challenges to meet to keep up the program quality, intent, and objectives.

1) We used evaluation forms for each seminar, which gave me a good deal of valuable feedback. I will certainly keep doing this, but I also feel I will need to do more to monitor the seminars for consistency of coverage, teaching effectiveness, and overall program quality. Keep in mind we have librarians from four units teaching the seminars, some with a lot of experience in this kind of thing, some with very little. Three things I will do toward this goal are a) continue to teach seminars and share handouts and scripts with others, b) occasionally attend seminars other librarians teach, and c) continue to hold practice sessions for newly created seminars, or for librarians who want to hold them.

2) How to increase attendance is a challenge. Administration loves to see high numbers, but, as mentioned, small class size is appropriate for this program. It would be gratifying to see the enrollment and attendance figures come closer together (as they did in the spring).

3) Besides asking for ideas for new seminars on the enrollment and evaluation forms, a broader needs assessment survey would be useful. Now that we have a program, we have a channel for the results of such a survey and could more easily use its

findings. We need to know what those that do not enroll are thinking.

4) Keeping the program vital with standard and also new offerings will be important, the main challenge being to offer what this clientele needs and make it appealing.

CONCLUSION

In conclusion, I would like to encourage any of you in the position to do this kind of thing to begin building toward it and see what happens.

- Go in with the assumption that grads and faculty DO need instruction, and that offering a well-rounded, realistic service will include individual, online, printed, and group instruction.

- Begin coordinating with librarians in other units who serve the same clientele and sharing a vision of what an instruction program for this group might look like and what it can do.

- Keep in mind the needs of this group for discipline-tailored, research-oriented instruction, and know that these needs might best be served in small-group situations, with some hands-on.

- Build contacts and a reputation for expertise in electronic sources through your course-related program or consultation services, because electronic resources are the "hook."

- Spend time producing the right kind of publicity and coordinating the program

- Be the ones they will turn to for instruction, and make them see it as their program to exploit and help you to improve.

NOTES

1. For example, Richard A. Dreifuss, "Library Instruction and Graduate Students: More Work for George," *RQ* 20 (Winter 1981): 121-123; Milton G. Ternberg, "Library Orientation for Business Students: A Case Study," *College and Research Libraries News* 44 (April 1983): 114-115; Marilyn Parrish, "Academic Community Analysis: Discovering Research Needs of Graduate Students at Bowling Green State University," *College and Research Libraries News* 50 (September 1989): 644-646; Mary I. Piette and Betty Dance, "A Statistical Evaluation of a Library Orientation Program

for Graduate Students," *Research Strategies* 11 (Summer 1993): 164-173; and Godfrey Franklin and Ronald C. Toifel, "The Effects of BI on Library Knowledge and Skills Among Education Students," *Research Strategies* 12 (Fall 1994): 224-237.

2.   Dreifuss, 122.

3.   Denise Madland, "Library Instruction for Graduate Students," *College Teaching* 33 (Fall 1985): 163-164.

4.   An interesting discussion of why this is so is given in Stephen K. Stoan, "Research and Information Retrieval Among Academic Researchers: Implications for Library Instruction," *Library Trends* 39 (Winter 1991): 238-257. It is also discussed in Constance McCarthy, "The Faculty Problem," *Journal of Academic Librarianship* 11 (July 1985): 142-145.

5.   Diane W. Kazlauskas, "Bibliographic Instruction at the Graduate Level: A Study of Methods," Report, University of Florida Libraries, 1987, 13p., Eric Document Reproduction Service, ED 311 932, microfiche.

6.   Pamela S. Bradigan, Susan M. Kroll, and Sally R. Sims, "Graduate Student Bibliographic Instruction at a Large University: A Workshop Approach," *RQ* 26 (Spring 1987): 335-340.

7.   Bonnie G. Gratch and Charlene C. York, "Personalized Research Consultation Service for Graduate Students: Building a Program Based on Research Findings," *Research Strategies* 9 (Winter 1991): 4-15.

8.   Anita Kay Lowry, "Beyond BI: Information Literacy in the Electronic Age," *Research Strategies* 8 (Winter 1990): 22-27.

9.   Usha Gupta, Lutishoor Salisbury, and Alberta Bailey, "SuperService: Reshaping Information Services for Graduate Students," *Research Strategies* 13 (Fall 1995): 209-218.

10.   Madland, 164.

11.   Kazlauskas, 10; and Gratch and York, 5.

12.   Kazlauskas, 10.

13.   Wayne Miller, "Report on the GTC Pilot Program, Winter 1996," e-mail dated 22 April 1996.

14.   Anne Lipow, "Outreach to Faculty: Why and How," in *Working with Faculty in the New Electronic Library, 19th National LOEX Library Instruction Conference, 1991*, ed. by Linda Shirato (Ann Arbor, MI: Pierian Press, 1992), 15.

15.   Marsha Forys, "The Electronic Library: A Faculty Seminar," in *Working with Faculty in the New Electronic Library, 19th National LOEX Library Instruction Conference, 1991*, ed. by Linda Shirato (Ann Arbor, MI: Pierian Press, 1992), 143-148; Mark Schumacher, "Instructing the Academic Search Service User: The Faculty Connection," *Research Strategies* 7 (Winter 1989): 33-36; and Susan Kendall, "Internet Training for Faculty at a Small University," *Computers in Libraries* 14 (February 1994): 57-60.

Reaching the Whole Population:
Adaptive Techniques for Reaching Students
Who Fall Through the Cracks

Linda Carder, Carl Pracht, and Robert Willingham

Introduction

Through the general studies program at Southeast Missouri State University, incoming freshmen are given a library orientation early in the semester. Transfer and nontraditional students are left out of this initial introduction, and other special needs students such as international, at-risk, and disabled students sometimes need more instruction than the 50-minute general studies orientation provides. The first segment of this article will describe the requirements and characteristics of three special needs groups: nontraditional students, international students, and hearing-impaired students. In the second segment, an adaptive technique based on Hersey's Situational Leadership Model will be described. This technique provides a framework for determining the student's level of experience and ability, so that instruction begins at the right place.

Nontraditional Students

Approximately 27 percent of the student population at Southeast Missouri State University is comprised of nontraditional students. A nontraditional student is one who is 25-years old or older, or is returning to school after an absence of a year or more.

Carder is bibliographic instruction coordinator, Pracht is reference librarian and ESL instructor, and Willingham is audiovisual specialist, Southeast Missouri State University.

Nontraditional students come to the college experience from a wide range of backgrounds and with varying degrees of library experience. The characteristics outlined here are common, but not all-inclusive. They are the tendencies that present challenges and barriers to these students and to the librarians who work with them to help them become independent learners.

1) **Not campus focused**—Unlike the 18- to 23-year-old for whom education is a central developmental task, adult learners are fulfilling several roles. They may have feelings of "regressing" or being "off task" when they begin their role as student.

2) **Influenced by work and life experience**—While adult learners' life and work experiences are sources of sophistication, there may also be a lack of understanding of formal education because their frames of reference are influenced by informal bases from their everyday lives.

3) **Low self-confidence**—Because of their multiple commitments, different perspectives, and needs to upgrade their academic skills, adult learners often express the feeling that they are marginal and do not belong. Adult learners often feel a sense of competition with the younger students.

4) **Sense of urgency**—Adult learners feel pressed to apply what they learn in school, because of both financial pressures and a need to justify using family

— Instructive Session 2 —

Loex-96 67

resources for education. They may think they are stealing time from family duties and therefore feel rushed when pursuing studies. Their families may be providing resistance rather than support.

What can a librarian do to help the nontraditional student overcome these barriers? Being aware of the special characteristics of the adult learner, both positive and negative, is the first important step, leading to strategies for overcoming the problem areas. In the student's initial re-entry to college, lack of self-confidence is one of the most important hurdles to overcome. Steltenpohl and Shipton[1] recommend starting nontraditional students out in homogenous groups in their first semester. BI sessions directed toward returning students should be offered at a variety of times to meet their varying schedules. The first BI courses specifically designed for nontraditional students at Southeast Missouri State University were offered evenings and Saturdays, and the advertisements were targeted specifically for that group. After a few years, the flyers invited everyone who had not received the initial GS 101 orientation, and yet the groups are still predominantly comprised of adult learners. When the groups are small and the majority are nontraditional students, they are more at ease about asking questions and trying out new databases. The BI instructor becomes a contact they approach with confidence when they experience problems in the library, because they know their questions are not considered stupid and that the instructor has some understanding of their needs and capabilities.

Another characteristic that the librarian can take advantage of with adult learners is their wide range of experience. As mentioned earlier, their frame of reference may be influenced by informal bases. For example, they may be aware of a political issue such as planning and zoning, abortion, or school voucher systems because it affects their lives in a personal way, and they may derive knowledge about these issues from family friends, neighbors, and the local media, but they may not know how to research the primary sources of information on these issues. Developing instruction on primary and secondary sources and including government documents in a unit can provide meaningful learning in which the adult learners can incorporate their own experiences into formal education.

The nontraditional student's sense of urgency is another difficult barrier on the road to becoming an independent learner. Students who are pressed for time tend to rely on classroom materials and use the library as little as possible, seeing it as an external drain on their time rather than an important part of their education. One remedy for this problem is to incorporate bibliographic instruction into classroom work. Collaboration with the teaching faculty is essential in accomplishing this. If the classroom instructor can bring the group to the library at the time BI instruction is needed, process and content are learned at the same time, and contact is made with a librarian in case follow-up is needed.

THINGS LIBRARIANS NEED TO KEEP IN MIND REGARDING INTERNATIONAL STUDENTS

1)   These students have traveled great distances and left family and friends to study at your school.

We need to realize that it is tough to learn a new language and to live in a new culture. These students deserve our respect and our help.

2)   All will suffer culture shock at various times while in your institution.

All international students will experience culture shock. At times, the frustration that results from culture shock will be directed toward you or your library.

3)   Many of these students would much rather ask a friend for information than a librarian.

This is often a normal reaction to encountering something new. Many foreign students do not realize that librarians are employed to assist them in the library.

4)   Many of your students will have varying attitudes towards the status of librarians as well as towards female librarians.

Some of these students do not realize that librarianship is a career that requires college degrees. It is also interesting how some foreign students treat female librarians differently.

5)   The idea of doing library research may be new and developing good library skills may seem irrelevant to them.

Libraries are not the same around the world. In many countries, libraries are study halls. Often foreign students do not realize that research beyond class lectures and textbooks is required.

6)   Most of these students would benefit from hands-on practice in your BI programs.

Immediate feedback is extremely important to reinforce learning. This feedback can also be helpful when determining if the students are understanding what is being taught.

7)   Librarians need to assess audiences immediately.

In order to avoid wasting class time, librarians must decide quickly if the planned activity is at the appropriate level and must be able to make changes to maximize learning.

8)   English skills can be easily taught in library activities.

The library component in most intensive English programs does not have to be limited to one library visit per semester. The library component is limited only by your own creativity. When I meet a new group of intensive English students, my goal during the first class is to seem more approachable to those students.

THE HEARING-IMPAIRED LIBRARY PATRON

There are approximately 24 million people in the United States who have some degree of hearing impairment. This amounts to about six to eight percent of the population. Since the enactment in recent years of laws and legislation decreeing that all individuals in this country shall have equal access to services provided by all public and private institutions, more and more people with one sort of disability or another are attending colleges and universities. With the new technology of hearing assistive devices, particularly the "all in the ear" hearing aids, the fact that one has a hearing impairment is not always obvious; hence, these people are frequently referred to as the "invisibly handicapped."

The term "hearing impairment" refers to both the deaf and the hard-of-hearing. Deaf people can hear only a little of the loudest noise, and maybe not even that, and cannot understand the speech of another person. Their own speech might be greatly distorted or unintelligible. Hard-of-hearing people, on the other hand, have limited hearing abilities and can understand another person's speech under ideal conditions. Their speech may be clear and easy to understand.

People normally learn to speak through imitation, that is, listening to other people speak and then repeating, or imitating, what they have heard. For young children with normal hearing, this manner of learning speech presents few problems and their speech will be clear because they can hear well. The problems in speaking generally begin when children lose hearing just when they are beginning to learn how to speak. Because they are unable to clearly hear the finer points of speech sounds, such as consonants that are difficult to discern and often sound like other consonants, they will frequently repeat what they thought they heard with the result that what they are saying is not understood by others.

Since the age of onset of one's hearing impairment frequently determines the quality of that person's speech, a hearing impairment is often categorized by when the person lost his or her hearing. A "prelingual" hearing impairment refers to those who lost their hearing before they have learned a spoken language. These people often have difficulty learning to speak because their ability to correctly hear and imitate speech sounds clearly has been taken away. On the other hand, the designation of a "postlingual" onset of hearing loss is reserved for those who lost their hearing after they have begun to learn to speak. This can include young children as well as the elderly whose speech patterns are usually well developed by the time they incurred their hearing impairments. Thus, one's speech and hearing ability are intertwined, being somewhat dependent upon one another for their respective effectiveness. The age of onset of a hearing loss often determines the degree of impairment to one's speech.

With the characterization of a hearing-impaired person as having an "invisible handicap," how can we recognize a hearing impaired person when we encounter one? There are several general characteristics or behavior traits which, when they occur together in the same individual, might indicate that we are dealing with a hearing impaired individual. These characteristics are

- lack of attention,

- frequent requests for repetition of what was said,

- irrelevant answers,

- frequent mistakes in carrying out oral instructions,

- uncommon listening behaviors such as cupping the ear,

- unclear speech or speech defects, and

- daydreaming.

In an information provider/receiver situation, whether in the classroom or at the library reference desk, Melanie J. Norton notes that "effective communication is the key to effective instruction."[2] Whenever communication breaks down, the librarian becomes frustrated about his or her inability to fully understand what the patron/student is trying to communicate and the patron/student gets frustrated when the message is not being understood. So, how does one feel when dealing with a hearing-impaired person apart from the frustration that the efforts at communication are simply not working? Feelings of awkwardness and/or being uncomfortable are not uncommon. They are normal and would be expected of a person who is honestly trying to assist a hearing-impaired individual. When faced with such a situation, there are questions librarians may ask of themselves:

1) How can communication be enhanced?

2) How can we know whether or not a message is being understood?

3) How will one understand a person whose speech is unintelligible?

The answers to these questions along with a basic understanding of how the hearing-impaired person hears and communicates with the available resources will determine how the librarian will respond in an encounter with the hearing-impaired patron/student. There are a number of things the librarian can do once he or she is aware that a hearing-impaired individual is present: 1) quickly identify the communication deficit; 2) develop a means of dealing with it; and 3) respond in an appropriate manner. Some of these tips for communicating are just common sense, while others require some knowledge of how the hearing-impaired person hears and communicates:

- Get the person's attention before communicating.

- Look directly at the person when speaking.

- Speak slowly and clearly without shouting or exaggerating lip movements.

- Use body language and facial expressions to supplement your communication.

- Maintain eye contact.

- If you are not being understood, try rephrasing a thought by using different words.

- Try writing down your thoughts.

- Keep hands away from face and mouth while speaking.

- Make sure that lighting makes your face clearly visible.

- Know that gum chewing, pencil biting, long mustaches, and similar obstructions of lips will lessen the effectiveness of your message.

Whenever communicating with another person is just not working, some change in communicating style or method would be in order. When one is attempting to communicate with a hearing-impaired person, some understanding of how that person can hear and communicate with the limitations he or she possesses can greatly lessen the frustration factor which often results from miscommunication. The librarian can then appropriately modify his or her mode of communication to fit the given situation with the more desirable results of more effective communication, a greatly enhanced comfort level of both the librarian and the hearing-impaired person, and more productive interaction.

SITUATIONAL LEADERSHIP

Situational Leadership Theory was developed by Paul Hersey. Leadership style is based on the client's readiness or level of experience, rather than the leader's preferred style. Examples of situational leadership theory can be found in teaching,[3] management,[4] nursing, and counseling.[5]

Using bibliographic instruction as an example, a student with little or no library experience would receive high direction and support from the instructor. The supportive and directive behavior of the instructor follows a progression through four quadrants: Telling, Teaching, Supporting and Delegating (see figures 1 and 2).

Quadrant 1

In Quadrant 1 the student is unready and unable to begin working independently in the library, and needs the necessary support and direction in order to move toward the goal of independent learner. This support usually comes in the form of individualized instruction, and an acceptance of the person at the person's present level, so that he or she can request assistance without fear of humiliation.

At this level, there is more telling than teaching going on because students are usually not ready to provide feedback at this point. Both support and direction on the instructor's part are high.

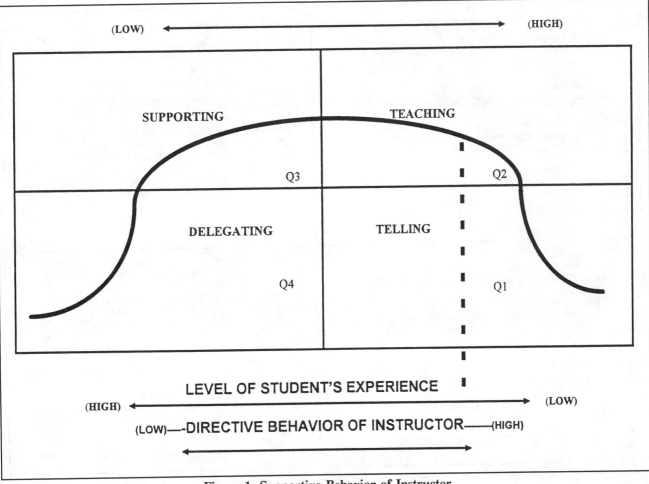

(LOW) ⟷ (HIGH)

SUPPORTING · TEACHING

Q3 · Q2

DELEGATING · TELLING

Q4 · Q1

LEVEL OF STUDENT'S EXPERIENCE

(HIGH) ⟷ (LOW)

(LOW)—-DIRECTIVE BEHAVIOR OF INSTRUCTOR——(HIGH)

Figure 1: Supportive Behavior of Instructor

Characteristics

This student is often overwhelmed by the dual task of having to learn the process of accessing information as well as course content. Online catalogs and other automated reference tools present a barrier rather than a supporting link to the task at hand. The student may be reluctant to reveal his or her lack of knowledge and may be reluctant to approach the reference desk. There may be an attempt to bluff through the situation. This becomes apparent when the student's request is obviously unreasonable. For example, the student may express indignation that a small academic library does not have all the sources that a research library has, or may claim that a CD-ROM database is not operating properly when a faulty search strategy is the problem.

In working with these students, it is important to realize they are learning new skills and that follow-up and reinforcement of concepts are important. If their initial experience with the librarian is positive, they will come forward with their information needs and will develop the confidence necessary to rise to the challenge. There must be a balance of challenge and support. If the student is over-challenged and under-supported, he or she will give up or regress to earlier

coping strategies. If there is too much support and too little challenge, the student will remain dependent on the instructor. It is important to be consistent and approachable so that the student will understand the librarian's function and make progress. Individualized and small group sessions are especially effective for these students. They are more likely to ask questions, participate, and receive support from other students. While this may seem to be a labor-intensive effort, if these sessions are well designed, they can work in the overall instruction program. Good teaching strategies for special needs students often make good strategies for orientation sessions. The suggestions made for working with foreign students and the hearing-impaired, for example, are good habits to cultivate in any classroom.

A special problem for many students who fall into this group is having to take on the role of beginner after being accomplished in other areas of life. For example, a student having difficulty in the library may be a supervisor or community leader. One way for the librarian to deal with this is to think of oneself as a consultant. The student will be less likely to perceive

APPROACHES DESK READILY PROBLEM BEHAVIOR MAY STEM FROM BEING FORCED TO ASK QUESTIONS RATHER THAN WORKING NDEPENDENTLY HIGH AWARENESS OF WHAT IS AVAILABLE KNOWS ADVANCED SEARCH STRATEGIES MAY REGRESS TO Q1 DUE TO EXTERNAL PRESSURES, IN WHICH CASE, BEHAVIOR WILL NOT BE CONSISTENT TRANSFERS SKILLS FROM DISCIPLINE TO DISCIPLINE AND FROM LIBRARY TO LIBRARY EASILY **READY/ABLE** Q3	"AVERAGE" FRESHMAN WILLING TO WORK INDEPENDENTLY AFTER BASIC INSTRUCTION HAS A DESIRE TO BE MORE INDEPENDENT MAY REGRESS TO Q1 AS A RESULT OF PRESSURE , PROCRASTINATION OR EXPOSURE TO UNFAMILIAR MATERIAL MAY HAVE DIFFICULTY TRANSFERRING LIBRARY SKILLS TO A NEW AND PROBABLY LARGER SETTING, BUT HAS A BASIC IDEA OF WHAT IS AVAILABLE IN THE LIBRARY HANDLES LEARNING PROCESS AND CONTENT AT THE SAME TIME MORE EASILY **READY/UNABLE** Q2
"INVISIBLE" BRING SUGGESTIONS FOR IMPROVING SERVICE PROBLEMS THEY EXPERIENCE CAN LEAD TO IMPROVED SERVICES BRING THEIR OWN FOCUS AND MOTIVATION WHEN THEY ASK "WHY DON'T YOU HAVE—" IT IS USUALLY SOMETHING YOU SHOULD HAVE **INDEPENDENT LEARNER** Q4	RELUCTANT TO WORK INDEPENDENTLY MAY REFUSE TO APPROACH REFERENCE DESK, BECOMES UPSET WHEN STRATEGIES DON'T WORK PROBLEM BEHAVIOR MAY STEM FROM RELUCTANCE TO REVEAL LACK OF KNOWLEDGE - BLUFFING HELPLESS - FEARUL - LOST - OVERWHELMED MAY CLEARLY STATE NEED FOR BASIC INSTRUCTION, WILL PROBABLY NEED FOLLOW-UP SESSIONS TO REINFORCE CONCEPTS CONFUSED BY LEARNING CONTENT AND PROCESS AT THE SAME TIME MAY NOT UNDERSTAND LIBRARIAN'S FUNCTION MAY BE ACCOMPLISHED IN OTHER AREAS OF LIFE AND RESENT TAKING ON ROLE OF "BEGINNER" OR STUDENT **UNREADY/UNABLE** Q1

Figure 2: Student Characteristics

himself or herself in a one-down position and will more readily join into a relationship with the librarian that is conducive to independent learning.

Quadrant 2

Quadrant 2 represents the "average freshman" who is ready to become an independent learner, but who needs instruction and occasional support from the reference librarian to develop the necessary skills. Library orientations and introductory library skills classes are the traditional ways of meeting the needs of these students, as well as occasional assistance from the reference desk. At this level, students are given increasingly challenging assignments requiring critical thinking and feedback. The instructor is moving from telling to teaching, still providing high direction and support, and the student is becoming a more active participant in his or her instruction.

Characteristics

At this stage, the student is willing to work independently after basic instruction, and prefers to do so. This student may have difficulty transferring skills from a small library to a larger one, or from public to academic, but will have a basic idea of what is available and where to find it. While facing various challenges, the student may regress to Quadrant 1 temporarily, but he or she has usually developed a preference for working independently. One of the problems common to this group of students is their tendency to not take the library orientation seriously because it comes early in the semester before they realize what skills they need to accomplish the course work. A positive orientation experience is important so they will approach the reference desk as the need arises. Some of these students may show up at small group sessions designed for adult learners to pick up what they missed earlier in the semester.

Quadrant 3

The Quadrant 3 student is ready and able to use the library independently, but may need occasional support as subject matter in senior-level and graduate courses becomes more difficult. The student is self-directed and motivated to learn the skills necessary to complete the task and is pushed by internal motivation rather than pulled by the external demands of the instructor or the required course material. The problems that Quadrant 3 students experience in the library can help the librarian make improvements in signage, purchase of appropriate materials, and databases for various disciplines. The instructor moves from the role of teacher to that of consultant, providing low direction, high support. More often the librarian is assisting the student in locating hard-to-find material and providing information on new databases or changes in the library.

Characteristics

These students transfer skills easily from library to library and from discipline to discipline. Their problems stem from being forced to ask questions at the reference desk due to idiosyncrasies in the organization of the collection. Quadrant 3 students often dislike having to ask questions rather than working independently. Occasionally, a Quadrant 3 student will regress to Quadrant 1 in an attempt to enlist extra help from the librarian. This is usually caused by external pressures due to multiple commitments. Understanding this enables the librarian to help the student stay on task and provide encouragement rather than resistance.

Quadrant 4

The Quadrant 4 student is an independent learner and is usually "invisible" to the librarian. This group consists of faculty members and students who seldom need the librarian's assistance. Like the Quadrant 3 student, observing their problems in the library often leads to improvements in service. The librarian's roles in working with these patrons is that of a delegator and consultant to lifelong learners. For example, a faculty member and librarian may discuss ways to improve instruction to students, which could include training teaching and graduate assistants. Direction and support are low because the independent learner is equipped with the internal motivation and skills. The librarian's knowledge of what is available at other institutions and what has become attainable through developing technology is a valuable source of information for the independent learner.

Characteristics

The independent learner brings his or her own focus and motivation. They are a valuable resource to librarians, because when they ask why the library does not have a particular source, it is often something the library should have. Like the Quadrant 3 patron, the independent learner prefers to work independently and can make useful suggestions for making the library more accessible. Observing the problems and delays experienced by these patrons and encouraging feedback

from them is a good way to improve services. This is especially true in the case of the independent learner who is physically challenged. This patron is able to articulate clearly the problems in the library that need attention.

It is challenging to decide which quadrant or level of experience the student falls into during a brief encounter at the reference desk. Identifying the student's degree of readiness is important, because it often determines the librarian/student's relationship from that point on. When working with foreign students, the hearing-impaired, or those who are intellectually advanced but inexperienced with libraries, it is easy to miscue and interpret their difficulties as incompetence rather than temporary barriers that can be overcome. For those cases in which the student's level of competence is not clear, it is always appropriate to start in a position of high rather than low support and direction and adjust one's teaching style as the student provides clues or progresses from that point. Once the librarian has an idea of where the student is, he or she can encourage growth by challenging the student to advance one step from the present position (see figure 3). For example, if a student is asking the librarian to find necessary materials for a class assignment, the librarian can use that as an opportunity to teach the student how to use the online catalog. If the student returns repeatedly for help on various databases, the librarian can provide simple handouts that enable the student to learn the basics independently. The goal is to keep the student progressing from Quadrant 1 to Quadrant 4 with the right amount of support and challenge.

NOTES

1. Elizabeth Steltenpohl and Jane Shipton, "Facilitating a Successful Transition to College for Adults," *Journal of Higher Education* 57:6 (1986): 637-658.

2. Melanie J. Norton, "Effective Bibliographic Instruction for Deaf and Hearing-Impaired College Students," *Library Trends* 41:1 (1994): 118-149.

3. Gerald O. Grow, "Teaching Learners to Be Self-Directed," *Adult Education Quarterly* 41:3 (1991): 125-149.

4. Paul Hersey, *Management of Organizational Behavior: Utilizing Human Resources*, 6th ed. (Englewood Cliffs, NJ: Prentice Hall, 1993).

CHALLENGES	SUPPORTS

POSITIVE

CHALLENGES	SUPPORTS
Freedom	Opportunity to Practice
Insistence on initiative	Safety
Expectations	Similarity
Direct Experiences	Clarity
Increasing Complexity	Warmth
Emphasis on participation	Empathy
Alternatives	Orientation
Requests for performance	Staff accessibility
Choices	Services availability
	Assistance
	Consistency
	Relaxed atmosphere
	Predictability

NEGATIVE

CHALLENGES	SUPPORTS
Humiliation	Smothering
Logistical frustrations	Creating dependency
Excessive anxiety	Authoritarianism
Demands without clarity	Low standards
Intimidation	Excessive advice-giving
	Removing responsibility

Figure 3: Challenges and Supports

5.   George S. Howard, Don W. Nancy, and Pennie Myers, "Adaptive Counseling and Therapy: An Integrative, Eclectic Model," *The Counseling Psychologist* 14:3 (1986): 363-442.

FURTHER RESOURCES

Allen, Mary Beth. "International Students in Academic Libraries: A User Survey. *College & Research Libraries* 54 (July 1993): 323-333.

Arfken, Deborah E. *A Lamp Beside the Academic Door: A Look at the New Student and His Needs.* Opinion Paper No. HE 018 701. Washington, DC: National Center for Research in Higher Education, 1981. ERIC Document Reproduction Service No. ED 261 603.

Ball, Mary Alice, and Molly Mahony. "Foreign Students, Libraries, and Culture." *College & Research Libraries* 48 (March 1987): 160-166.

Baumgarte, Roger. *Cognitive Development as a Goal of Freshman Seminar.* Report No. HE 020 521. Washington, DC: National Center for Research in

Higher Education, 1987. ERIC Document Reproduction Service No. ED 283 494.

Beck, Susan G. "Technology for the Deaf: Remembering to Accommodate an Invisible Disability." *Library Hi Tech* 13:1-2 (1995): 109-122.

Chickering, Arthur W. *The Modern American College.* San Francisco: Jossey-Bass, 1981.

Chickering, Arthur W. *Education and Identity.* 2d ed. San Francisco: Jossey-Bass, 1993.

Cross, K.P. Adult Learners: Characteristics, Needs, and Interests. In *Lifelong Learning in America.* Ed. by E. Petersen. San Francisco: Jossey Bass, 1979.

Goldman, Warren R., and James R. Mallory. "Overcoming Communication Barriers: Communicating with Deaf People." *Library Trends* 41:1 (1992): 21-30.

Hagemeyer, Alice Lougee. *The Legacy and Leadership of the Deaf Community.* Chicago: American Library Association, 1991.

Hagemeyer, Alice Lougee. "We Have Come a Long Way." *Library Trends* 41:1 (1994): 4-20.

Hardy, Richard E., and John G. Cull. *Educational and Psychosocial Aspects of Deafness*. Springfield, IL: Charles C. Thomas, 1974.

Hollander, Pat. "Deaf-Advocacy at Queens Borough PL." *American Libraries* 26:6 (1995): 560-562.

Kasworm, Carol. "Lifespan Differences between Student Groupings." *Journal of College Student Personnel* 23 (September 1982): 425-428.

Koehler, Boyd, and Kathryn Swanson. "ESL Students and Bibliographic Instruction: Learning Yet Another Language." *Research Strategies* 6 (Fall 1988): 148-160.

Knowles, Malcolm. *The Adult Learner: A Neglected Species*. Houston, TX: Gulf Publishing Company, 1973.

McDaniel, Julie Ann. "They Can't Hear Us Does Not Mean We Can't Serve Them. *Journal of Library Administration* 16:4 (1994): 131-141.

MacDonald, Gina, and Elizabeth Sarkodie-Mensah. "ESL Students and American Libraries." *College & Research Libraries* 49 (September 1988): 425-431.

Marlow, Christine. "Identifying the Problems and Needs of Nontraditional Students at Your Institution." *NASPA Journal* 26:4 (1989): 273-277.

Maxon, Antonia B., and Diane Brackett. *The Hearing Impaired-Child: Infancy through High School Years*. Boston: Andover Medical Publishers, 1992.

Muro, Gertrude, and Alice Wise. *Meeting the Student's Needs: A Transdisciplinary Approach*. Report No. JC 890 093. Washington, DC: National Center for Research in Junior Colleges, 1988, ERIC Document Reproduction Service No. ED 304 173.

Natowitz, Allen. "International Students in U.S. Academic Libraries: Recent Concerns and Trends." *Research Strategies* 13 (Winter 1995): 4-16.

Roark, Mary L. "Challenging and Supporting College Students." *NASPA Journal* 26:4 (1989): 314-319.

Sanford, Nevitt, ed. *The American College: A Psychological and Social Interpretation of the Higher Learning*. New York: John Wiley & Sons, 1966.

Tannenbaum, Robert, and Warren H. Schmidt. "How to Choose a Leadership Pattern." *Harvard Business Review* 36:2 (1958): 95-101.

Tannenbaum, Robert, Irving R. Weschler, and Fred Massarik. *Leadership and Organization: A Behavioral Science Approach*. New York: McGraw-Hill, 1961.

Van Cleve, John V., ed. *Gallaudet Encyclopedia of Deaf People and Deafness*. New York: McGraw-Hill, 1987.

Vernon, McCay, and Jean F. Andrews. *The Psychology of Deafness: Understanding Deaf and Hard-of-Hearing People*. New York: Longman, 1990.

LIBRARY INSTRUCTION FOR THE LIBERAL ARTS: DIALOGUE, ASSIGNMENT DESIGN, ACTIVE LEARNING, AND OUTREACH

Janet McNeil Hurlbert

Basing a library instruction program upon curricular issues and pedagogical principles is not easy even at a small liberal arts institution when technology pushes us to teach the mechanics of information retrieval. The focus of Lycoming's instruction program rests with the idea that information provides the format for conversations and dialogue between students and the information they are reading or researching, and that the setting that enables students to learn best is a collaborative one that prepares them to live in community with each other now and in the future. Our library instruction places assignment design at the crux of the program, supported by active learning techniques and renewed by outreach to the campus community. I will present information about the instructional environment at Lycoming College and discuss the instructional guidelines for our program and the framework for assignment design. Since any healthy instruction program requires thoughtful evaluation, I will conclude with a discussion of the challenges and dilemmas yet unresolved in the Lycoming program.

Instructional Environment

Lycoming is a small, undergraduate, liberal arts college with professional programs in business, communications, nursing, and an education minor for those wishing to gain a teaching certificate. Our students

Hurlbert is associate professor, head of instructional services and archives, Snowden Library, Lycoming College, Williamsport, Pennsylvania.

number approximately 1,500, the majority being between the ages of 18- and 22-years old who have come to us from Pennsylvania and surrounding states. There is limited diversity on campus (both students and faculty), a faculty-student ratio of 1-14, and student SAT scores in the 950-1150 range. About 18 percent of our students go on to graduate school, and a high percentage stay in the area to work after graduation. Of equal significance to the library instruction program is that in recent years the academic dean has sponsored teaching effectiveness workshops that have not only enhanced the techniques that we can apply to our own instruction, but also have provided a common experience shared by librarians with faculty.

Snowden Library's staff consists of five librarians: director, head of collection management and systems, head of instructional services and archives, two instructional services librarians, 5.5 library technicians, and student assistants. In addition to coordinating the instruction program, the three instructional librarians assume the additional public service responsibilities of supervising document delivery/interlibrary loan, the public service aspects of being a partial U.S. documents depository, coordinating archives, designing and maintaining the library home page, and covering the reference desk days, evenings, and Sundays.

The library is a five-floor complex that houses a 160,000-volume collection with 950 current journal subscriptions, numerous CD-ROM databases, First-Search, Dow Jones News Retrieval, and campus connections to the Internet. A basement-level instructional laboratory has a table arrangement separate from four individual computer stations and a fifth station for demonstrations and projection, allowing students to work in groups both at the tables and computer stations. Not having individual stations was primarily a budgetary consideration, but has proven most helpful in reducing the distractions that computer connections to the Internet bring. In addition, students may do group work with print sources away from the computers.

Snowden Library Instruction Program

Our library instruction program is an active and continuously evolving one over the past decade. At the present time we teach approximately 150 individualized instruction sessions per year, which increasingly includes technology workshops for faculty and staff. These classes range in size from 12 to 35 students with normal class size being about 22 students. The most enviable bonus of our schedule is that many sessions are one hour and 50 minutes or 65 minutes in length, or are held during science lab periods. We value our long-term faculty relationships, many of which began through our new faculty lunch when faculty first arrived on campus. Library instruction is stressed during this luncheon session, and faculty experienced in working with the program discuss ways in which they have designed information assignments.

Our official administrative goals are as follows:

- to support the curriculum offered at Lycoming College with library instruction which addresses specific informational assignments while incorporating the broader curricular objectives of information analysis, critical thinking, and creativity in the use of information;

- to involve librarians and faculty members jointly in the creation of information-based assignments, the ultimate goal being an integrated process with information tasks woven throughout the duration of the course;

- to promote life-long information literacy in each individual student;

- to acquaint students in each discipline with the unique body of information within that field and how it is organized;

- to provide students with an active classroom experience in the library, emphasizing hands-on activities and active learning techniques;

- to provide students with a balance of automated and print resources that support individual assignments;

- to create ladder learning for students in which library instructional approaches are used in increasingly sophisticated ways as the students continue through the college curriculum, especially within a discipline; and

- to provide a role model through individual work with students for information searching that not only displays the use of local campus resources, but also draws upon national and international resources as well.

Such formal objectives are supported by these instructional guidelines which serve us in the day-to-day workings of the library instruction program.

Design of the assignment is crucial

The manner in which students work with the information process is vital to the success and learning that takes place. Although a minor objective for the session might be to deliver information to 25 people at one time, ideally the classroom instructor and librarian have worked equally hard to create an assignment that will communicate their mutual goals for students both within the workshop itself and as the assignment progresses. The thrust of these goals is creating a dialogue between the student and the information used through relevant approaches to finding information and critically examining it. A true conversation with information involves generating, interpreting, sending, listening, and actively responding to ideas and information. Students need to make connections between past and present, between self and the outside world of knowledge, and determine what information is needed for future conversations. There is also the realization that information can be used in a variety of ways through a variety of assignments—there are many ways to converse. Most importantly, students need to make connections between course content and the students' present or future lives.

A first practical planning consideration is how the information component can be integrated with the substance and routine of the course. Although a true research or term paper has value, often it is difficult to integrate this type of assignment throughout a course; students feel it is external to the real subject matter. Also, students bring with them many preconceived, and difficult to discourage, ideas about how to do a term paper. As we enter into an era where plagiarism runs rampant, and the Internet brings yet more possibilities for plagiarism, the only meaningful defense is a carefully structured assignment.

Here are some components of assignment design:

- Consider methods that may already be functioning in a classroom when trying to integrate the information process into as much of the course content as possible. Internal electronic discussion lists and journals are two ways to extend the value of any assignment.

- Librarians can serve as a clearinghouse for successful assignment ideas. It is always surprising how little faculty may know about teaching techniques used by their colleagues. Librarians can suggest applications of assignments used by others that have proved effective. Even an occasional newsletter sharing library instruction ideas and quoting faculty on the success of certain methods is a good way to communicate because faculty are usually willing to listen to each other.

- "Channeled choices" provides an overall structure for an assignment, then allows individual choices to be made by the student as the project progresses. An example of this might be a sociology class studying healthcare reform The instructor and librarian have determined the overall topic—healthcare. The students would first discern the voices speaking to them about healthcare issues—healthcare professionals, politicians, consumers. Students, or students working in groups, choose one of these voices and solve a particular problem posed by the teacher. Usually if students are given choices within an assigned category, they respond as well as, if not better than, to the notion of "pick a topic that interests you."

- Good assignment design reduces or eliminates plagiarism by having students involve themselves in the assignment. Start with a personal reaction or individualized activity, pose problems to be solved through current materials, and require manipulation of information and critical thinking.

- Assignment design is dependent upon constant evaluation. If library instruction is part of the total assignment, a mechanism for evaluating the two at the same time proves beneficial to both the librarian and the instructor. Some of our best suggestions for improvement have come from students' writing paragraphs in answer to pointed questions about their reactions to assignments.

Look for long-term results

Information is a process as opposed to a system of searching, finding, and reporting. Instructional success must be viewed by the capabilities of students at the end of four years, or possibly the end of a course, *not* at the end of an individual instruction session. "Time on task" is probably one of the most important elements of long-term success with the average student. Working with information and the related supporting skills needs to be repeated, and repeated in different disciplines at different times and from different angles. This process approach also applies to faculty working with the library instructional program. Faculty relationships represent a partnership developed over a series of semesters and years as librarian and classroom instructor experiment with content and techniques to ensure that the flow among library, classroom, and information is integrated.

Absolute commitment to active learning techniques, writing and speaking across the curriculum, and learning models

Seeing the library as a laboratory and/or the sessions as workshops further communicates the time-on-task concept as well as emphasizing active learning techniques. When librarians participate fully in teaching effectiveness workshops and seminars to further their skills, they discover opportunities not only to share the experience with professors, but to build on this common experience when designing assignments and the teaching methods to implement them.

Another aspect of active learning is to have worksheets and/or something in which students apply what they learned. It is essential for students to practice and explore further what they have learned and need to do. This provides self-instruction in automated resources, and the student feels that he or she is moving ahead on the actual assignment. Through interacting with students as they work on these worksheets, desk reference becomes an extension of the instructional classroom and a personal way of modeling information behaviors.

Taking advantage of instructional aspects within many campus settings

Promoting library instruction itself or the concept of the instruction program is a responsibility of each librarian utilizing his or her contacts in campus settings. On our particular campus we have found opportunities to include instruction in workshops conducted by the Career Development Center, prepare the tour choir for trips abroad, present programs for the Institute for Management Studies, and involve the library in the symposium series.

Theoretical Framework for Instruction

Applying theory to the information process is an ever-changing and challenging aspect of library instruction. The library literature contains much in this area, but it is often helpful to explore other materials that faculty are more familiar with as well.

Seven Principles in Action: Improving Undergraduate Education provides a basis for the whole instruction effort as several of the principles remind us to encourage cooperation among students, encourage active learning, emphasize time on task, and respect diverse ways of learning.[1] Bruffie promotes the whole concept of starting dialogue through collaborative learning techniques, certainly the way in which conversations about information can take hold. He encourages students to "plan and carry out long-term projects in research teams" and "puzzle out" difficult problems.[2] Ruggerio offers a look at critical thinking challenging us to not let the undergraduate overvalue subjectivity and indulge feelings.[3] What better way than to use information assignments as the basis of critical thinking experiences.

A librarian's relationship with the classroom instructor determines the choice of learning model and how far the models may be pursued. Something as straightforward as American Library Association's *Evaluating Information: A Basic Checklist* furnishes ideas for worksheets on critical thinking,[4] or Eisenberg and Bergowitz's *Information Problem-Solving: The Big Six Skills Approach* can be applied and modified for almost any classroom situation.[5] Blandy and Libutti donate an approach to the information process using levels of competence, serving to remind us that the technology layer (search structure, operation, search protocol) is below the scholarly layer (dialogue with points of view, communicate discoveries, develop individual viewpoints).[6] On our own campus, Professor Fredric Wild has worked with me on developing and implementing a Developmental-Information Model which will be discussed in the next section of this article.[7]

The manner in which any models or approaches are taught in the classroom is based on active learning. Active learning exercises in themselves are not the end goal; the techniques must serve the informational or learning goals established for the workshop. Johnson, Johnson, and Smith's *Active Learning: Cooperation in the College Classroom* generates ideas for classroom use.[8] Fulwiler's *Teaching with Writing*[9] and his other similar publications along with O'Keefe's *Speaking to Think/Thinking to Speak*[10] expand the ways in which the library instruction classroom can enhance writing and speaking across the curriculum on liberal arts campuses while promoting critical thinking and reaching more learning styles. One of the most helpful concepts is covered in Angelo and Cross's *Classroom Assessment Techniques* with its emphasis on using active learning techiques to assess how much the student is retaining at different intervals in the teaching situation.[11]

The Developmental-Information Model

Professor Wild, one of our mass communication professors, who has worked with the library instruction program since its inception, has a background in learning theory and has developed an information model consisting of four positions in the information process. Although the model is still being tested, it has not only served his classes well, but has been a source of inspiration for assignments in the classes of faculty in other disciplines. Here are the four positions:

- Position One: Connecting with Information

- Position Two: Encountering Multiplicity

- Position Three: Finding a Voice

- Position Four: Engaging in Dialogue

Assignments developed for each of the four developmental levels should be able to fulfill the following functions:

- to make the student's personal dialogue with information the center of the educational process;

- to engage students in active-learning experiences involved with collecting, evaluating, and using information that model for students how to solve problems in whatever their fields of study;

- to enable students to discover through the experience of researching and using information how making decisions is a process of evaluating options and making choices within particular contexts;

- to establish a sense of connectedness between past and present and the ability to make ethical choices founded on this awareness; and

- to build interpersonal skills and create community among students, instructors, staff, and other users of information.

The appendix illustrates assignment samples for each of these positions. Although the assignments were used in an oral communications class, they could easily apply to different disciplines with writing assignments as the final product.

Challenges and Dilemmas

Any healthy instruction program needs constant evaluation, but there are also perplexing issues that remain unsolved. Our program at Lycoming is no exception. Staffing, the curriculum, and campus dynamics and politics all interact with the instruction program. On our campus our library professional staffing will remain the same size in the foreseeable future, and this will probably be true of support staffing as well. The tension between creative ideas, taking time to research teaching theory and literature, and outreach versus the amount of staff time available frustrates the instructional services librarians. This is magnified when a new instructional services librarian begins employment with us. Our salary range attracts beginning candidates who have not taught before and may not have had much academic library experience. Obviously they need to be mentored and carefully initiated into teaching as well as to their other duties—the time to do this balanced with immediate course load creates more of a survival atmosphere for all of us. This leads to a consideration of how much work is too much, and if it is too much, how limitations can be set.

There are several perplexities about our program in general. Specific evaluation of a whole program has taken a back seat to keeping the program running. Although we feel comfortable with our program and the assignment-type evaluations, we have nothing to administratively prove that the program is successful other them impressionistic comments. Combined with this are curricular issues. Is a formalized information literacy requirement worth the campus political effort to validate the program? Also, a beginning point for the program is a dilemma since there is no extended freshman seminar program or common core that runs through freshman English. An added dimension is now how our program and the newly expanded instructional role of our computer center will mesh in terms of instructional outreach for teaching new information technologies.

Conclusion

An active library instruction program must seek to clarify for students the real meaning of the use of information and the information search—not only as a basis for projects and term papers, but as a basis for dialogue with others, and as a basis for finding the answers to questions relevant to students' lives. The force supporting this process is the design of the assignment preferably using collaborative learning with supporting skills related to automated and print resources taught through active learning. The library contributes to a liberal arts education by providing students over a period of time with the intellectual instructional environment needed to become educated users of information delivered in all formats.

NOTES

1.   Susan Rick Hatfield, ed., *Seven Principles in Action; Improving Undergraduate Education* (Bolton, MA: Anker Publishing Company, 1995).

2.   Kenneth A. Bruffie, *Collaborative Learning. Higher Education, Interdependence, and the Authority of Knowledge* (Baltimore: Johns Hopkins University Press, 1993).

3.   Vincent Ruggiero, *Beyond Feelings: A Guide to Critical Thinking*. 3d ed. (Mountain View, CA: Mayfield Publishing Company, 1990).

4.   *Evaluating Information: A Basic Checklist* (Chicago: American Library Association, 1994).

5.   Michael B. Eisenberg and Robert E. Berkowitz, *Information Problem-Solving: The Big Six Skills Approach to Library & Information Skills Instruction* (Norwood, NJ: Ablex Publishing Corporation, 1990).

6.   S.G. Blandy and P.O. Libutti, "As the Cursor Blinks: Electronic Scholarship and Undergraduates in the Library," *Library Trends* 44:2 (1995): 279-305.

7.   Frederic M. Wild, Jr. and Janet McNeil Hurlbert, "Time, Place, and Community: A Developmental Strategy for Enabling College Students to Connect Course Content with 'Things That Matter,'" unpublished paper, 1995.

8.   David W.Johnson, Roger T. Johnson, and Karl A. Smith, *Active Learning: Cooperation in the College Classroom* (Edina, MN: Interaction Book Company, 1991).

9.   Toby Fulwiler, *Teaching with Writing* (Upper Montclair, NJ: Boyton Cook Publishers, 1986).

10.   Virginia O'Keefe, *Speaking to Think/Thinking to Speak: The Importance of Talk in the Learning Process* (Upper Montclair, NJ: Boynton/Cook Publishers, 1995).

11.   Thomas A. Angelo and K. Patricia Cross, *Classroom Assessment Techniques*, 2d ed. (San Francisco: Jossey Bass, 1993).

POSITION ONE: CONNECTING WITH INFORMATION

Theoretical Application and Objectives:

Students to evaluate material intuitively, without extensive analysis or internalization. Student is asked to establish his or her own criteria for deciding which story or piece of information is interesting and most relevant to the topic at hand and then to shape this information in some way (through writing or speaking) in conversations involving an exchange of ideas. Emphasis is upon connecting the student's own feelings with the experience of another person discovered through research.

Information Objectives:

• Become familiar with primary and secondary sources.

• Gather facts and identify stories.

Procedures:

• Students conduct a survey of peers to gather contemporary impressions of a past decade which has been assigned to them.

• Students conduct selective and guided research to understand the mindset of another person through role play.

• Students work in assigned groups, using informational resources, to select individuals from the decade.

• Each group conducts a discussion through role play based upon a contemporary issue which was also dominant in that particular decade.

Examples:

The librarians and instructors choose the decade of the 1930s, which includes the Depression and the approach of World War II. After reading several reference sources giving an overview of the era, students are asked to select individuals representing major segments of society, such as the performing arts, science, business, or politics, for the role-play activity. A typical group discussion might include Margaret Burke-White, Henry Ford, Walt Disney, Charles Lindburgh, and Eleanor Roosevelt. The theme for discussion could center around the meaning of success, what is true creativity, the impact of home on adult contributions to society, overcoming failure, or significant achievements. Often a moderator chosen from a noted figure of the current decade, such as Richard Nixon, adds further perspective to the discussion.

Wild/Hurlbert Developmental-Information Model 1996

POSITION TWO: ENCOUNTERING MULTIPLICITY

Theoretical Application and Objectives:

At Position Two, students build upon what they have practiced in Position One. Instead of allowing personal reactions to information to serve as the primary guide for deciding what to include or to exclude from a conversation, in Position Two the instructor encourages students to consider what information must be included or explained to enable the audience to understand and to use what is being communicated. The student is asked to consider what must be done to promote at least some kind of *understanding* (not persuading) on the part of the audience. The emphasis, in other words, is upon understanding, not persuading.

Information Objectives:

• Look at information within the general population and consider their stereotypes.

• Begin to question information.

• Locate, sort, compare, and classify information, and formulate further questions. Compare information to stereotypes.

• Form opinions from information.

Procedure:

• Students conduct a survey of peers to gather contemporary impressions about a particular population group in contemporary American society that has been assigned to them.

• Groups of students conduct research from an outsider's objective perspective.

• Students identify contemporary issues and challenges facing this group of people in contemporary American society.

• Students present these findings in the form of a panel discussion.

Example:
   The instructor assigns each small group of students to a specialized population such as Latinos, the disabled, American Indian, and persons living in the inner city. After students determine the four basic challenges of each of these groups, such as education level, employment, family structure, and stereotypes, they prepare and present a panel presentation for the class.

Wild/Hurlbert Developmental-Information Model 1996

POSITION THREE: FINDING A VOICE

Theoretical Application and Objectives:
   At Position Three, students have their own perspectives about the information they have collected, and they have some idea about what needs to be done in order to share this information with other people. The student's aim is to take a stand, and then persuade. To do this, the student must have some personal connection with the information (Position One) and be able to explain it to other people (Position Two).

Information Objectives:
•   Identify multiple viewpoints.

•   Critically analyze information, identify voices/viewpoints, and deal with conflicting information.

•   Select and defend this information.

Procedure:
•   Students conduct a survey of peers to gather contemporary impressions about a right that most Americans consider basic to us as citizens. This right is presented to them in the form of a case study.

•   Students must analyze this right and decide what the two sides are using an insider's "subjective" perspective.

•   Students argue in a debate context ways in which a group's understanding of a basic right or value should be interpreted and applied.

Example:
   The instructor develops scenarios or uses contemporary news accounts which illustrate basic rights such as the right to bear arms, privacy, or free speech. Each student group is assigned a right, and then must use various undergraduate legal materials to understand the fundamental issues which surround the right in general.

Then each group is encouraged to appreciate and examine divergent points of view through appropriate reference materials which analyze the right from other perspectives—philosophical/religious, psychological/sociological, cultural, and historic viewpoints as well as to support their arguments by selecting spokespersons or groups and current events. To help students prepare more adequately for the concluding debate, sides on the particular issue may be given to students just before the debate—usually this works better if handled by a "drawing" rather than by assignment.

Wild/Hurlbert Developmental-Information Model 1996

POSITION FOUR: ENGAGING IN DIALOGUE

Theoretical Application and Objectives:
   Position Four asks students to work with information intuitively much as they did at Position One and to integrate the skills they have developed in Positions Two and Three in presenting information to various audiences in order to explain or to persuade. The emphasis at Position Four is on integrating the personal experience of students with the information they had researched and with the analyses they have performed in order to discuss and resolve problems in community. The student engages in a "conversation about things that matter" from three perspectives at once: from a subjective perspective; objectively, from the point of view of a detached observer; and from the point of view of a person who has an opinion that he or she wishes others to consider.

Information Objectives:
•   Give responsibilities for choosing information sources, selection of information, and analysis to students.

•   Begin silent conversations with information and relate this information to self.

•   Internalize the information and be able to communicate and defend spontaneously.

Procedures:
•   Students conduct a survey of peers to gather contemporary impressions about an issue of importance to students in their own time and place.

•   Students research the topic according to basic methods established in other projects.

- Students engage in an extended roundtable conversation about this issue that requires integrating personal experiences with researched information.

Example:

The instructor assigns a general topic such as education, and discusses with the class certain life questions associated with this broad topic for which there are no answers. Within the field of education this might be "What is a good education?" or "What makes a good teacher?" Students then take more responsibility for choosing their research paths and methods, but they are also given outcome expectations: They must find statistics, quotations, key articles, and so on and utilize these in their discussion contribution. Specific instructions prove effective in stimulating the various roundtable groups (usually eight students in each). The students must talk non-stop; everyone must participate and do so by offering various portions of their research. The topic "education" has worked particularly well because students have all had experiences on a personal level and now can develop different perspectives based on their research.

— JANET McNEIL HURLBERT —

USING LIBRARY PARAPROFESSIONALS TO TEACH
LIBRARY SKILLS IN AN EFL PROGRAM

Rebecca Jackson

Five years ago, librarians at the Gelman Library at George Washington University (GW) began exploring alternatives to the practice of having librarians teach library skills classes to the three levels of English as a Foreign Language (EFL) courses that are regularly taught on campus. Librarians taught an average of 25 classes per semester, and, with all their other responsibilities for instruction, this added number became too much of a burden.

In addition, EFL classes require that fundamental skills be taught. As a result, librarians found themselves teaching the same things, class after class, with very little evidence that their instruction was providing students with the skills they needed.

In 1991, the acting user education coordinator wrote a proposal to the director of the library, requesting that funding be provided to hire several graduate students to act as library skills teaching assistants for the EFL classes. At the time, the proposal did not stipulate whether these students would be graduate students from GW or library school graduate students from the two library programs in the area. The library accepted the proposal and $800 was granted to the coordinator to fund the new program.

At the same time, the user education coordinator, along with the subject specialist for EFL, began meeting with the director of the EFL program and several other EFL instructors. The purpose of these meetings was to review the objectives for the three courses and to review what materials and information would be taught in each class. As in most schools,

Jackson is user education programs coordinator, Gelman Library, George Washington University, Washington, DC.

many of the EFL instructors were part-time adjuncts and, therefore, knew little about the library. The librarians and the permanent EFL instructors felt that instruction in the use of the library needed to focus on a few skills that would be fairly easy to comprehend by both the students and their instructors.

That year the library introduced a new online catalog system to the public that included the combined catalogs of the seven universities that are a part of the Washington Research Library Consortium. In addition, there were several databases loaded with the online catalog, including several Wilson indexes and ERIC. The whole system is called ALADIN.

Up to 1991, the main focus of the EFL classes had been to teach students how to use the print *Readers' Guide to Periodical Literature* and then how to find the periodicals in the library using an in-house-produced print listing. Because the librarians were finding that students were gravitating to the periodical indexes on the ALADIN system, we decided to revamp the whole teaching module for EFL. Instead of teaching the print *Readers' Guide*, we would teach the use of the GENL database on ALADIN, which included *Readers' Guide, Social Sciences Index, Humanities Index,* and *Business Periodicals Index* combined in one database. We also decided to teach the students how to find the Library's periodical holdings using the ALADIN system, rather than the print listing.

I started as user education programs coordinator in November of 1991, in the middle of all these changes. We planned on hiring the graduate students to begin teaching in the spring semester, since this was a lighter teaching semester than the fall. I started just at the point when we were ready to start advertising for the teaching assistants.

With the assistance of our library student liaison, we began interviewing students. About ten students applied and we planned to hire five or six. As a surprising bonus, the head of our information desk indicated an interest in teaching and his part-time assistant also applied. I saw a definite advantage to having someone from the library teaching the classes, and determined that the information desk head could afford to take time from his regular responsibilities to take on this additional job. We hired three graduate students from outside the Library and the two library staff members.

The next task was to begin training the new library instructors. The EFL subject specialist, another librarian, and myself planned two half-day workshops for training. The EFL subject specialist revised the objectives for each of the three EFL levels that come into the library for instruction and totally revamped the workbook that we had been using. We wanted to make the workbook an outline for the class, so that the library instructors could follow it as they began their teaching experience.

In the training sessions, we focused on exactly how to use the workbook in the classes. We demonstrated using the online catalog in class to perform keyword searches as well as to find periodical holdings information. As a further aid in the teaching, we made up a set of generic transparencies that the library instructors could use. We gave the new instructors a tour of the library as they would give the EFL students. We also discussed teaching strategies and the special needs of foreign students in U.S. university libraries. We encouraged the new instructors to ask open questions in class and not to be afraid to say they did not know an answer to a question.

As for the logistics of scheduling classes, they went through several changes throughout the semester. At first, the EFL subject specialist planned to receive the calls from the instructors, arrange for scheduling the classroom, and assign the class to one of the new instructors. As the semester progressed, we found that we could more easily refer the instructors to the head of the information desk who became the de facto coordinator, arranging for classroom scheduling and assigning classes to the instructors. The library instructors were supposed to make contact with the EFL instructors whose classes they were teaching before the class, to make sure the times were right and to see if there were any special needs to be taken into consideration for the class. In reality, this became problematic, as many of the EFL instructors were hard to reach.

Throughout the semester, the EFL subject specialist and I observed at least one session for each of the library instructors, and we arranged for consultations with them periodically. At the end of the semester, we met with them as a group to discuss how the program went and what changes they felt should be made for the program to succeed. We also met with them individually, so that we could get candid feedback. In addition, we developed evaluation forms for the EFL instructors; those who did not fill them out were called for feedback.

As a result of the various forms of feedback, as well as our experiences during the semester, we recommended that the program be continued, but that some changes be made:

1) We felt that non-librarians, with the proper training, were quite good at doing these classes. In fact, they offered some advantages we had not considered beforehand. For one, they were graduate students, as were many of the EFL students, so the EFL students felt a little like they were learning from their peers. In addition, several of the instructors were themselves foreign students and so had a real understanding of the EFL students' needs and difficulties. Finally, because two of the instructors were often at the information desk, the EFL students recognized them and therefore talked to them more easily about their needs after the class, when they were actually working on an ALADIN search.

2) We did feel, however, that we wanted to have only Gelman staff teaching these classes. Partly this was a result of the fact that Gelman staff who work at public service desks already know the library. But more important was the difficulty of scheduling the outside students to teach. It was often difficult contacting them and even harder to work the EFL classes into their own schedules. Because of these problems, the two information desk staff ended up teaching more than their share of the classes.

3) We found that new library instructors became more confident if they taught more classes. We therefore recommended that we train just enough instructors so that they would teach about eight to ten classes during the semester.

For that fall semester, we recruited five Gelman staff members to teach the EFL classes. These staff members went through another eight-hour training session, this time incorporating a short videotaping session into the training, so they could actually review themselves teaching. The head of the information desk continued coordinating the scheduling. Considering the increased number of classes in the fall, there were relatively few problems. The most significant problem was one that was to be expected—sometimes staff's "real" jobs got in the way of their teaching responsibilities. Halfway through the semester, I contacted all the supervisors of the new library instructors to make sure that it was still feasible for the staff member to teach the classes and to reinforce the priority of classes.

As for the EFL instructors, few of them had any complaints about the new instructors. Most of them noted the first semester that the library instructors were new and that in time their teaching skills would probably improve. We have been running this program for over four years now, the EFL instructors are used to the library staff teaching the classes, and I have not had any complaints in over two years.

A year ago last summer, we made what was to me a significant change in the program, but probably one not noticed by the EFL instructors. At that time, the head of the information desk left the library. Instead of simply replacing him, we changed the position completely. Now that position is titled instructional services support supervisor and the grade of the position was raised significantly, so that now it is one of the highest-level non-librarian positions in the library. The new title reflects the fact that for the past several years the information desk has been responsible for most of the basic ALADIN instruction that occurs on a one-on-one basis. The person in that position has responsibility for developing and maintaining the instructional point-of-use materials for the ALADIN system. In addition, that person has almost total responsibility for the coordination of the EFL instruction, as well as any other tours that are done for other classes. That position has always reported to me directly, but now the ties between that position and mine are far more complex.

Fortunately for me, the person we hired for that position is excellent. She had worked in the library almost five years before taking this position, the last two years as a supervisor at the periodicals desk. She was also one of the staff who had been teaching the EFL classes since the time we started working only with Gelman staff. We had almost a complete turnover in the staff who teach the EFL program; the new supervisor recruited people from all over the library and handled their training. She also hired two new assistants at the information desk; one of them is also working with the EFL program. In the fall of 1995, she started offering the EFL instructors the option of scheduling two library classes instead of one. Several of the EFL faculty took her up on the offer; in some cases, the second session was a follow-up, scheduled after the students had done some work in the library. In a couple of cases, she worked with the students to

teach them how to use our campuswide information system and the World Wide Web.

I have since taken over the coordination of the EFL program as a subject specialist. This means I have developed a close relationship with several of the permanent EFL faculty. They are all delighted with the program and think that our supervisor has done an excellent job of training the staff who teach and maintaining the consistency of quality teaching. They continually talk about what a great person Ami Cutler is and what a good job the library instructors are doing.

In addition, the staff who do the library instruction have benefitted. They are learning new skills and adding variety to their jobs. We have trained some staff who are not public services staff, and they seem to love the opportunity to get out and work with our patrons; in addition, they have a better idea how what they do in their "regular" jobs affects how our users get the information they need. In short, most of them have found their teaching experiences a welcome addition to their work at Gelman.

I have included two appendixes that I thought might be most helpful to you if you are interested in undertaking a program like this. Appendix 1 explains some of the points to remember in working with international students and in giving presentations. These are the points we focused on in the training sessions. Appendix 2 is a listing of what we included and still include in the staff training for the program. There are some general tips at the end of this handout, lessons we learned and wanted to pass on to others who might be interested in starting such a program.

Most of the library staff and EFL instructors feel this program has been a great success. It has freed librarians to spend more time on outreach within their subject areas. It has given the staff who do the teaching a broader, more exciting experience of working in the library. It has allowed us to offer the EFL program a multi-level approach to teaching their students to do research. As a result of the success of this program, I am considering ways we might expand the teaching to include some of our freshman experience classes, which at this point are only getting a basic tour of the library and whatever research skills training that their advisors in the course feel they can provide. Of course, I have been fortunate both in the strong support I have gotten from the library administration and in the people who have been in the crucial positions as schedulers and teachers. However, I think with careful planning and a positive recruitment program, other libraries would be equally successful in initiating such a program.

APPENDIX 1: POINTS TO REMEMBER ABOUT WORKING WITH INTERNATIONAL STUDENTS

1. Public service (reference, information, circulation, instruction) is a uniquely Western concept with which most foreign students are unfamiliar.

2. Tell them to bring their first assignments to the reference desk for help and direction.

3. The ideas of call numbers and even being able to retrieve their own materials are also foreign to many.

4. Part of what we are working for in the instruction classes is to build a positive relationship with students—to make them feel comfortable with you and the library.

5. A positive or negative experience with one library representative may influence a student's perception of an entire staff.

6. Be sensitive to the emotional state of the students. Not only are language problems real and frightening, but there may also be financial pressures, strange foods, lack of close friends and family, and worry about what's going on back home.

7. Students may not want to admit that they don't understand something, so you have to make a special effort to make sure they do. Often they will nod their heads and say they understand, but if you ask them "What did I say?," the answer will probably be, "I don't know."

8. Make no assumptions. Ask open-ended questions that will require something other than a yes or no answer.

9. In many Asian countries, students do what they are assigned, and they are usually not assigned creative or imaginative tasks. Often they will not do any research papers until they are in graduate school.

10. Foreign students will probably read English much better than they speak it or comprehend it, so using blackboards or handouts to emphasize important points is recommended. If you notice anytime that they look lost or confused, write what you are saying on the board.

11. Speak slowly, enunciate clearly. Direct your voice toward the individual or group. Don't shout. It isn't that they can't hear you; they can t understand what you are saying.

12. Eye contact is very important. Constantly check with your eyes for understanding. If you see confusion, stop and repeat. And rephrase; don't just use the same words.

13. Repeat important points and check for comprehension. Give several meanings for important words within the sentence.

14. Use standard English. Avoid library jargon (stacks, circulate, citation), slang, and colloquial English.

15. Use simple vocabulary. For example, instead of the verb "to circulate," use "borrow" or "take home."

16. Try to use fairly simple sentence structures. The less subordination in a sentence, the easier it is to understand. Example:

> NOT: I understand that you have to write a thesis on a topic of a scientific nature which requires the use of several journal articles.

> BUT RATHER: I understand that you have to write a paper on a topic in science. You will need to use several journal articles to find information about your topic.

17. Use your body to help communicate. Gestures are particularly effective. Be animated.

18. Periodically ask questions to check for understanding. Instead of asking, "Do you have any questions?," ask "What questions do you have?"—and then give them time to respond (count to ten silently).

19. Remember that these students are the best from their own countries. They are very bright and probably feel more frustrated at their communication problems than you are. Treat them with the same respect you would treat any other bright, eager student.

— REBECCA JACKSON —

APPENDIX 2: TEACHING TIPS

1. Tell 'em what you're gonna say.
   Say it.
   Tell 'em what you said.

2. The fewer barriers between speaker and audience, the better. Elevation, distance, podiums, and other obstacles between speaker and audience all serve to impede communication.

3. People listen to a speaker who

- is enthusiastic,

- speaks on a subject of importance to them and gives them something of value in a language they can understand,

- makes them feel comfortable and puts them in an enjoyable mood,

- recognizes when it's time to take a break, and

- presents material in digestible amounts.

4. Talk to the students. They are composed of individuals. Talk to them as individuals, conversationally.

5. If you are nervous, look for the friendly faces.

6. At the start, let the room come to order, look people in the eyes, and begin. Don't start speaking until you and the class are ready.

7. Keep your perspective—don't take the class too seriously and even try to enjoy it a little.

8. Know your material and prepare well.

9. Focus on the message, not what the audience might be thinking about you.

10. Conduct early participatory activity. Perhaps get their names and where they are from.

11. The most fundamental rule for successful presentations is to start where they are, not where you are.

12. Avoid lengthy formal definitions; instead, use brief paraphrased definitions, with specific examples.

13. Be careful with jokes and humor.

14. Listen intently to their questions and comments. Repeat them back before responding to make sure the question is understood.

15. Remember, a presentation is like any performance. Don't be alarmed if you have butterflies at the start.

16. As a presenter you are representing the whole library, not just yourself.

17. The power of a smile is tremendous.

18. Be and stay positive.

19. Assume that the main burden of responsibility to communicate is yours and that your duty as an instructor is not to impress, baffle, or overpower your listeners, but to help them understand your message and the library.

20. Don't use qualifiers very much, hopefully, generally.

Using Visuals

1. Talk to the students, not the screen or equipment.

2. The rule is to make sure people never sit in a perfectly dark room.

3. Remove visuals when they have served their purpose.

4. Test equipment in advance. Know how to change bulbs in overheads.

5. Have equipment in place.

6. Stand so that you do not block the audience from seeing your visuals.

7. Make sure the visual can be seen clearly by the whole audience.

Potential Problems

1. Side conversation: keep your eyes on the person(s) talking; move around to the talkers

2. Equipment doesn't work: have alternatives in mind.

PLANNING FOR DIVERSITY:

A LIBRARY INSTRUCTION PROGRAM

FOR STUDENTS WITH SPECIAL NEEDS

Sharyl McMillian-Nelson and Marilyn Graubart

In this program, we define students with special needs as international students, minority students, and students with physical disabilities. The diversity program covers sensitivity training for staff, library instruction, and collection enrichment. We will discuss all three aspects but focus on library instruction. The program was funded by a grant received from the University of Missouri-Kansas City (UMKC).

[At the beginning of the session, we passed out copies of the grant announcement (see appendix 1) to all attendees, divided into small groups, and allowed everyone ten minutes to discuss how they would respond to this kind of proposal. At the end of the session, we discussed their ideas.]

[MARILYN GRAUBART]

We both had different reasons for applying for a grant, "Planning for Diversity," offered by the University of Missouri-Kansas City. I had recently returned from a development leave in Israel where I had studied orientation programs for international students in Israeli universities. I visited seven university libraries in Israel, met with the librarians, and attended some of the orientation programs. It was interesting to observe that all of the libraries had library guides

McMillian-Nelson is library instruction reference librarian, and *Graubart* is business reference librarian, University of Missouri-Kansas City, Kansas City, Missouri.

written in several languages. Also, many of the librarians who conducted the orientation sessions were bilingual, and spoke to the students in their native languages. When I returned to UMKC, I wrote up my findings and shared them with the public services staff. I saw the grant as an opportunity to adapt and develop some of the ideas from my Israeli experience to our library.

[SHARYL MCMILLIAN-NELSON]

As the coordinator of the library instruction program, I also had reasons for being interested in the grant opportunity. We were already doing a basic library orientation for English as a Second Language classes and new international students, but I saw a need for more in-depth instruction. Like Marilyn, I felt that having the library guides translated into other languages and having interpreters present at library programs would be beneficial.

We also wished to provide better reference service for students who use the adaptive technology workstations provided for persons with visual impairments. Offering workshop opportunities for students with visual impairments seemed important. My main concern was library instruction, but other library staff were also consulted for their ideas. As a result, two additional concerns were listed: sensitivity training for library staff and collection enrichment.

[MARILYN GRAUBART]

In writing our grant proposal, we listed three major goals and objectives:

1) Improve the ability of students to conduct library research independently by expanding the library instruction program to better serve persons with physical disabilities and international students.

2) Improve library services by increasing the sensitivity and understanding of the staff toward all of the diverse groups which use the library.

3) Improve access to information and enhance the library's collection, better serving persons with physical disabilities.

[SHARYL MCMILLIAN-NELSON]

In the original grant proposal we requested $10,000; $8,000 was awarded with funds coming from the original diversity award pool and the Office of the Vice Chancellor for Student Affairs, the University Libraries, the Applied Languages Institute, the Office of Affirmative Action, Minority Students Affairs, and the Student Government Association. As part of the grant, the UMKC Counseling Center agreed to provide staff sensitivity training, thus making it possible to meet all of the goals outlined in the proposal.

$1,500 was awarded for collection enrichment. The library was already purchasing multicultural materials. Therefore, the focus of this grant component was on materials for sight-impaired library users. Materials were of two types: 1) large-print reference works (dictionaries, a thesaurus, and a medical dictionary/health manual) and 2) electronic databases that could be added to the adaptive technology workstation. Items in the latter category included an encyclopedia, a standard English dictionary, and a four-language dictionary to be placed on the workstation. These allow users to enlarge the print as much as necessary to read and print.

We had requested $2,000 for sensitivity training for full-time library staff. These services were provided without charge by the UMKC Counseling Center staff. Workshops were offered, with each person receiving six hours of training, divided into two sessions. There were two main goals we hoped to accomplish through the sensitivity training workshops: 1) to help staff gain sensitivity and 2) to increase skills in interacting with persons who were different from themselves. Many interactive activities were planned as part of these sessions. Student panels, comprised of one or more international students, one from a racial/ethnic minority group, one with a physical disability, and a representative from the campus gay and lesbian organization, were an important focus of the second training session.

The library instruction component was the most expensive and labor-intensive part of implementing the grant. Of our request, $6,500 was directed toward library instruction. The implementation occurred over two semesters.

Preparation of materials for the sessions began in the fall of 1994. We began weekly planning meetings. Minutes of each meeting were recorded on e-mail and sent to supervisors and administrators. The first step of implementation involved preparing two general library guides: "Finding Books and Articles" and "A Guide to the library." Large-print and Braille versions of these guides were produced within the library.

The two guides were translated into the five major languages of UMKC's international student population: Chinese, Bahasa Malay, Thai, Arabic, and Korean. Copies of the guides written in English were sent to the Language Link Corporation in Kansas City, Missouri, for professional translating. Translated guides were sent to us "camera ready." After attaching the library's graphic, we sent them for printing.

In the spring of 1995, preparation for the sessions intensified. We created a four-page glossary of library terms. We prepared materials to go into packets to be distributed to participants. Session outlines were prepared (see appendix 2).

The plan was to conduct library instruction sessions for the international students by language. Each session would have an English-speaking library instructor and a translator. One of our administrators recommended holding an additional session in English with no interpreter. This session would be available in case an international student was unable to attend her or his designated session, an international student's language was not one of the top five, a student preferred an English session, or for our noninternational students. Sessions were advertised as being open to all UMKC students, faculty, and staff.

We arranged similar workshops for persons with hearing or sight impairments. A session also would be offered for hearing-impaired students with a sign-language interpreter. We held two sessions for persons with sight impairments. Additional guides were produced for students with visual impairments that pertained to use of the adaptive technology workstations. Copies of standard library guides were printed in large print and Braille.

After consulting with library administrators, the decision was made that, despite the cost, no session would be cancelled even if no one registered in advance. This proved to be a good decision; some sessions with no sign-ups did have several attend.

[MARILYN GRAUBART]

In order to ensure that the program would be a success, it was necessary to network both on and off campus, and to market and advertise the program extensively. We began with the library staff. Because of the many administrative details such as reserving a room for the sessions, making all of the staff aware that students would be calling or coming in to sign up, and securing help in hanging advertising posters in the library and on campus, we worked with the library staff and student assistants in reference extensively.

We wanted the other reference librarians to feel a sense of ownership in our program, and we hoped that in coming years, if we repeated the program, they would join us in conducting library instruction for these groups. Therefore, we encouraged them to attend any sessions of interest to them.

Because many international students work in circulation, we had a special meeting with circulation students, explained our program, asked for their suggestions, and invited them to attend a session. We also suggested they invite their friends.

We met several times with the director and staff of the Office of International Student Affairs. The director was the person who told us which were the major languages of our international students and put us in contact with the translation service we used. The staff was helpful in giving us additional ideas about international students' library interests. They also indicated to us what times during the semester their students would be most likely to use the library. The staff agreed to send an e-mail message which we prepared about the program to all international students. They also arranged for us to attend a meeting of the International Student Organization, which consists of the officers and active members of the individual international student groups. This meeting was similar to the one we had with the students who work in the library. We asked them what international students expect from the library, told them about our program, invited them to attend, and asked them to bring their friends.

Many of our international students live off campus, and we contacted the managers of several apartment buildings where these students live and secured their permission to put up posters advertising the program on their bulletin boards. The coordinator of services for students with disabilities helped us locate all of the students registered with his office. He personally contacted some of the students, told them about our program, and invited them to attend.

We used many different methods to market and advertise our library instruction. Some of these, in addition to the ones I have already mentioned, included hanging large posters in the library and all over the campus, placing table tents on the tables in the cafeteria, placing ads in the student newspaper, writing an article for a campus publication which goes to staff and faculty, and sending notices to ESL teachers and the Applied Language Institute, which coordinates the English-language study for international students. We prepared separate posters and ads for the sessions for international students and the sessions for students with disabilities. All of our notices asked students to RSVP by phone, e-mail, or in person.

One of the questions we asked on our evaluation forms for the program was how the person learned of the sessions. It was interesting to us to note that all of the marketing tools we used were mentioned, and no one was heavily chosen. Many students wrote that they learned about the program from a friend who heard about it from one of the various sources I mentioned.

[SHARYL MCMILLIAN-NELSON]

At each session, we did the following: 1) introduced ourselves and the translator, 2) discussed our goals for the session and encouraged questions, 3) discussed the contents of the packets, 4) covered information in the "Guide to the library" in detail, 5) demonstrated the library catalog, 6) demonstrated a CD-ROM index, 7) discussed how to find a book and a periodical in our library, 8) discussed what to do if an item is missing from the shelves or is not held by the library, 9) described more advanced research tools and announced workshop opportunities available to learn them, and 10) had time for last-minute questions and evaluations.

Conducting the sessions taught us a number of important lessons. First, the instruction sessions on the adaptive technology workstations for persons with sight impairments were attended only by library staff. Although we were disappointed that others did not attend, these sessions proved excellent training for reference personnel, and enabled us all to provide better instruction to sight-impaired users of the equipment whenever they came to the library. Since this was needed, we feel that the sessions were worthwhile.

The session for students with hearing impairments was attended by one student. The session went well, and we learned a great deal from the sign-language interpreter. She taught us that additional information gathered prior to the session would be useful. Examples of questions to ask include: "Do participants use sign language? What type? Do they lip-read? Would some sort of adaptive technology be helpful?" In discussions with the interpreter prior to our session, she pointed out the importance of having the interpreter stand in a well-lit area. Since we would need to turn off the lights during part of the demonstration, we arranged to have a small light directed at the interpreter so she could still be seen.

To allow the language interpreters to prepare for the sessions with the international students, we sent them the session outline and a sample packet in advance. Some noted that the "Glossary of Library Terms" was helpful. In addition, we arranged to meet with the language interpreters for a half-hour prior to each session. This allowed the instructor and the interpreter to negotiate how frequently to stop for translation. It varied among the sessions, but none of the sessions were done word-for-word. Both the library instructor and the interpreter stood facing the group. We discovered that the students' abilities to communicate in English varied greatly, and the interpreters proved excellent in determining their needs. Many students asked their questions in their native languages, and the interpreter translated the questions to English for the library instructor. We found these sessions with the interpreters to be dynamic and interactive!

Because we expected to repeat these programs in the coming years, it was important to evaluate them. We had a participant evaluation form for each session. The form solicited information regarding the session attended, the participant's status (for example: freshman, sophomore, graduate student), their number of years at UMKC, their major areas of study, how they learned of the event, how useful they found the session and the guides, and how well the information was presented (see appendix 3). The results were positive. The majority thought the session and guides were extremely useful (4-5 on a scale of 0-5). The majority indicated the material presented was at the right level of difficulty, although several students at the Chinese and English session thought the information was too basic. At sessions with interpreters, participants indicated they found the guides and interpreters extremely helpful. At the English session, several students expressed doubt that interpreters would be needed. (We suspect this occurred because many of the students who attended this session had advanced English skills.) One surprise was that many who attended these orientations were graduate students rather than undergraduates. One session attracted a visiting professor. On the whole, we were pleased with the evaluations, and were eager to continue the program.

[MARILYN GRAUBART]

Everything we have been telling you has been about the program during the first year. We were able to secure funding from the library and have repeated the sensitivity training (for new employees hired since the last sensitivity training) and the library instruction,

and have purchased additional materials. We prepared a budget of approximately $3,000 to cover these areas. The languages of the majority of our international students have not changed, and the information in our guides has remained nearly the same also, so we did not have to budget for new translations. The counseling center has agreed to continue providing the sensitivity training at no cost to the library. Most collection development has been absorbed into subject funds administered by the subject specialists.

We met with members of the library administration to discuss continuation of the program. They agreed with us that the diversity program matches well the strategic plans of the university and the library which emphasize the importance of diversity. We all believe that the program has enhanced the image of the library in the academic community.

Together, we developed some new ideas and suggestions for changes in the program. We plan to recommend to the Office of Student Affairs that they include information on the library's diversity programming in material they distribute to prospective students. International students who work in the library are among the first people patrons entering the library encounter. In the future, they will be required to attend library instruction for international students. This training should make it easier for them to answer questions about various library services. It may also help them become student ambassadors to their friends encouraging their attendance. We see this as one method to increase the attendance of international students.

We plan to integrate diversity programming into the ongoing activities of the library. For example, the staff development committee, a standing library committee, will offer a yearly program highlighting diversity.

[SHARYL MCMILLIAN-NELSON]

Between the time when we submitted the proposal and the time we received a letter saying our application was awarded, we considered what we would do if we did not receive the award. One thought for implementing the plan without the requested funds was to use students and staff with language ability for interpreters and translators. We feel fortunate we were able to use professionals for these tasks. Coordinating these efforts with volunteers would be a formidable undertaking, but we mention it as a possibility for anyone wanting to implement such a library instruction program without additional funding. The translating service we use has two people involved in each translation. One does the initial translating; another reviews it. We would recommend this to anyone attempting to use volunteer services as well, as a quality control.

[MARILYN GRAUBART]

Development of the grant gave us several opportunities for publication. I combined information from the report I prepared on my Israeli experience with the initial work we did on the grant to publish an article, "Orientation Sessions in Israeli Academic Libraries" in *Research Strategies*.[1] An article describing the sensitivity training and library instruction for students with physical disabilities was published in an electronic journal, *Information Technology and Disabilities*[2] as well as in *Library Hi Tech*.[3]

[SHARYL MCMILLIAN-NELSON]

[We concluded our presentation with a discussion of the following questions.]

Discussion questions:

1) Do you have any questions concerning our program?

2) Have any of you developed library instruction programs for special groups or are you aware of similar programs at other libraries?

3) What ideas did you list on your handouts (see appendix) while "brainstorming" at the beginning of this session?

NOTES

1. Marilyn Graubart, "Orientation Sessions in Israeli Academic Libraries," *Research Strategies* 13 (Summer 1995): 165-175.

2. Marilyn Graubart, "Enhancing Library Services for Patrons with Disabilities through Staff Sensitivity Training and Specialized Bibliographic Instruction," *Information Technology and Disabilities* (1995): 2. [Online Journal] Available gopher://sjuvm.stjohns.edu:70/11/disabled/easi/easijrnl/itdv02n4.

3. Marilyn Graubart, "Serving the Library Needs of Students with Physical Disabilities," *Library Hi Tech* 14:1 (1996): 24-27.

Exercise: *If the following announcement came to you, what would YOU do with it? How might you adapt the award to a library setting?*

An Award to
Diversify the University's Curriculum

Faculty members who propose creative ways to integrate diversity issues into their curriculum may qualify for an award to implement the ideas.

$10,000 will be available annually to one or more faculty members to fund proposals for modifying existing courses to foster a greater understanding of diversity.

To Apply:

Submit a proposal describing an innovative modification of your course or the introduction of new material that would promote a greater sensitivity to and appreciation of diversity. Interested faculty should submit a detailed description of their plans, the goals or results to be achieved, and an itemized budget needed to implement the proposal. No request should exceed $10,000.

Guidelines:

Diversity may include, but is not limited to, ethnicity, cultural pluralism, gender, race, sexual orientation or age. A combination of diversity issues also is acceptable.

Funding will be awarded to projects that can be implemented in one academic year. Priority will be given to new projects that can be repeated or adapted in subsequent semesters, have expansive value to other courses, and directly benefit student learning.

Excerpts taken from award announcement at the University of Missouri-Kansas City, 11-4-93
sam 5/13/96 file: announcm.loe

— SHARYL MCMILLIAN-NELSON AND MARILYN GRAUBART —

Outline of Library Instruction Sessions

I. Introduction:

    A.   Instructor, translator, and participants introduce themselves. Participants say their name, area of study, and what they hope to learn from session.

    B.   Summarize outline of session. Provide packet with all handouts. Briefly go through what is included in packet:

        1.   Guide to the Library
        2.   Library Guide to Finding Books and Articles
        3.   Library Guide to Interlibrary Loan
        4.   Glossary of Library Terms
        5.   Guide to LUMIN
        6.   List of databases
        7.   Evaluation form
        8.   Blank Sheet of Paper for taking notes
        9.   Pencil

    C.   Encourage participants to ask questions if something is unclear, or to help explain a concept to other participants in a different way.

II. Library Services:

    A.   Discuss information included in "Guide to the Library" handout.

    B.   Discuss Interlibrary Loan procedures, as detailed in "Library Guide to Interlibrary Loan" handout.

III.   Research Methods:

A.   Designing a "research strategy"

   1.   Deciding on a topic and a focus.
   2.   Learning about terms and concepts by using general and subject specific dictionaries and encyclopedias.
   3.   Gathering information by looking at specialized Reference sources for statistics, biographies, etc., and by searching for books and articles.

B.   Demonstrate LUMIN, (automated catalog for finding books and other library materials). Handout included in packet. Types of searches to demonstrate:

   1.   title
   2.   author
   3.   subject

C.   Use of "controlled vocabulary" used in many library tools. (Specific example: Library of Congress Subject Headings used in LUMIN).

D.   Using "periodical indexes" to find articles in journals.

   1.   Using print indexes:

      Pass around samples of Wilson indexes: Humanities Index, Social Sciences Index, Education Index, Applied Science and Technology Index, etc. Discuss procedures for using, locating journal abbreviations in list at front of index, etc.

   2.   Using cd-rom indexes:

      Demonstrate use of one or more cd-rom indexes, based on subject interests of participants.

3. Exercise:

Provide participants with a topic, and have them write down suggestions for keywords and search terms. Try out a search on a cd-rom incorporating their suggested terms.

4. Other electronic sources of information:

 a. First Search
 b. Eureka
 c. Site Search
 d. Nexis/Lexis
 e. other cd-rom tools
 d. Internet

IV. Putting it all together:

A. Considering the "value" of information gathered:

1. Is the journal "scholarly?"
2. Date of material published
3. Qualifications of author
4. Looking "critically" at the content

B. Using information gathered in an appropriate manner:

1. DO incorporate ideas read.
2. DO respond to them in a critical way.
3. DO support your ideas with those of other authors.
4. DON'T plagiarize! Use quotations marks to indicate direct quotations from sources. Provide citations for sources of ideas even when not directly quoting. DO NOT copy sections from a book, making only minor changes to wording.

V. Conclusion:

A. Summary/Wrap-up
B. Answer questions
C. Reminder of evaluation forms!

[sam/mg: 3/6/95; rev 3/13/95]

APPENDIX 3:

International Student Library Instruction Sessions
Evaluation Form

Personal Data:

Language Session you attended _____ Date _____

Please check one: Freshman ____   Junior ____
                 Sophomore ____   Senior ____   Graduate ____

How many years have you been a student at UMKC? ____ Major area of study _____

How did you hear about this event? _____

Evaluation of session: *(Circle one number for each question.)*

How useful did you find today's library instruction session?

    Not very useful   0   1   2   3   4   5   Extremely useful

How helpful did you find it to have the library guides translated into your native language?

    Not very helpful   0   1   2   3   4   5   Extremely helpful

How helpful did you find it to have a language translator assist with the instruction?

    Not very helpful   0   1   2   3   4   5   Extremely helpful

Did you feel the information presented was...

    Too basic/easy 0 1   2   3   4   5   Too advanced/difficult

Did you feel the librarian presented the information in a way that was...

    Confusing/unclear 0   1   2   3   4   5   Easy to understand

What did you like best about the session?

What do you wish had been done differently?

Would you recommend this program to a friend? yes _____   no _____

[sam 3/10/95]

100 LOEX-96   — SHARYL MCMILLIAN-NELSON AND MARILYN GRAUBART —

INTEGRATING INFORMATION LITERACY
INTO THE CURRICULUM

Karen L. Michaelsen

The Seattle Central Community College Library has been recognized for its successful instruction program. However, the program has served an increasing number of students in an environment of academic, economic, and technologic challenges. If we do not change we will fail to serve our students effectively. This article describes one college library's struggle to remain successful while facing these challenges.

Our college is located in the heart of a large urban area and serves Washington State's most diverse population of students. We serve approximately 10,400 students (6,150 full-time equivalent). Nearly 60 percent of our regular students are preparing to transfer to four-year programs, while the other 40 percent are enrolled in professional-technical, English as a Second Language (ESL), high school completion, and personal enhancement programs. The final report of the Northwest Association of School and Colleges applauded our "strong institutional focus on educational assessment and student learning outcomes," and "the many examples of cross-disciplinary collaboration and the exemplary coordinated studies classes."[1]

The college first offered "Effective Library Techniques," a three-credit research course, in 1971. This course has evolved over time, adapting to new technologies and new pedagogies. The course curriculum underwent a major revision in the early 1990s as a result of collegewide teaching initiatives. The work of Deborah Fink[2] was an important influence in the re-

Michaelsen is instruction librarian, Seattle Central Community College, Seattle, Washington.

vision of our curriculum. Librarians Kelley McHenry and Jennifer Wu collaborated with English instructor and author J.T. Stewart in developing the course to be responsive to the college's curriculum theme of cultural pluralism.[3] They developed our first link with English 102 (documented research papers). Since then we have developed other links with history and ESL classes in the belief that linking content courses to our library curriculum is most effective for students. This effort continues.

The definitions of successful programs presented at the 1996 LOEX conference included lists of attributes that successful programs share. Our program has a number of these attributes: our instruction is linked to the goals and educational philosophy of the college, we receive library and college administrative support, we are actively supported by many of our faculty, we have stated goals for our instructional sessions, we evaluate our instructional programs, we incorporate active learning techniques, and our curriculum evolves to incorporate changing technology. These attributes have been recognized in our 1993 curriculum review report, a 1995 accreditation self-study, and student evaluations of reference service and courses.

These measures of our success have been gratifying, but we were killing ourselves. One quarter we taught five sections of Library 101. Over time, the number of one-hour instructional sessions had also greatly increased. (In one year 5,500 students were served in course-integrated instruction.) All this took place with only three full-time librarians and part-time support. We had reached our limit. We knew there had to be a better way.

As a group we were concerned that we were spending so much time preparing for and teaching classes, that while some of our students were receiving a high level of instruction, others received only superficial instruction, and some students were not being served at all. Some students were getting the same kind of instruction repeatedly and not at successively higher levels. We started doing mini-surveys at the beginning of sessions to find out how many students had already had library workshops before and adjusted our presentations on the fly, using students who had previous experience to help lead small-group exercises.

We felt that some instructors were relying heavily on us to provide instruction that they could and should be teaching and reinforcing in their own classrooms. We believed that if they could do the groundwork in class, we could do higher-level instruction in the library. Other faculty were simply operating as if the library did not exist. They might rely heavily on textbooks or their own private libraries. Some faculty seemed to believe that we have nothing to offer their students and undermined our work by sending their students to other nearby libraries.

We knew we could not simply keep teaching without continuous review and revision, but we did not have a plan. We began to develop our understanding of information literacy and the role of college faculty in supporting students to find and use information effectively. The following activities and projects helped us to change our thinking about what we teach and how we teach it.

The Information Literacy Taskforce was a statewide project of the library media director's Council for Washington State Community College Libraries, led by Debra Gilchrist (see her article in this publication). The process included faculty librarians as well as library directors. We met to define what it means for our students to be information-literate. The resulting document was a means of communicating the need to make information literacy an outcome for all Washington community college students.[4]

The librarians on our campus had already asked the campus outcomes assessment committee to include information literacy on the list of student outcomes. Once this was accomplished, however, we started to wonder: How could we ensure that all students had a chance of becoming information literate as a result of their college experience? Two projects grew out of this concern.

The first project was a curriculum development grant project titled "Information Literacy Resources Project," (see appendix 1). The project was arranged by student learning objectives for fostering information literacy. The collection contained handouts and strategy development worksheets, curriculum plans, and subject guides. This collection was made available to faculty outside the library as well as to part-time librarians to provide ideas on how to develop the defined abilities. All who used the collection were encouraged to add their materials as they were developed.

A second curriculum development grant provided the resources to write a faculty guide, "Integrating Information Literacy across the Curriculum" (see appendix 1). The idea of integrating information literacy across the curriculum is not an original one; Jan Kennedy Olsen and Bill Coons reported at the 1989 LOEX conference about their project at Cornell University. They talked about targeting core courses in the curriculum to be vehicles for information literacy instruction.[5] Robert Baker wrote that "Teaching faculty are not requiring their students to independently find, use, and evaluate information as an integral component of the courses they teach."[6] Baker further challenges us to persuade faculty to collaborate with us in developing their curricula to integrate information literacy.

Perhaps what we are really trying to do is to reintegrate information literacy into the curriculum. Bibliography has traditionally been a core seminar in many graduate programs, while undergraduates have rarely been served well in this area. In the past few decades, the bibliographic instruction movement has attempted to fill this need. In a way, this has relieved undergraduate faculty from the responsibility to teach students how information is communicated and used in their discipline. The faculty guide was meant to help faculty incorporate information literacy outcomes into their own curricula, where it naturally belongs. The purpose was to inform faculty of the importance of information literacy for their students and how information literacy can be a vehicle for teaching their own disciplines. The guide went out to many Washington community college librarians and to faculty on our campus. The guides were made available to faculty by request and through faculty workshops.

In the year since it has come out, this guide has been used more by librarians to develop faculty programs promoting collaboration with librarians, rather than by the faculty to whom it was originally addressed. In a survey of the people who received copies, librarians were most inspired by the guide: while the faculty expressed more interest in the handouts than in the framework in which they were presented (see appendixes 2-5).

Shortly before the 1995 accreditation team visit, we were hiring a fourth full-time librarian. In order to integrate our new team member, we wanted to take time to reflect on who we were and where we were going. That winter we had a library faculty retreat, spending a day off campus defining what we could do to change how we plan, how we operate, and how we get the job done. We knew that even without the new hire, we could not continue at the same rate of growth we had experienced in the past and continue to be effective.

Clearly, our library instruction program was growing out of control. We had marketed our services so well that we were devoting too much of our time to direct instruction. Because of our work with the information literacy projects, the faculty guide, and with the campus outcomes assessment committee, we knew it was time for a change. Since all librarians share the responsibility for instruction, we also knew that the entire group needed to plan, execute, and evaluate any significant changes. The library instruction retreat took place in fall of 1995. We wanted to reinvent our program, not just fix it.

During the retreat we used a brainstorming process to establish our new goals and objectives for library instruction. Built into the process was the goal to evaluate our effectiveness. This was not meant to be a one-time evaluation, but to fold evaluation into our planning to help us with future program design (see appendix 5).

In defining these goals we also brainstormed to list activities we were already doing that helped further these goals. We brainstormed once again to list new activities we could develop. We recognized that in developing new activities we needed to give up current ones that would not support our new priorities.

The areas we agreed to address included the need to develop strategic positions in campus planning committees and meetings to be sure that library instruction programs and resources are included in the conversation. We wanted to reach all students and provide increasingly higher levels of instruction according to students needs, and to get away from one-shot basic instruction. We wanted to target core courses in each program to link specific information-literacy goals to the curriculum of those classes as a way to deliver instruction to all students. We wanted to provide different kinds of instruction: CAI, multimedia, tool and strategy workshops, as well as course-integrated instruction.

Central to our plan was the need to evaluate the effectiveness of the new activities we introduce. We are relying heavily on the ACRL's 1991 publication on the new model statement of objectives for academic bibliographic instruction.[7] This is an important publication for any library wishing to develop or redesign an instruction program. The recent Library Instruction Roundtable publication on evaluating library instruction includes sample questions, forms and strategies for practical use.[8]

We are beginning to execute some of our ideas; we are planning a promotional library open house for faculty and staff in the fall and developing faculty guides for library programs and services. We are struggling with what to measure and how to measure it. We are beginning to look at each goal and to consider what we should ask and whom we should ask it of. We are designing a benchmark library survey. We are considering using focus groups to get faculty involved in conversations about what the library could be doing to support their curricula, and we are preparing to contact the state's college and university reference departments to ask about their experience with community college students and how we might better prepare our transfer students.

In our efforts to develop the best program for our students we have recognized a number of roadblocks which must be common to college libraries. Many faculty are faithful supporters of the library. For us they include members of our library advisory committee, those who have taught linked courses with us, and those who have faithfully brought their classes for content-integrated library instruction. However, many faculty operate as if we do not exist. How will we reach them?

Students as well as faculty may resist our mission. We need somehow to convince students that becoming information literate is important to them as life-long learners and as effective employees and citizens. In linked classes sometimes students who think they know it all feel they have been trapped: "I don't need this class, I can get anything I need off the Internet." How do we reach these students?

Finally, if we don't have support of administrators and other faculty, it will be hard to do our jobs. We don't just need new machines and new software; we need technical support and continuing education to manage them. We also need to be advocates for student learning, developing curriculum and pedagogy that work in a changing environment. We need to be advocates within our institutions, active in the budget development process, active in campuswide curriculum and program planning and review process, active in developing resource-sharing relationships in our regions and states, and advocates for a culture that values learning and recognizes the need to help people be independent information users.

We hope to keep on track in addressing these issues through annual planning retreats to consider where we are and where we are going. We plan to continue using classroom research methods to get direct student responses to our teaching effectiveness. We plan to maintain a highly visible profile on our campus as advocates for library programs and services. Finally, we plan to attend local, regional, and national conferences to share with and learn from others in facing these issues.

Notes

1. Northwest Association of School and Colleges (NASC), "Visiting Team Recommendations and Commendations for Seattle Central Community College." Seattle Central Community College, photocopy, 1995.

2. Deborah Fink, *Process and Politics in Library Research; a Model for Course Design* (Chicago: American Library Association, 1989).

3. Kelley McHenry, J.T. Stewart, and Jennifer Wu, "Teaching Resource-Based Learning and Diversity," In *New Directions for Higher Education* 78 (Summer 1992): 55-62.

4. LMDC: Library/Media Directors' Council (CMDC), "Information Competency: An Initiative for Integrated Learning." A position statement of the Washington State Library/Media Directors' Council, photocopy, 1993.

5. Jan Kennedy Olsen and Bill Coons, "Cornell University's Information Literacy Program," in *Coping with Information Illiteracy: Bibliographic Instruction for the Information Age*, Library Orientation Series no. 20 (Ann Arbor: Pierian Press, 1989).

6. Robert K. Baker, "Working with Our Teaching Faculty," *College and Research Libraries* 56 (April 1995): 377-379.

7. ACRL, Bibliographic Instruction Section. *Read This First: An Owner's Guide to the New Model Statement of Objectives for Academic Bibliographic Instruction* (Chicago: American Library Association, 1991).

8. Diane D. Shonrock, ed., *Evaluating Library Instruction: Sample Questions, Forms, and Strategies for Practical Use* (Chicago: American Library Association, Library Instruction Roundtable, 1996).

— KAREN L. MICHAELSEN —

APPENDIX 1:

Information Literacy Resources Project

ABSTRACT

The information Literacy Resources Project consists of four binders containing materials which the library teaching staff use to compile custom packets for classes, orientations, and workshops. These binders contain photocopy masters of informational handouts and assignments currently used in the SCCC Library's Information Literacy Program. In addition, the binders contain sample syllabi, tests, review materials, and final projects for Library 101 for the information of any instructor who is preparing to teach this course. These binders are also available to any district instructors wishing to integrate information literacy into their own curricula. Copies of many of these materials are available in WP51 files to facilitate adapting them to the particular needs of instructors. New materials will be added to this collection as they are developed. (Spring 1993)

Integrating Information Literacy Across the Curriculum: an Instructor's Guide

ABSTRACT

The object of this guide is to enable faculty in any discipline to integrate information literacy learning objectives into their courses. Faculty across the district will learn about resources and services available to them through their libraries to help them develop meaningful course objectives to promote information literacy. The materials in this guide include sample learning objectives, guidelines for creating library assignments, suggested assessment techniques, and sample workshops which can be adapted to almost any course. Finally, faculty will be challenged to reach beyond textbooks to guide students to information sources outside the classroom.

Promoting information literacy helps students gain critical skills through the discovery and use of appropriate information sources. This requires them to develop their curiosity and discover for themselves the nature of information in formats relevant to their course work and appropriate to their learning styles. It teaches them to develop information seeking strategies, to challenge the credibility of sources, and to develop confidence in using resources available to them both in and beyond the library.

All of this is increasingly important when information technology is changing rapidly. Students who do not develop good abilities as information consumers now will be disadvantaged in their personal and work lives later. The more information seeking and evaluating abilities they develop in the relative safety of the college environment, the better prepared they will be to succeed in their future educational, social and work environments. (Spring 1995)

Karen Michaelsen, Seattle Central Community College, LOEX 5/96

INTEGRATING INFORMATION SEEKING SKILLS INTO YOUR CURRICULUM

The abilities of recognizing a need for information, identifying what is needed and how to find it, and evaluating and assimilating it when it is found are all critical skills for our students. They must master this process in order to succeed as responsible citizens in a democratic society and to compete in an ever-changing work place.

As we have taught more library research classes linked with other courses around the college, we librarians have come to recognize that students learn these abilities most effectively in the context of the different disciplines. They are using information to answer questions and to solve problems.

If you hand a student a textbook and ask them to learn the material it contains, they are practicing a certain kind of learning: they should be getting an overview of the subject, they may be learning to identify what the author thinks is important, they may be learning to identify what you the instructor want them to learn, and they are learning to memorize and perhaps summarize the contents. I do not mean to dismiss the value of a good textbook, but students do a different kind of learning when they are asked to find answers to questions and to solve problems by finding information. They are practicing critical thinking skills and they are practicing your discipline by learning about the reference and periodical sources for your discipline, they are learning the language of your discipline, and the ways scholars in your discipline do research and communicate their results.

For each program and subject area there is a faculty librarian who acts as a liaison to the library's programs and services. That person is a valuable resource to you in planning and designing exercises, activities, and workshops which require your students to practice these skills and abilities. That library liaison is there to help you discover what information learning objectives are appropriate to your classes. That person also is interested in what your students are doing so that decisions to purchase materials in your subject area are consistent with what you and your students need. Your library liaison is also an important resource for developing library assignments that work.

Call your library reference desk to find out who is responsible for your subject area.

Karen Michalesen, Seattle Central Community College, LOEX 5/96

DESIGNING EFFECTIVE LIBRARY ASSIGNMENTS

Effective library assignments accomplish three important things: they motivate students to use the library to find information they need for your class; they introduce students to resources which are important to your subject; and they encourage students to use the library for their own needs and apply what they have learned in your class to further their personal goals. This is a real contribution to developing your students' critical thinking abilities and life long learning.

Library faculty are happy to help you develop library assignments which will support your teaching and assist students' learning. The following guidelines are offered to help you in thinking about how to integrate information literacy into your curriculum.

1. **Define your objective:**

   Relate your assignment to the information literacy objectives you have identified for your course. What do you want to accomplish? Do you wish your students to be acquainted with the key resources in your subject area? Do you want them to do the groundwork for a term project or research paper? What do you want the students to do with information once they have found it?

2. **Develop the assignment:**

   Focus your assignment on the process of finding information which explains a phenomena, clarifies a viewpoint, defines an issue, or answers a question. Depending on your subject area and the level of your students, you might want to focus on a particular kind of information (dictionaries, encyclopedias, periodicals, books, or other media) or perhaps to find information in a variety of sources.

   Require your students to exercise critical thinking. Pose a problem or question which asks students to develop a strategy to complete the exercise. Once students have found the information, also ask them to evaluate or comment on it. They should analyze it, question it, and compare it to information found in other sources.

   Ask students to find information which they can use. Avoid exercises which ask them to find information in particular resources such as in a treasure hunt. Students are easily frustrated when all of the students in your class are looking for the same material. The first student who pulls that item off the shelf makes it hard for all who follow to find it again. Instead, ask a question which might be found in a number of places and which is relevant to the objectives of your course.

3.   **Test your assignment:**

Do the assignment yourself. Make sure your students have a reasonable expectation of successfully completing the assignment. Many students come to the library seeking a particular book or article their teacher believes is in the library. Get to know what the library has for your students and work with the librarian who is responsible for your subject area to develop the resources for your students. Students who are doing research on specialized topic may find that there are resources outside of our collection that they need. The reference librarians can help these students to identify where the information is located and they can often borrow the material from another library. The material may also be readily available locally.

Show the assignment to a colleague in your department or in the library.
Someone who knows your subject well may have important suggestions to make and a librarian may see practical problems that you overlooked.

Ask your students for feedback on the assignment. Be open to their suggestions and comments. The next time you use the assignment it will be stronger and more effective and more likely to achieve your objectives.

Success breeds success. Students who successfully complete your library assignment will be more willing to use the library on their own. Sample assignments conclude this section.

Tips for effective library workshops:

If your curriculum requires significant library use, we encourage you to request a library workshop. Call the Reference Desk at your library and make an appointment to bring in your class. Be very clear about what your objectives are and share your library assignment with the person who will be presenting the workshop. It is possible for you to bring your class into the library and to work with them without the assistance of the librarian, but please make an appointment for this as well. We want you and your students to have a positive experience and if we have more than one class in the library at the same time, this is difficult to achieve.

Prepare your students for the workshop. Explain to them why the library workshop is important for them to be successful in your class. Give them the assignment before the workshop so that they are thinking about what they need to know and can ask relevant questions.

Follow the workshop with class discussion of your students experience in the library and make sure that your students have a chance to use what they have learned. Communicate both problems and successes to the librarian who gave the workshop. This information is important to developing future workshops for you and others.

Karen Michalesen, Seattle Central Community College, LOEX 5/96

REVIEWING THE LIBRARY COLLECTION FOR YOUR DISCIPLINE

Your Name:

Your discipline or program:

The courses you teach:

Library of Congress call number ranges related to your discipline or program:

Your Library Faculty Liaison:

Please examine the following sections of the library collection for material relevant to the courses you teach or the program in which you work. Do not spend a lot of time, but quickly get a sense of what is on the shelf. Think about how your students might use the materials. Do you know of materials appropriate to your students' level which should be in the collection? Please briefly note your impressions and suggestions in the space provided.

Periodicals Collection:

Relevant titles:

Suggested titles:

Reference Collection:

Important works:

Suggestions:

Main Collection:

Overall impression:

Suggestions:

AV Collection:

Important discoveries:

Suggestions:

NOTES:

Please return to the library during the next week and spend more time working on this exercise. Your input is important information that we can use when we are purchasing materials and will make it possible for us to improve our services and resources for you and your students. Please keep in touch with your library faculty liaison.

Return this form to your library faculty liaison when completed.

Karen Michaelsen, Seattle Central Community College, LOEX 5/96

Seattle Central Community College

LIBRARY INSTRUCTION PROGRAM GOALS

1996 AND BEYOND

- Promote information literacy

- Empower students to be independent learners

- Develop diverse instructional delivery

- Increase collaborative instruction relationships

- Provide access to diverse resources

- Improve outreach and visibility of library

- Evaluate effectiveness

Karen Michaelsen, Seattle Central Community College, LOEX 5/96

A Program that Works: Library Research Course for Early Childhood Students at SUNY Cobleskill

Nancy Niles

SUNY Cobleskill is a two-year college with programs in early childhood education, agriculture, business, foods and hospitality, and liberal arts and sciences. In 1987, a one credit course in research skills (LIBS 101) was approved as an elective and has been taught by the instruction librarian each semester since then. Many faculty members in the Early Childhood Division saw the usefulness of such a course, and advised their students to take LIBS 101, since many early childhood students transfer to four-year colleges for degrees in elementary education. In 1990, the early childhood faculty asked if it were possible to have all entering early childhood students take LIBS 101. Unfortunately, I was the only instruction librarian and was already teaching over 150 course-related sessions plus LIBS 101. Therefore, offering the course to 200 additional students was not feasible.

As a compromise, the Learning Resource Center (LRC) agreed to design an independent study library skills course for the early childhood students. We designed a workbook that introduced students to the LRC, the tools needed for researching topics in education, and a simple search strategy for doing library research. After a one-hour orientation session and slide-show tour, students had five weeks to read the workbook and complete a search assignment. The search assignment was reviewed by a librarian and returned to the students with evaluative comments. Each student took a mastery

Niles is instruction librarian, State University of New York, College of Agriculture and Technology at Cobleskill, Cobleskill, New York.

test at the eighth week, with one retest available two weeks later for students who did not pass it the first time. Beginning with the second year of the program, students were also required to complete an in-house-designed computer tutorial for early childhood research.

Statistics for the eight semesters the course was offered revealed an alarming drop in numbers of students passing the course, from 90 percent the first year to 61 percent in 1994 (see table 1). More important, observations from reference librarians and early childhood faculty during those years confirmed that students were merely passing the test; they had not developed any usable research skills. Even students who passed the course admitted that they did not really know how to do research when faced with an information problem. Clearly our efforts were not successful.

What Went Wrong?

I believe that so many students failed the independent study course because the design of the course did not take into account the type of student majoring in the early childhood program. Over the span of just a few years, students admitted to the early childhood major were less and less prepared for college-level work. These students were not self-motivated, independent learners. Over half of the students entering the program were placed in remedial math and remedial writing courses. An independent study course was not a wise choice in methodology for the students in the program.

TABLE 1: PERCENTAGES OF STUDENTS PASSING EACH SEMESTER					
	1990-91	1991-92	1992-93	1993-94	1994-95
Fall	90	81	79	63	61
Spring	72	80	64	30	50

The independent study course also lacked a meaningful connection to the early childhood curriculum. Students did not have actual curriculum-based research needs to motivate them to learn how to do research. The search assignment was essentially meaningless for students, as evidenced by the frequent incidence of cheating (two or more students handing in identical searches). Although students were aware that they needed to pass the course to graduate, they did not take it seriously. In addition, since early childhood faculty rarely required students to do any extensive library research, the implicit message was that the course had no real value for students.

Another important missing instructional element was that there was no real-life modeling of research behaviors. The workbook did outline the steps in the research process, and the search assignment was designed to lead students through those steps, yet interviews with students revealed that they did not read the workbook or use it as a guide for the search assignment. They saw the search assignment as a series of unrelated steps and frequently changed topics with each different search tool required by the search strategy.

In essence, the course was a sham. In no way could it be construed as developing adequate information skills for college-level research needs. We considered giving up and telling the early childhood faculty that we were eliminating the course.

A New Approach

Since the library faculty's primary goal is to help students become information literate, we decided to have one more try. We approached the early childhood faculty with a new proposal. Rather than give up, we suggested that a full-semester credit course be developed and tied to the content of an introductory course that all early childhood students took the first semester. By our calculations, such an undertaking would require teaching eight sections of the class, assuming class size could be limited to 20.

As it turned out, there was no introductory course that *all* students took the first semester. The introductory course that we had hoped to target, "Introduction to Early Childhood Programs" (ECHD 130), was of-

fered in both fall and spring; half the first-year students took it each semester. Despite our desire to have all students take the library skills course their first semester at college, it appeared that the research skills course, "Library Research Skills for Early Childhood" (ECHD 131), would also have to be taught both Fall and Spring, with half the students taking it each semester together with "Introduction to Early Childhood Programs." Actually, pairing the library skills course with this particular course was ideal, since the professor who taught the course assigned a position paper requiring research skills far more advanced than those of the first-year students. Students in that class had required extensive reference help in past semesters.

The dean of the Early Childhood Division took our course proposal to the administration, requesting adjunct pay for the librarian to teach four sections of ECHD 131 each semester. Both were approved. The adjunct salary was then used to pay a part-time librarian to take my normal ten hours of reference each week and to teach LIBS 101, my one-credit elective course.

The New Course Syllabus

Several members of the early childhood faculty had described the difficulties their students experienced in reading an article from an education journal and summarizing the main points, so for the first three weeks I focused on critical reading skills (see appendix 1). Students practiced reading journal articles, identifying main concepts, and writing short summaries (abstracts) of the articles. For the first two weeks, I provided reprints of articles for the critical reading exercises; once we had covered using Infotrac's Academic Index and the print version of the Education Index, I required students to find, read, and summarize their own articles. I also introduced APA style and required students to cite all their sources using that format. For the first half of the semester, students used their research topics from their ECHD 130 course as applications topics for learning about search tools and strategies in our class.

Besides weekly assignments that gave students practice using various research tools such as the online catalog, print and CD-ROM databases, OCLC's First-

TABLE 2: SUCCESS RATES BY SEMESTER

	Passing	Failing
Fall 1995	51%	49%
Spring 1996	76%	24%

TABLE 3: GRADE DISTRIBUTION BY SEMESTER

	A	B	C	D	F
Fall 1995	10	14	8	4	27
Spring 1996	27	13	15	2	15

Search, and Netscape, students completed a major "Research Scenarios" project (see appendix 2). Each student selected five scenarios illustrating "real life" information needs of teachers and students. These scenarios required a synthesis of the skills and ideas we had covered during the semester. During the last few weeks of the semester students worked in class on the scenarios; many students also asked for individual help outside of class.

Even though I was explicit about the need to work independently, many students handed in scenarios identical in part or in total to those of other students. Students found to have shared work received F grades (and had to repeat the course the following semester). The number of students who cheated, added to the students who left school without formally withdrawing and the students who just plain did not do the work, created the impression that the course was not successful—at least if teaching success is based solely on numbers (see Fall 1995 results in tables 2 and 3)—since only 51 percent of the students passed the course. Grades of C or above are required in courses in the major, so any grade below a C means the student must repeat the course.

Anecdotal reports from the reference desk and the early childhood faculty, however, presented a slightly different picture. Faculty indicated that students who took the new course were much more capable of independent research than in previous semesters. Evaluations from students also said that they found the course to be useful not just for their early childhood courses, but for other classes as well.

Improving Student Success

The second semester, I incorporated several changes based on the experiences of the first semester. (One of the rewards of teaching ECHD 131 has been the fun of creating, trying out, changing, and improving the course and course materials.) First, I included instruction in e-mail. At the end of the previous semester, I realized that many early childhood students had not learned the fundamentals of using computers, so early in the spring semester I covered PC Mail and computer basics. I then used class distribution lists to send messages to entire class sections. I also sent and received many messages to and from individual students. Topics of our electronic correspondence varied from my observing to a student that I had missed him in class to providing individual help with assignments for other classes.

Next, I spent more time on the World Wide Web and databases searchable through the Internet. Since our library now had a home page (<http://www.cobleskill.edu/ lrc/service>) with links to OCLC's FirstSearch and a list of links by subject area, I scheduled three class sessions on using the Internet. I also revised the scenarios project to include more use of Internet resources. I even gave an extra-credit assignment of subscribing to a listserv for early childhood educators for several weeks and reporting on the topics of discussion.

I made a special effort to contact by phone or e-mail students who had missed classes and encourage them each to come to another session to make up the missed class. I formally withdrew students who were obviously no longer attending class. This action was not just for housekeeping purposes; any student who stops coming to class but who does not fill out a course withdrawal form must receive an F as a final grade. It looks much better for the instructor to have fewer students receiving F grades, whatever the reason. Ten percent of the students who failed the previous semester had actually dropped out of the class or out of college entirely and had never formally withdrawn.

Finally, I discussed, probably *ad nauseam*, the seriousness of cheating and its consequences. Cheating was minimal the second semester.

Next semester, instead of the scenarios project, I will ask students to work independently or in pairs on a specific topic. Students can opt for presenting their research via home pages they create or by using Powerpoint. If students choose home pages, they will describe effective search strategies, list the best print sources, and provide links to some useful Web sites. Students preparing Powerpoint presentations will cover effective search strategies, the most useful search tools, and Web sites and summarize key elements of the topic.

So Why Am I Not Satisfied?

It is gratifying to be able to claim success with this one group of students on our campus. It would be far more satisfying—my professional dream come true—to have a successful information literacy program where *every* student at our college acquires these skills. In order for that to happen, however, something different has to occur. I know I cannot, nor do I even think I should attempt to, duplicate this course within every major at Cobleskill, especially considering the fact that one of our five librarian positions has recently been eliminated.

The time has come to be honest about the real effectiveness of our BI program. In claiming that my BI reaches 1,500-some students or that I teach over 150 classes, I am only perpetuating the illusion that most of our students learn how to do research. In truth, they do not, as question after question at the reference desk bears out. By teaching this course, I am essentially excusing faculty from their absolutely critical roles in teaching information literacy. Much of what I taught students in this course could be integrated naturally and seamlessly with the content of early childhood courses, *if* the faculty themselves had those skills and that knowledge.

I believe that BI has arrived at a critical juncture, at least on our campus, and, I suspect, at many other campuses. Until now, BI librarians have been heavily involved in promoting our own expertise, convinced, and usually rightly so, that classroom faculty could not provide the best research skills instruction to students. However, it has become obvious that traditional course-related BI is a hit-or-miss situation, and I am no longer willing to allow the misses to occur, not when information skills have become so critical to success in any occupation our students might enter.

Add-On or Add-In?

We have approached a fork in our instructional road. One path would mean creating a content-area research skills course for every major, thus maintaining control over instruction. To do this we would need more librarians to teach these courses. Several colleges have taken this approach. SUNY Plattsburgh, for example, has a required library skills course in the general education curriculum. Most of their librarians teach sections of the course, with adjuncts hired specifically to teach additional sections. A variation of this scenario is to create a set of Web-based or multimedia tutorials that all students must complete. This strategy amounts to the old workbook approach, only using newer electronic media. The library would still be viewed as responsible for the instructional program and we would still be working in isolation from the curricula.

The other alternative is to first train faculty, bringing their research skills up to speed. Faculty and instruction librarians could discuss which skills should be taught or reviewed and reinforced at what points in the curriculum. In this approach, the librarians would be giving up much of the control over the teaching of information skills, trusting faculty to introduce whatever information skills they decided were important in each course. Librarians might be involved in some of that instruction, but would spend a more significant amount of their time working to help faculty maintain cutting-edge knowledge of information technologies and sources.

I prefer the second alternative, encouraging more faculty to weave information skills into their teaching, while also providing Web-based or multimedia instruction for faculty to assign or incorporate as needed. Even if I could do a better job at teaching information skills, would it not be better for students to have those skills introduced, demonstrated, and required by their professors? Isn't that really what information literacy/resource-based education is all about? I certainly am not advocating elimination of my instruction program, but I do envision an exciting new role for myself (and all instruction and reference librarians)—that of consultant when the information needs of the students exceed the limitations of the faculty member's information skills and knowledge. Then truly will our expertise be recognized, sought out, and appreciated, by faculty and students alike.

— NANCY NILES —

ECHD 131 Library Research Skills for early childhood 1 credit

Instructor: Nancy Niles Office: LRC103B Phone: 5849

Course description:

Students will develop the critical thinking and research skills that are essential for students in education and human services. Students will use print and electronic resources and tools to locate, select, and evaluate information on topics directly related to ECHD 130 course content and assignments. *To be taken consecutively with ECHD 130 Introduction to early childhood Programs.*

Required text: *Library Research Guide for early childhood Students (bookstore)*

Note: Students must obtain computer user accounts for this course. This should be done at the bookstore before the third week of classes.

Course outline:

Class 1: Introduction: rationale for course; course requirements; attendance policy; relationship to ECHD 130

> Handout: Article: "Misbehavior or Mistaken Behavior"
> Assignment: Read article, identify key points; summarize in 2-3 sentences.

Class 2: Critical reading skills; identifying key points and audience; general indexes; e-mail.

> Read: Library Research Guide pages 19-22
> Handout: "Using Infotrac's Academic Index and National Newspaper Index"
> Assignment: Find article on topic using general index; identify key points; summarize in 2-3 sentences; cite as for bibliography.

Class 3: Critical reading skills; basic (BROWSE) searching on Education Index

> Read: Library Research Guide pages 23-25
> Handout: "Basic Searching on the Education Index on CD-ROM"
> Assignment: Find article on topic using Education Index; identify key points; write one paragraph practicing citing article using APA style.

Class 4: Advanced searching on Education Index; popular and professional information sources (reference, periodicals, books).

> Read: Library Research Guide pages 10-12
> Handout: "Advanced Searching on the Education Index CD-ROM"
> Assignment: "Education Index—Part 2"

Class 5: Searching multiLIS; using controlled vocabulary and other strategies.

> Read: Library Research Guide pages 13-19
> Handout: "Basic Searching on MultiLIS"
> Assignment: "MultiLIS Assignment #1."

Class 6: Advanced searching on multiLIS; searching other campuses. Research Scenarios major project introduced.

> Handout: "Advanced Searching on MultiLIS"
> Assignment: "MultiLIS Assignment #2"

Class 7: Using FirstSearch online search service.

> Handout: "Searching WorldCat and Article1st on FirstSearch"

Assignment: "FirstSearch Assignment"

Class 8: Searching the ERIC database online.

Read: Library Research Guide pages 26-27
Handout: "Searching ERIC on FirstSearch"
Assignment: "ERIC Assignment"

Class 9: Searching the Internet for information on education, child care, human services.

Due: Rough copies of scenarios 1 & 2
Handout: "Using Windows and Netscape"
Assignment: "Netscape Exploration for Teachers"

Class 10: More on the Internet; listservs and electronic discussion groups in Education.

Handout: "List of Discussion Groups in Education"
Assignment: "Visit a Discussion Group"

Class 11: Work on research scenarios.

Due: Rough copies of Scenarios 3 & 4
Read: Library Research Guide pages 31-32
Handout: "Grading Guide for Research Scenarios"

Class 12: Work on research scenarios.

Due: Rough copy of Scenario 5

Class 13: Work on research scenarios.

Due by Friday at 5 pm: All 5 Scenarios in Final Copy Form

Class 14: Course evaluation. Powerpoint in the Classroom.

Attendance policy:

Since our class meets only once each week, it is essential that you attend every class. Each class involves learning new research strategies or the use of new tools. **More than three absences (meaning you have missed almost 1/4 of the course) will seriously jeopardize your ability to complete this course successfully.**

Grading policy:

Grades will be based on weekly assignments and the preparation and submission of a portfolio of short research scenarios. These scenarios will address real-life information needs, integrating course content from ECHD 130 Introduction to early childhood Education and research skills learned in this course.

Weekly assignments: 60 percent of grade	10 assignments/60 points each	= 600 pts
Portfolio: 40 percent of grade	5 scenarios/80 pts each	= 400 pts
	Total possible points	= 1000

Sections: All sections meet in the LRC Library Instruction Room. or the Computer Classroom.

Cheating and Plagiarism:

All assignments should be your own work. "Working together" means you can help each other to learn but **not** share answers. All the class assignments are designed to help you to understand and practice the skills taught in the course. Copying someone else's paper is self-defeating. Students found to have shared work will receive no credit for that assignment and may be brought before the early childhood Ethics Committee.

ECHD 131
RESEARCH SCENARIOS ASSIGNMENT

INSTRUCTIONS: One half of your final grade will be based on your performance on five research scenarios. You are to do **5** scenarios, choosing one out of each of the following pairs of SCENARIOS. Each scenario will be worth up to 100 points. We will be working on them to some extent in class during the final weeks, but they are **ALL DUE THE FRIDAY OF THE NEXT TO THE LAST WEEK OF CLASSES AT 5 PM**. You should demonstrate your knowledge of Library Research Skills AND early childhood Education. Use APA style for citing sources. Your work must be typed or word-processed.

ALL WORK IS TO BE YOUR OWN. ANY EVIDENCE OF SHARED WORK OR COPIED WORK WILL BE CONSIDERED CHEATING.

SCENARIO 1

You work in a medium-sized day care center where a growing number of the children have significant behavior problems. There are 25 teachers and staff. The director has asked you to be in charge of creating a small library of journals and books for the teachers to help them deal with the children's behavior. She has given you a budget for purchasing up to 10 books and subscribing to up to 5 journals or magazines. Find the BEST 10 books and BEST 5 periodicals about teaching young children with behavior problems. The director wants a sentence or two annotating each title you are recommending **AND a paragraph explaining how you did your research.**

OR

You have applied for and received a grant of $800 from the state Department of Social Services to set up a borrowing library for parents at your child care facility. You will use the money to purchase books and videos which parents can borrow on the honor system. You want to buy the best books and videos on parenting skills, children's health, or child development that you can find. Use the resources of the LRC and the Internet (including FirstSearch) to develop a list of the materials you plan to purchase. The state requires specific titles and brief descriptions of the materials you buy with the grant money (i.e., an annotated bibliography).

SCENARIO 2

You are applying to another college for transfer. That college has a library skills course required of all students in their first year. Transfer students are usually required to take that course **UNLESS** they can document that they already have the research skills covered in the course. The college will accept an essay in which you describe what you know about library research (process, indexes, tools, etc.) It is suggested that you pick a topic and describe how you would go about researching that topic in a narrative essay.

OR

You are applying for a professional position in your field. On the application form there is a question about your information skills. It asks you to describe your information skills and to give specific examples of the types of research you have done and types of information tools you know how to use. You are limited to two typed pages.

SCENARIO 3

The LRC is trying to decide whether to keep the Education Index on CD-ROM or to get rid of it and offer searches about topics in education through ERIC on FirstSearch. They want the opinions of some early childhood students so the Dean of the early childhood Division has asked you to prepare a brief comparison of the **ADVANTAGES AND DISADVANTAGES** of using ERIC on FirstSearch and using the Education Index on CD-ROM *and a recommendation from the perspective of the student.*

OR

ERIC can be searched using FirstSearch or AskEric on the Internet. Do the same subject searches on each and compare the results you get with each program. Write a one page evaluation of the **ADVANTAGES AND DISADVANTAGES** of each type of searching. **Use specific examples.**

SCENARIO 4

Finding ONLY children's books by subject is easy on multiLIS, but it is difficult to find children's books using WorldCat on FirstSearch. Develop a search strategy for finding children's books by subject to use with FirstSearch. Prepare a handout for other early childhood students on how to search for ONLY children's books on **BOTH** multiLIS and WorldCat. This handout will be distributed to all students and used in classes.

OR

You have been hired to teach at one of the local schools. The school's collection of audiovisual materials (filmstrips, recordings, videos, etc.) is very limited. Pick one of the following topics (or use one of your own topics) and compile a BRIEF annotated list of audiovisual materials about your topic which you could borrow from the LRC **or** borrow through your school's interlibrary loan (in other words, use both multiLIS and WorldCat to find titles).

TOPICS: SCIENCE   WEATHER
                  COOKING OR NUTRITION   HOLIDAYS
                  FOLKLORE/FOLK SONGS   USING THE LIBRARY
                  NUMBERS/COUNTING   TRAINS
                  NATIVE AMERICANS   ANIMALS

SCENARIO 5

You have a connection to the Internet and the World Wide Web through your computer at your home day care business. You want to set up a home page to help link parents to useful information on parenting, preschoolers, children's health, etc. Describe at least 10 links you would have on your home page. Provide the name of the Web site and a one-sentence description of the information at each site.

OR

For your practicum, your supervising teacher has asked you to create a list of really interesting Web sites having to do with Science. She wants you to make sure the sites are appropriate for kindergarten-grade 3. Select the best 10 sites and describe them. (You may first want to find out what topics are usually taught in science for those grades.)

A Comparison Between User Education Practice in Australian University Libraries and a Model of Effective User Education Programs

Mehri Parirokh

This article is a report of a study that aimed to investigate how far user education practice in several university libraries in Australia matches a model of characteristics of effective user education programs. In this research, effective programs are identified as those that are capable of promoting independence in students in accessing and using information. The information from cases was collected through interviews with 34 user education librarians in the target libraries and a review of instructional materials including their home pages. The results show that user education in the academic libraries studied in this research does not closely match the characteristics of the model. The data also reveals that the model cannot fit completely into the practice. The necessary conditions for running ideal and comprehensive programs do not exist. The findings suggest a need for a change in teaching approaches and attitudes of some of the academics, more emphasis on the provision of self-instruction programs, more staff development programs with emphasis on teaching/learning issues, and the provision of consistency between aims and practice.

Parirokh is a doctoral candidate at the School of Information Library and Archives, the University of New South Wales, Sydney, Australia.

Introduction

Australia is an island continent with 7,682 million square kilometres, six states, and two territories. It has 43 higher education institutions of which more than half are large universities that provide services for between 10,000 to 40,000 students. Since the 1960s higher education experienced much growth and development. While the number of higher education institutions and students constantly increased, the quality of higher education has been a matter of concern. Several government reports not only have highlighted the role of higher education in social, cultural, and economic life of Australia, but also they have specified the direction of higher education.[1] In this new direction the quality of higher education in the teaching/learning process has been taken into particular consideration. Academic libraries have been known as an integral part of higher education for enhancing quality and preparing independent individuals.[2] Through providing user education programs, they try to play their parts in enhancing the quality of higher education and promoting independence in students in accessing and using information effectively.

As contributors to higher education, academic libraries are also concerned about the quality of their user education programs and about the promotion of students' independence in accessing information. It therefore seems interesting to compare some user ed-

TABLE 1: GENERAL INFORMATION ABOUT THE CHARACTERISTICS OF UNIVERSITIES (N=5)

Universities	no. campuses	no. faculties	no. libraries	no. user education librarians	no. students
University 1a	2	5	1	6	
University 1b	2	4	3	9	21, 500
University 1c	3	7	3	8	
University 2	3	9	3	11	20,706
University 3	1	12 schools	1	9	17,370
University 4	7	15	25	28	29,600
University 5	4	11	5	20	26,534

ucation practice to some acknowledged criteria for effectiveness. A review of the relevant literature on education and psychology suggests that several elements should work together in an educational environment to enable learners *to learn how to learn* and achieve independence in learning. A review on the user education literature, which emphasizes the incorporation of learning theories in practice, indicates that several models prescribe that programs should be designed and assessed with respect to students' learning styles.

METHOD OF THE STUDY

Based on King, Morris, and Fitz-Gibbon's recommendations in regard to the critical characteristics of educational programs generally, a model was constructed. This model not only takes into consideration learning skills of learners, but also pays attention to other conditions that should be considered for providing an effective user education program. The researcher attempted to prepare a comprehensive "Model of characteristics of effective user education programs." This model has been used as a framework for discussion in this research study and as a basis for constructing the data collection tools. Because of time limitations, this presentation, which is a report of the comparison between user education practice in some Australian university libraries and the model, focuses solely on reporting the research findings on some of the components of the model. These components are underlined in a copy of the model (see appendix 1). To examine how far user education practice matches the characteristics of the model, a study was undertaken in five government-funded university libraries in Sydney, Australia. Two units of data collection were chosen: 1) librarians involved in user education practice were interviewed (see appendix 2) and 2) instructional materials prepared by the target libraries including their home pages on the Web were also reviewed.

RESULTS OF ANALYSIS

Thirty-four user education managers and librarians were interviewed. Ten managers responded to the general questions and 26 practitioners (of which two are the managers who are also involved in teaching) provided more specific responses. The reports of interviews were sent to the interviewees for confirmation. To provide a theoretical framework for the study, the elements of the model derived from the literature are categorized according to the recommendations by King, Morris, and Fitz-Gibbon: "context of programs," "activities of programs," and "theory in action."[3]

CONTEXT OF PROGRAMS

This feature of programs refers to a picture of the environment and the setting of the programs. Under this feature, general characteristics of universities are introduced.

General Characteristics of the Universities

As table 1 shows, user education programs are designed and implemented in environments that have different characteristics in terms of the number of campuses, faculties, libraries, user education librarians, and the students for whom those libraries should provide services.

ACTIVITIES OF THE PROGRAMS

This category includes important attributes relating to the way in which programs are implemented. Under this category, subcategories such as cooperation between librarians and academics, instructional materials, staff development, and evaluation of user education are discussed.

TABLE 2: THE LEVEL OF COOPERATION OF ACADEMICS WHO HAVE CONTACT WITH LIBRARIANS (N=26)

Scale	very good	good	moderate	no relevant response	total
Frequency	6	11	6	3	26

Cooperation between Academics and Librarians

Table 2 reveals that most of the librarians (17 out of 26) indicated that the level of cooperation is "very good" or "good," and six librarians perceived it as "moderate."

Although these responses show the positive attitudes of academics towards cooperation, according to librarians, those who contact the librarians and value user education are a small number of total number of academics. They complained that the majority of academics do not cooperate with the librarians and do not value user education.

Staff Development

In three of the universities, staff development is identified as a shortcoming. According to the information presented in table 3, three universities provided their staff with the opportunity of attending formal courses that focused on teaching techniques. In-house programs seem to be the most common staff development activities. Four libraries value the skills and expertise of those librarians who studied education and consider them as a source for the improvement of programs. Three library systems plan to arrange staff development programs in 1996 with the cooperation of some experts in education. It seems that in most libraries training for enhancing skills in accessing information and using technology have been provided internally. Based on table 3 and on the lack of sufficient staff development programs with a focus on teaching techniques, it can be concluded that there is not a close association between the staff development activities and the model.

Instructional Materials

Based on the model, various kinds of instructional materials should be used to motivate learning and to provide various learning conditions for students. Table 4 shows the frequency of instructional materials that librarians in the sample use. As can be inferred from this table, most librarians distribute handouts in their classes. Overhead transparencies are other common instructional materials. Power Point has been used by

17 out of 26 respondents to prepare slides for lessons/lectures to prepare slides for their presentations.

TABLE 3: STAFF DEVELOPMENT ACTIVITIES (N=26)

Activities	Frequency
Training courses	6
'Training the Trainers' course	2
'Basic Methods of Instruction' course	1
Site visit	2
Seminars	2
Workshops	1
Electronic discussion groups	1
In-house training:	
general	7
observation	3
review of programs and materials	4
networking	2

TABLE 4: VARIETY AND FREQUENCY OF INSTRUCTIONAL MATERIALS USED BY LIBRARIANS (N=26)

Instructional Materials	Format	Frequency
Handouts		21
Overhead transparencies		16
Workbooks/manuals		9
Instruction Sheets/pamphlets	printed	7
Information sheets	printed	7
	electronic	6
Subject guides	printed	7
	electronic	5
Library guides	printed	7
	electronic	7
Demonstration	computer screen	11
	Power Point	17
Printed reference sources and tools		4
Orientation tour on video		2
Video presentation		2

Moreover, some of the libraries (Universities 2, 4, and 5) put more emphasis on preparing workbooks and all libraries attempt to provide information about the library, library services, and information resources available in the library or on the Internet on the library's home page on the World Wide Web. Two libraries have also provided instructions on the use of the catalog on their home pages (Universities 3 and 4). Based on the subjects of interest to the faculties within the universities, four of the library systems and one

Aims	information literacy	lifelong learning	independent learning	promote information access skills for all of their students
Universities				
university 1a	X	X		
university 1b	X		X	
university 1c	X		X	
university 2	X			
university 3				X
university 4		X	X	
university 5	X		X	

branch library within one of the universities have classified the information sources and tools available on the Internet. However, since access to the Internet is not possible for all students, there is limited access to the libraries' home pages. Although table 4 shows that a variety of instructional materials is used in the target libraries, all the librarians do not use a variety of materials. Therefore, it can be concluded that there is not strong agreement between the practice of some of the librarians and the model.

EVALUATION OF USER EDUCATION

Overall Evaluation of Programs

Based on the responses, only one university has done an overall evaluation. However, three universities acknowledged it as an issue worth dealing with in 1996.

Evaluation of Particular Programs

The information collected indicates that two librarians, out of 26, have "often" evaluated their programs, seven of them have done it "sometimes," two librarians have "rarely" dealt with it, and 11 librarians have "never" done any evaluation. Informal feedback from academics and students is the most common method of obtaining information about the quality of their programs. The majority of librarians, 17 out of 26, request students, colleagues, and academics to give informal feedback. Some problems mentioned in the interviews were lack of time allocated by the academics and lack of librarians' time for doing evaluation, lack of evaluation skills, lack of a policy for evaluation, and lack of academics' interest in

evaluation. These shortcomings prevent librarians from carrying out sufficient evaluation. The information indicates that user education practice falls well short of the model that recommends the regular formal evaluation of programs and students' achievements.

THEORY IN ACTION

This category deals with the theory underlying programs. Under this category, subcategories such as "aims and objectives" and "teaching methods and focus" are discussed.

Aims and Objectives

According to the respondents, the overall aim of user education in their libraries has not been documented. Nevertheless, describing their overall aims, they indicated that they all consider that their user education programs will have long-term benefits for students.

A summary of the overall aim of the libraries is presented in table 5.

The model derived from the literature recommends that the overall aims of user education should be documented. As mentioned earlier and based on the responses, the libraries studied in this research have not documented their overall aims. In this particular case, therefore, user education practice falls short of the prescription of the model. In terms of the stated aims, there is a strong association between the overall aims of the libraries and what is recommended in the model which focuses on long-term benefits of user education for students.

TABLE 6: THE NUMBER AND THE PERCENTAGES OF OBJECTIVES WHICH MATCH THE MSO AREAS (N=26)

MSO areas	no. of responses	percentages of responses
1) How information is identified and defined by experts	4	9
2) How information sources are structured	13	30
3) How information sources are intellectually accessed	18	42
4) How information sources are physically organized and accessed	8	19

LIBRARIANS' OBJECTIVES IN SETTING THE PROGRAMS

Apart from the overall aim of user education, since each particular program should have its own objectives, librarians were asked to specify the objectives which they consider for their programs.

The stated objectives can be compared with the Model Statement of Objectives (MSO) which have been set by the Instruction Section (then Bibliographic Instruction Section) of the Association of College and Research Libraries (ACRL). MSO directs librarians' attention towards designing programs that are more process-orientated. With this approach, according to the MSO model, libraries would be able to develop programs that are more user-oriented and aiming "to prepare individuals to make effective lifelong use of information, information sources, and information systems."[4] The model categorizes the process of information gathering into the following four areas:

1) How information is identified and defined by experts;

2) How information sources are structured;

3) How information sources are intellectually accessed; and

4) How information sources are physically organized and accessed.

To explore to what extent the objectives stated by the librarians match the objectives set in MSO, the objectives stated by the librarians were compared with the elements included within each area. The following table is a summary of the result.

The majority (42 percent) of the responses match the components of the third area. Thirteen percent of them pay attention to the second area and nine percent

are related to the components of the first area. It seems that, since programs with particular attention to the last area are arranged centrally (i.e., library system arranges programs that help students become familiar with the library, library services and the physical arrangement of materials in the library), the last area was not addressed by most of the responses. Based on the information presented in table 6, it seems that there is a moderate match between the objectives of each program and those of MSO and ultimately the model.

Teaching Methods and Focus

In order to examine the teaching methods of librarians and the focus of their classes against the purpose of this research, it seems imperative to have a logical framework (i.e., a learning model). Based on the literature on learning theories,[5] if the focus of teaching is on the process of learning and if it incorporates the following process in its practice, it would enhance independent learning and can help students have control over their learning process through metacognition:

• to take into consideration the cognitive structure of the mind and to prepare the learner's mind for understanding the new concepts (awareness),

• to help the learner to confront the learning situation (the problem) and to analyze it (analyzing the situation),

• to help the learner to relate new concepts to the previous knowledge (presenting the concepts in class sequentially; assimilation),

• to provide the chance of trial and error for learners through practice (implementation), and

- to help learners to analyze the outcome, to become aware of the learning process (evaluation), and to use the new knowledge or awareness in a new learning situation.

These stages were considered as the basis for developing the model of learning shown in figure 1, which was developed by the researcher.

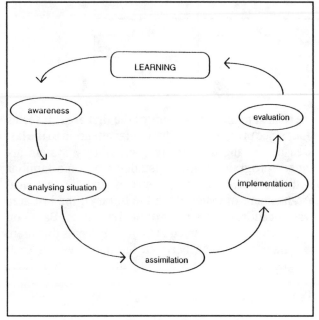

Figure 1: Learning Cycle model.

Application of Learning Cycle Model in User Education Practice

To identify the elements that should be incorporated into an effective user education program in terms of teaching/learning issues, the literature on user education that focused on the application of learning theories in user education practice[6] was reviewed. Each stage of the Learning Cycle model was compared with those elements; then they are categorized under five stages of the Learning Cycle model as in figure 2.

To come to some conclusion it seems necessary to compare overall teaching practice of librarians with the Learning Cycle model. Table 7 reveals that assimilation is more incorporated in teaching practice than other stages of the Learning Cycle; analyzing the situation, providing awareness and implementation have the second, third, and fourth ranks, respectively. Evaluation of the acquired information has the last rank in this table.

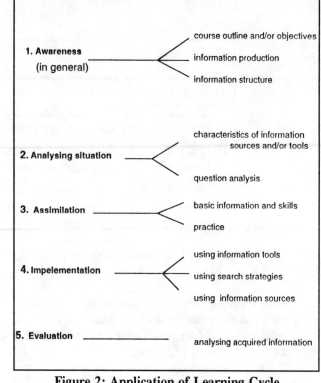

Figure 2: Application of Learning Cycle Model to User Education.

TABLE 7: COMPARISON BETWEEN LIBRARIANS' TEACHING PRACTICE AND LEARNING CYCLE MODEL (N=26)

Learning Cycle stages	Number of responses which deal with the elements of each stage of Learning Cycle model
awareness	17
analysing situation	25
assimilation	35
implementation	12
evaluation	10

Moreover, the teaching style of librarians may increase students' "awareness" of their learning styles and provide active learning, if it focuses on

- discussing the course outline or objectives in class,

- providing some examples and relating them to the students' knowledge and information needs,

TABLE 8: FREQUENCY OF TEACHING STYLES THAT LIBRARIANS USE (N=26)

Styles of teaching	discussion	group-work	question/answer technique	examples	sequential presentation of concepts
Frequency	1	1	20	16	9

- providing the chance for discussion, group work, or question/answer activities, and

- presenting concepts sequentially (i.e., the teacher begins from basic and simple concepts and moves to more complicated ones).

Information provided in tables 7 and 8 leads to the conclusion that, in general, there is a positive relationship between the model and teaching practice of the librarians. However, since the practice opportunities are not provided the effect of other elements in teaching methods might be decreased.

PROMOTION OF CRITICAL THINKING AND DECISION MAKING

The teaching practice of librarians can also be analyzed from another perspective. The importance of the two elements (i.e., the promotion of critical thinking and decision making), in enhancing meaningful learning and in preparing independent learners has been discussed in the literature. The collected data can be examined in terms of the extent to which the promotion of critical thinking ability has been taken into consideration. The elements that enhance critical thinking ability were identified in the literature by some writers.[7] These elements were examined against librarians' practice. Table 9 is the presentation of the result.

TABLE 9: LIBRARIANS' USE OF TECHNIQUES TO ENHANCE CRITICAL THINKING IN STUDENTS (N=26)

Activities	Frequency	Percentages
Analysis of search strategies	23	28
Question/answer technique	20	24
Critical study of characteristics of Information sources and tools	13	16
Question analysis	12	14
Evaluation of acquired information	10	12
Problems solving	5	6

Awareness about information, the characteristics of information sources and tools, and critical thinking and decision-making abilities help students to choose on these fronts:

- the suitable terminology that matches their information needs,

- the most appropriate: information sources or tools,

- the most effective search strategy, and

- the most appropriate information out of the acquired information.

Problem-solving opportunity, which is a kind of practice, is a situation in which students are required to be critical and to make decisions about the above-mentioned information-access process. Question analysis and question/answer techniques are suitable vehicles for the promotion of critical-thinking skills. These techniques help students to ask questions and decide for the best possible answer. The information in table 9 reveals that critical thinking is taken into consideration by librarians in their teaching. Although all of the elements do not have the same frequency, they are all used by librarians.

It can be concluded that, in terms of incorporating critical thinking in their practice, there is a positive association between teaching practice of librarians and the model. Problem solving, which is the stage in which students can implement what they have learned is not highly regarded. Table 7 also reveals that only 12 out of 26 librarians claimed that they provide the chance to practice.

CONCLUSION

It seems that user education practice in the academic libraries studied in this research does not closely match the characteristics of the model. Although librarians incorporate all the elements of the model in their practice, it seems that they do not use them at the same level. For example, in terms of teaching practice, most of the skills that should be taught are included. However, they all do not take into consideration the needed techniques and approaches in teaching at the same measure. Librarians complained about the existing problems such as the lack of staff development programs. This problem probably has a significant effect on reducing the effectiveness of programs. Staff development is a critical factor for making their programs effective. If librarians are expected to enhance learning quality, they need to be familiar with learning theories and teaching techniques. Lack of sufficient formal evaluation is another basic problem. If librarians are able to undertake formal evaluations they will recognize the shortcomings of their programs and they will try to improve them.

To look from another perspective, the data reveal that the model cannot fit into the practice very well. The necessary conditions for running ideal and comprehensive programs is not available. At the top of these obstacles that prevent the creation of such an ideal environment is a lack of a clear policy within the institutions in regard to their stated missions. Although increasing the quality of education is addressed in the higher education literature and in the mission statement of the institutions, librarians complained about the teaching methods of some of the academics that are not in line with the institutions' mission and have a direct effect on user education programs. Moreover, a lack of appropriate and sufficient facilities is another problem that makes programs less effective.

The findings of this study suggest that a change in teaching approaches and attitudes of academics for providing more effective programs may be necessary. New trends in library systems in terms of providing a self-instruction environment are promising. However, more emphasis on the production of good-quality self-instruction materials, in print and in electronic format, is another suggestion. The ideas of some of the librarians about students' learning styles and the necessity of using a variety of instructional materials, the language that they use about the aim of their programs in terms of promoting independent learning skills, lifelong learning skills, and so on reveal that some of them are familiar with the philosophy behind their practice and some teaching/learning theories in education and psychology. These ideas should be reinforced in these librarians and be established in others through appropriate staff development programs.

It seems that, in terms of increasing the quality and promotion of more capable graduates, one area that needs the highest appreciation is the overall policy within a library system and an institution at-large. According to the managers of information services interviewed in this study, long-term benefits of user education programs are the aim of academic libraries. Based on this aim, objectives, facilities, and user education activities, viz, librarians' attitudes, teaching methods, evaluation, academics' and administration support, and so on should be in agreement with the stated policy. Moreover, if the problem of higher education (i.e., most of the academics do not encourage students to use information), cannot be solved, even if librarians provide the most appropriate programs, their programs cannot cover all students.

Some of the libraries have planned to arrange staff development programs and the evaluation of their programs in 1996. Some of them are attempting to make some changes and to examine some innovations in regard to providing a self-instruction environment. It seems that a more promising future in terms of the provision of programs could be predicted. A further investigation seems necessary to explore the effect of these innovations and changes in their attitudes on their programs.

NOTES

1.   Report of the Committee on Australian Universities (Canberra: Commonwealth Government Printer, 1958); *Tertiary Education in Australia: Report of the Committee on the Future of Tertiary Education in Australia to the Australian Universities Commission* (Melbourne: Australian Universities Commission, 1964); *Commentary on Higher Education: A Policy Discussion Paper, December 1987* (Sydney: New South Wales Higher Education Board, 1988); and Philip C. Candy, Gay Crebert, and Jane O'Leary, *Developing Lifelong Learners through Undergraduate Education* (Canberra: Australian Government Publishing Service, 1994).

2.   Candy, et al., 104.

3.   Jean A. King, Lynn Lyons Morris, and Carol Taylor Fitz-Gibbon, *How to Assess Program Implementation* (London: Sage, 1987).

4.   "Model Statement of Objectives for Academic Bibliographic Instruction by ACRL Bibliographic Instruction Section," *Read This First: An Owner's Guide to the New Model Statement of Objectives for Academic Bibliographic Instruction*, ed. by Carolyn Dusenbury, et al., 5 (Chicago, IL: ACRL/BIS, 1991).

5.   C.E. Weinstein and G. Van Master Stone, "Learning Strategies and Learning to Learn," *The International Encyclopedia of Education*, 2d ed., ed. by Torsten Husen and T. Neville Postlethwaite, 3,325-3,329 (Oxford: Pergamon 1994); Philip C. Candy, *Self-Direction for Lifelong Learning: A Comprehensive Guide to Theory and Practice* (Oxford: Jossey-Bass, 1991); Ference Marton and Roger Saljo, "Approaches to Learning," *The Experience of Learning*, ed. by Ference Marton, Dai Hounsell, and Noel Entwistle, 36-55 (Edinburgh: Scottish Academic Press 1984); and Lora Idol, Fly Jones Beau, and Richard E. Mayer,

"Classroom Instruction: The Teaching of Thinking," in *Educational Values and Cognitive Instruction: Implications for Reform,* ed. by Lora Idol and Beau Fly Jones, 65-111 (Hillsdale, NJ: Lawrence Erlbaum Associates, 1991).

6.   Rao Aluri, "Application of Learning Theories to Library Use Instruction," *Libri* (August 1981): 140-152; Rao Aluri and Mary Reichel, "Evaluation of Student Learning in Library-Use: Instructional Programmes Based on Cognitive Learning Theory," in *Second International Conference on Library User Education. Oxford, Keble College, 7-10 July 1981*, ed. by Peter Fox, 87-91 (Loughborough: INFUSE, 1982); Rao Aluri and Mary Reichel, "Learning Theories and Bibliographic Instruction," *Bibliographic Instruction and the Learning Process: Theory, Style and Motivation. Papers Presented at Twelve Annual Library Instruction Conference Held at Eastern Michigan University May 6-7, 1982*, ed. by Carolyn A. Kirkendall (Ann Arbor, MI: Pierian Press, 1984): 15-27; Leon A. Jakobovits and Diana Nahl-Jakobovits, "Learning the Library: Taxonomy of Skills and Er-rors," *College and Research Libraries* 48 (May 1987): 203-214; Leon A. Jakobovits and Diane Nahl-Jakobovits, "Measuring Information Searching Competence," *College and Research Libraries* 51 (September 1990): 448-462; Carol Collier Kuhlthau, *Seeking Meaning: A Process Approach to Library and Information Services* (Norwood, NJ: Ablex, 1993).

7.   Mona McCormick, "Critical Thinking and Library Instruction," *RQ* 22 (Summer 1983): 339-342; Sonia Bodi, "Critical Thinking and Bibliographic Instruction: The Relationship," *The Journal of Academic Librarianship* 14 (July 1988): 150-153; Elizabeth J. McNeer, "Learning Theories and Library Instruction," *The Journal of Academic Librarianship* 17:5 (November 1991): 294-297; Nancy Niles and Trudi E. Jacobson, "Teaching Critical Thinking in Libraries: A Continuing Education Course," *Research Strategies* 9 (Fall 1991): 198-201; Gayle Piorier and Susan Hocker, "Teaching Critical Thinking in a Library Credit Course," *Research Strategies* 11 (Fall 1993): 232-241.

Activities

- Cooperation between academic staff and librarians should support programs

- Staff development should have continuous nature and focus on promoting librarians' skills and knowledge about teaching/learning theories and methods.

- A variety of instructional materials should be used.

- Programs' improvement should be taken into constant consideration through regular formal evaluation of programs and students' achievement.

- All levels of research skills from information identification and orientation to advanced information access skills should be covered.

- Assignments and exercises should be incorporated with the students' real needs, based on problem solving techniques and related to objectives of the programs.

- Should be aimed at using technological innovations for teaching purposes and teaching effective access and use of electronic information.

- Programs should be closely linked to the students information needs through close cooperation with academics.

- A variety of learning situations should be used (e.g., one-hour classes, credit courses, workshops, self-instruction materials, etc.),

Theory in action

- Overall aims should be written and should focus on long-term educational benefits of user education programs for individual and society such as promoting independent learning, information literacy or lifelong learning skills. Each particular program should have its own objectives.

- Teaching should focus on the process of learning and meaningful and active learning should be promoted.

- Programs should be based on promoting critical thinking and decision-making skills in information gathering techniques.

APPENDIX 2:
QUESTIONS PUT TO LIBRARIANS

1. Have you developed overall aims of your programs?

2. In your user education programs has there been any cooperative effort between instructor and academic staff?

3. Have you evaluated your user education programs?

4. What kind of instructional materials have been used in your user education programs?

5. What preparation have your user education staff had for teaching?

6. Which teaching methods have been used in your programs? How have students been involved in teaching/learning activities?

7. What do you expect students can learn out of your user education programs?

8. How far students should be independent in doing research and accessing information?

9. How can user education programs promote independence in students in accessing information and doing research?

10. What improvements should be considered for less effective user education programs?

ACCEPTING THE CHALLENGE OF CHANGE:
A CREDIT COURSE FOR THE 90S

Gayle Poirier

INTRODUCTION

A library skills course has been offered each semester at Louisiana State University (LSU) since the early 1930s. Its continued success can be contributed to many factors, among them the strong support from the library administration, flexibility and dedication of talented instructors, a constant evaluation of the program, a basic student interest in learning library skills, and good rapport with faculty and students. The course is approximately six to seven weeks long and meets twice a week for one hour, or once a week for two hours in the evening. Two sessions of seven to eight sections each are offered each semester; three to four sections are offered during the summer session.

History

In the early 1930s, Ella V. Aldrich established a Department of Books and Libraries within the College of Arts and Sciences at Louisiana State University. Her textbook, *Books and Libraries,*[1] was specifically written for "BKLI 1001: Introduction to the Use of the Library," which was then required of all freshmen. Several editions of the text were published between 1936 and the 1970s. Up to 54 sections a year were taught by four or five full-time instructors.

In the 1970s, the revised edition of the text, *Books, Libraries and Research,*[2] was used for the

course, which was renamed "BKLI 1001: Books and Libraries." Although the course was no longer required of all freshmen, it remained as a graduation requirement for majors in the fields of journalism, criminal justice, and rural sociology. An average of 26 to 34 sections a year were taught by two reference librarians assigned to teach two sections each nine weeks, plus selected reference librarians teaching one section each nine weeks.

The course was renamed "Introduction to the Use of the Library" in the 1980s when the Department of Books and Libraries moved to Middleton Library, the present main library on campus. In the 1982/83 term, the course was given its present name, "LIS 1001: Library Research Methods and Materials." Selected reference librarians were assigned to teach one section each nine weeks; two reference librarians were responsible for two sections each nine weeks. Including sporadic evening sections, 26 to 34 sections a year were scheduled.

In January of 1990, the course was transferred from arts and sciences to the School of Library and Information Science. When the criminal justice degree was deleted in 1990/91, a dramatic loss in enrollment occurred in the course, even though rural sociology and journalism majors still required the credit. The last edition of the text, *Library Research Skills Handbook,*[3] was written in 1991 to include the online catalog and online database searching. In 1996, 31 to 36 sections a year were taught by one full-time and two part-time reference librarians assigned to the course.

Poirier is head, library instruction unit, Louisiana State University, Baton Rouge, Louisiana.

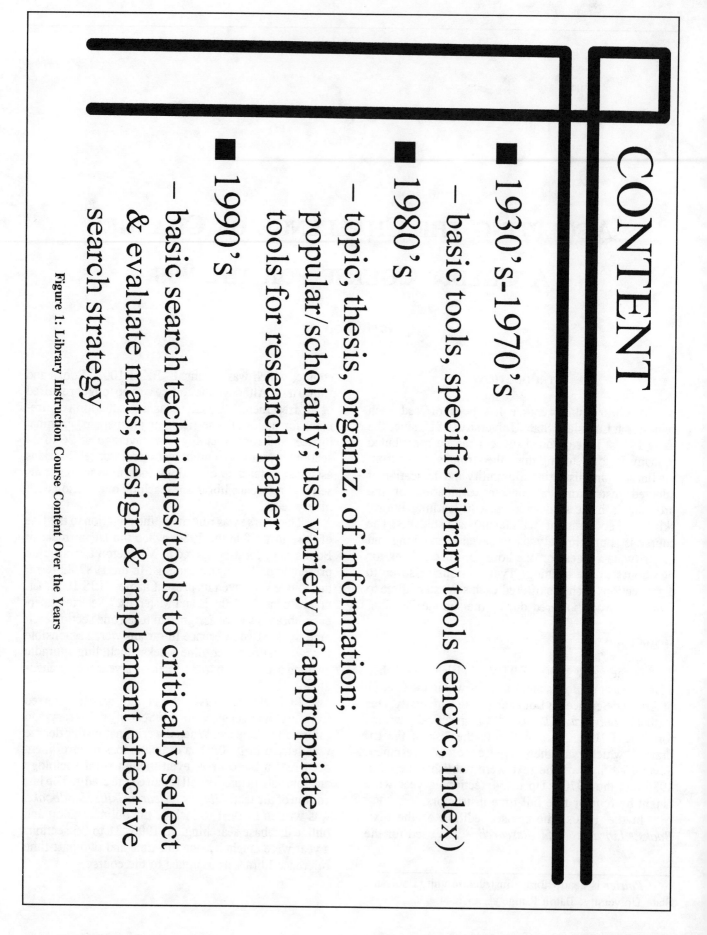

CONTENT

■ 1930's-1970's
  – basic tools, specific library tools (encyc, index)

■ 1980's
  – topic, thesis, organiz. of information;
    popular/scholarly; use variety of appropriate
    tools for research paper

■ 1990's
  – basic search techniques/tools to critically select
    & evaluate mats; design & implement effective
    search strategy

Figure 1: Library Instruction Course Content Over the Years

Course Content

Early library instruction centered around the text, which quickly developed into a workbook format including chapters on "The Book," "The Card Catalog," "Indexes," "Reference Books," a "History of the Social Sciences," "Literature," and "Making a Bibliography." Course content consisted of basic instruction on the parts of the book, the catalog, reference materials, periodicals, and so on. Specific types of reference works such as encyclopedias, and dictionaries, and so on were examined and studied. Emphasis was placed on card catalog access, subject headings, filing rules, and subheadings (see figure 1).

In the 1970s, emphasis shifted to understanding the access, evaluation, and organization of information, rather than just on the types of resources available. Instructors used a pathfinder or an annotated bibliography as a requirement.

The 1980s course stressed resource methods as a means to finding information. Students were taught how to discriminate between popular and scholarly sources and to understand how information is organized. Additions to the syllabus included instruction in finding biographical, book review, and literary criticism sources. When the online catalog appeared in 1986, electronic search techniques were introduced through live demonstrations in the classroom.

Beginning in 1992, a course packet with handouts, examples of source pages, and class exercises was prepared by the unit head and used by several instructors. The course was again revised in the fall of 1992 to reflect the rapid acquisition and availability of CD-ROM and online databases. The research paper requirement was discontinued and emphasis was placed on teaching the access, selection, evaluation, retrieval, and documentation of a wide variety of information sources. More electronic sources were demonstrated, including LEXIS/NEXIS, the libraries' LAN, and the integrated online catalog, which has developed into a statewide network over the last few years. The Internet was introduced in 1995, with basic instruction for using e-mail and demonstrations of various search techniques and search engines.

Assignments

Early classes relied heavily on textbook exercises and problems, such as arranging call numbers in shelf list order, filing rules, and compiling an annotated bibliography. A self-guided library tour was required. By the 1970s, annotated bibliographies or pathfinders were used to demonstrate the students' knowledge of the course content. Review questions at the end of textbook chapters were used heavily, along with problems or

exercises in the text. In the 1980s, note cards and a term project were introduced and became the focal point of the course. Either a term paper of two to three pages and ten worksheets from the text were used or an annotated bibliography was assigned to select an appropriate research topic, focus on a thesis statement, design an effective search strategy, and use a variety of appropriate tools to access materials on a specific topic. Critical thinking activities were encouraged both in class and in assignments.

Throughout most of the 1990s, a cassette library tour guided students through the physical arrangement of the various departments, and an online catalog assignment replaced the card catalog exercise. More hands-on activities with step-by-step instruction were included, especially for the increasing electronic sources such as LEXIS/NEXIS and the libraries' LAN. A search strategy assignment substituted for the paper, and provided evidence of the student's knowledge of the material. By 1994, typical course requirements included assignments for the online catalog, reference, periodicals, documents/statistics, and the cassette tour. In 1995, assignments included the online catalog/reference sources, printed indexes, and electronic indexes. In 1996, assignments included an online catalog/reference sources, periodicals, background sources, current events (including LEXIS/NEXIS, the LAN, and the Internet), and a final search strategy.

Exams

Several combinations of exams have been used throughout the years: a midterm and comprehensive final; two quizzes plus a comprehensive final; a midterm, a take-home (search strategy) assignment plus a written comprehensive final. Most instructors combine multiple choice, matching, true-false, and short open-ended questions on exams. During the early years, exams were standardized with input from all instructors to maintain consistency. With the turnover of instructors during the eighties and early nineties, instructors developed their own exams and some used quizzes instead of the midterm. With the current staff of one full-time and two part-time instructors, a decision has been made to return to the standardized exams with input from each instructor.

Sections Offered

Figure 2 reflects the number of sections offered from 1982 through the present semester. Prior to the 1980s when the course was required for all freshmen, up to 54 sections a year were offered; in 1979, 33 sections were offered. The number of sections de-

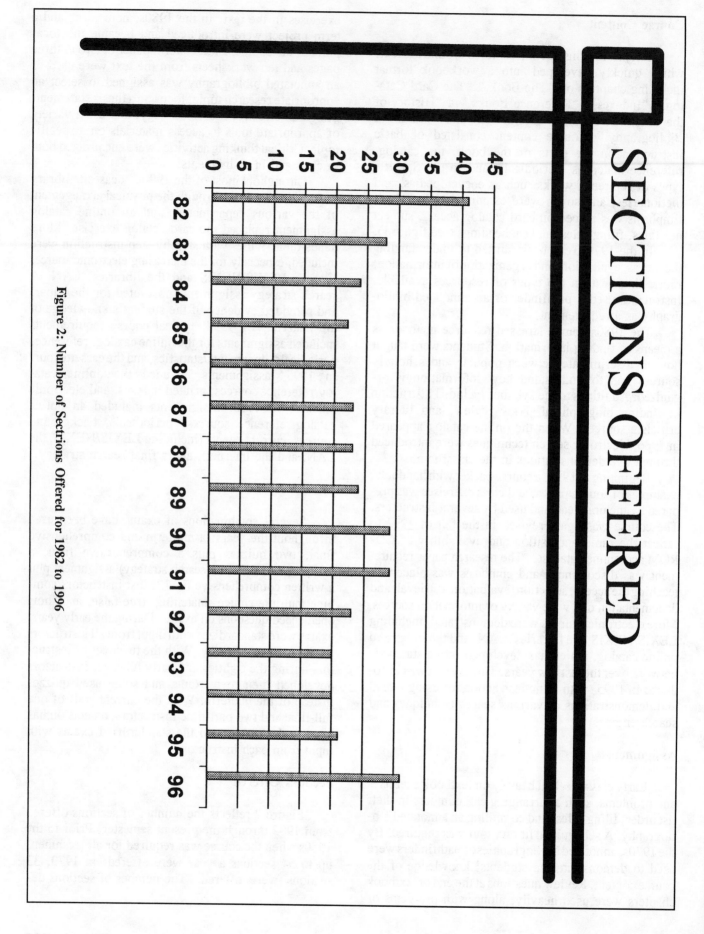

Figure 2: Number of Sectrions Offered for 1982 to 1996

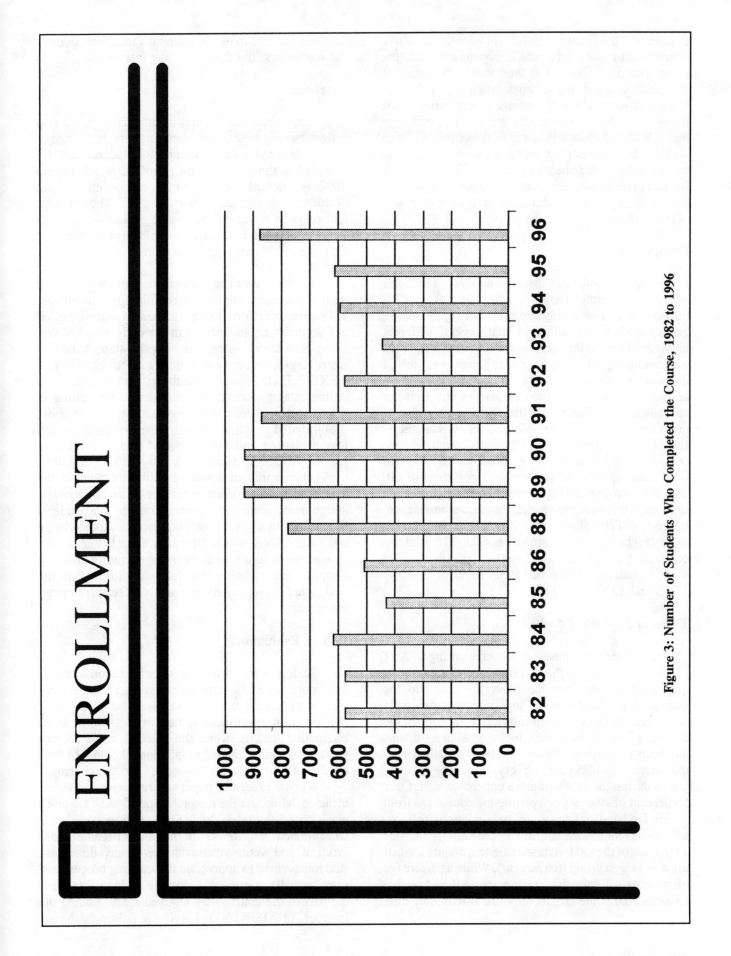

ENROLLMENT

Figure 3: Number of Students Who Completed the Course, 1982 to 1996

creased with the change from full-time dedicated course instructors to using reference librarians on a rotating basis with no assigned full-time instructor status. It increased again in the nineties when two reference librarians were given the primary responsibility of offering two sections each nine weeks on a permanent basis. With the change in status of the criminal justice majors, the number of sections were reduced to accommodate the reduced enrollment. The increased interest in electronic resources during the last few years has encouraged additional sections, including two evening sections.

Enrollment

Figure 3 indicates the total number of students who actually completed the credit course from 1982 through the current spring semester. The figures shown are somewhat misleading in that several different methods of tabulating were used until the 1990s, when a decision was made to base enrollment statistics on the number of students officially enrolled at midterm and at the final exam time instead of the first- or second-day enrollment and the final exam time as previously determined. In 1979, 33 sections taught by five instructors produced 991 students completing the course. A major decision was made during 1994 to limit enrollment to 35 in each section instead of 50. This allowed the instructor more time to work with individual students and resulted in greater attendance, interest, and completion rate. In 1995/96, 31 sections were taught by three instructors, with 876 students completing the course. The average class size in 1996 was 31 students, as opposed to up to 50 in the early 1980s and 1990s.

Types of Students Enrolled

In 1989/90, the university began requiring an ACT of 30 for admission to the university, bringing a higher quality of student into the university and into the course. While freshmen and sophomores traditionally have been the largest group enrolled in the course, the number of upperclassmen including graduate students has been increasing. Figure 4 indicates statistics for the current 1995/96 year and is typical of the growing trends during the 1990s of more upperclassmen. Over 55 percent of students completing the course are from Junior Division; majors from mass communications, which still requires the course for graduation, comprise 11 percent of the total. Arts and sciences majors formed the next largest group (ten percent). While a percentage of students still take the course because they "needed an extra hour," the largest response to why they took

the course seems to be "to learn how to use the library, the computers, the databases, the Internet."

Retention

Course retention figures as shown in figure 5 also reflect varying methods of tabulating data, but nonetheless are indicative of the number of students actually completing the course. The retention rate from the 1990s is reflected from the number of students enrolled at midterm and at the final exam time. The statistics and remarks made on the course evaluation indicate that students are pleased with the course content and find the information given extremely useful in their academic studies.

The increase in numbers of students staying after midterm to complete the course might be attributable to two major factors: the assignments were simplified and somewhat standardized in the early nineties with three consistent instructors; step-by-step, hands-on instruction for electronic sources such as the Internet, LEXIS/NEXIS, the LAN databases, and the integrated online catalog made assignments more interesting as the students selected their own research topics. Without the burden of an actual research paper, students seemed less pressured and more relaxed and interested in learning the basic techniques and skills, which they could then apply in actual real-life situations in the assignments. The research project or search strategy assignments seemed to demonstrate to the students themselves that actual learning, practical knowledge had taken place. It also prepared them better for the final exam by allowing them the opportunity of taking a topic of their choice, and following through in the design and implementation of an actual search strategy for research.

Course Evaluations

Student evaluations of courses are required by the university. The LIS instructors have used the evaluations as a practical means of measuring both the quality of instruction and the achievement of course objectives. Evaluation results from the 1980s, while overall positive in nature, tended to fall along the lines of "too much work for a one-credit course" and "too boring."

When the research paper was required, comments included "eliminate the research paper!" and "too much work for 1 hour credit." Once assignments were consolidated into fewer in number, became more practical, and were written with step-by-step directions, students seemed to appreciate the learning process and some actually commented that the assignments were the part of the course they enjoyed most. Adding the Internet, LEXIS/NEXIS, LAN, and online databases

CLASSIFICATION	Day 1 #	Day 1 %	Retention	Day 2 #	Day 2 %	Retention	Midterm #	Midterm %		Final #	Final %	Retention	# of Students per Section
Freshman	395	44		408	44		396	45		392	45		
Sophomore	231	26		225	24		210	24		205	23		
Junior	130	15		130	14		124	14		126	14		
Senior	152	17		154	17		147	17		143	16		
Graduate	9	1		10	1		11	1		10	1		
Other													
TOTALS	917			927			888			876		99%	28
Undergrad	626	69		633	69		607	68		597	68		
Upperclass	291	32		294	32		281	32		279	32		
Drops													
Adds													
COLLEGE/SCHOOL													
Agriculture	23	3		28	4		24	4		24	3		
Arts & Sciences	101	11		103	11		94	15		84	10		
Basic Sciences	48	5		45	5		46	5		44	5		
Business Adm.	8	1		6	1		7	5		9	2		
Design	6	1		5	1		6	1		6	1		
Education	10	2		9	1		10	2		10	2		
Engineering	18	2		26	3		22	3		21	3		
Evening School	23	3		23	3		22	3		21	3		
General College	60	7		57	7		70	8		67	8		
Graduate School	9	1		10	2		11	2		10	2		
Junior Division	500	55		511	56		480	55		477	55		
Mass Comm.	93	11		102	12		97	11		96	11		
Music													
Social Work													
Other													
GRADE DISTRIBUTION													
A													
B													
C													
D													
F													
W													
I													

Figure 4: Statistics for 1995/96 Year

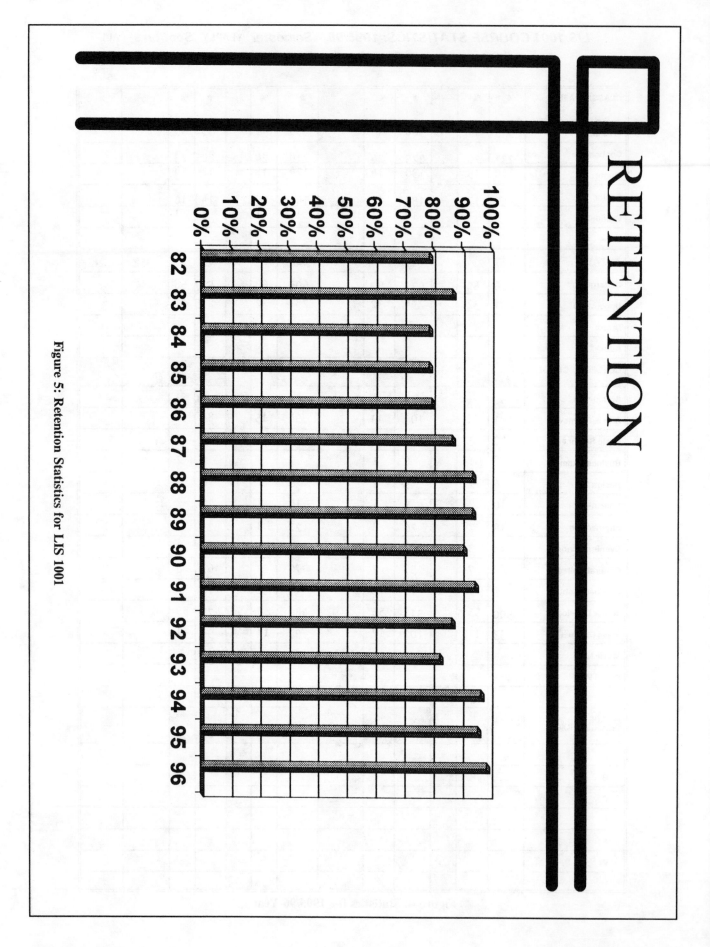

Figure 5: Retention Statistics for LIS 1001

**Louisiana State University Libraries
Course Evaluation Questionnaire**

1994-1995 Year

* Adapted from the actual results.

	Percent
1. Why did you take this course?	
Needed help in doing research	24
Required for major	26
Recommended	17
Needed an extra hour of credit	28
Other	7

        to speed up research
        was told it would help with Internet
        going to Graduate School; thought it would help
        to get over fear of the librry
        work in the library and wanted to learn more
        looked easy
        no experience with huge library like this
        to effectively learn to use the library
        thought it would be useful

2. Overall evaluation of the course:
  As a result of having completed this course,

	Strongly Agree	Agree	Disagree	Strongly Disagree
I developed a better understanding of what the library had to offer.	60%	38%	2%	
I can now easily locate information.	63%	35%	2%	
I can locate a variety of materials.	59%	38%	2%	

	Highest				Lowest	
	1	2	3	4	5	6
3. How would you rate this instructor compared to others at this university?	47%	33%	11%	3%	3%	1%
4. How would you rate this course compared to other at this university?	30%	32%	19%	12%	5%	3%

Figure 6: Comments from Spring 1996 Semester

5. **What were the most useful features of this course?**

   - handouts
   - LOLA (the online catalog) because that's pretty much what Middleton Library is all about.
   - Internet
   - Learned how to find magazine articles and use the electronic indexes to my advantage.
   - Letting us use what we learned quickly on assignments and making everything cumulative.
   - Everything.
   - Staying up with technology by utilizing the Internet and learning how to e-mail and LEXIS/NEXIS.
   - Learn new information about the library.

6. **What suggestions for improvement do you have to offer?**

   - I think the course should be longer.
   - None.
   - Perhaps a class library tour.
   - Make the class a whole semester because it has a lot of material.
   - A classroom with computer terminals so that students may follow along with the instructor.
   - Cover less material and be more thorough. Make everything clear.
   - Doing fun things on the Internet.

Figure 6: Comments from Spring 1996 Semester (continued)

sparked new interest in students and fewer complaints about the assignments. A sample of comments from the Spring 1996 semester is shown in figure 6.

The Future

We are very optimistic about the future of LIS 1001 seems very bright: the increased interest in electronic sources, including the Internet, full-text databases, and the integrated online catalog, indicate that students of all ages and backgrounds understand the need to correctly access information, select appropriate sources, and then evaluate them discriminately in the research process. LSU is developing a strong interest in the writing-across-the-curriculum concept, with English instructors using the Internet in teaching writing skills.

The library has strong support among university faculty and staff for instruction in library skills, both on a formal and informal basis. Reference staff liaisons with departments encourage enrolling in the course. Satisfied students who complete the course voluntarily

tell their friends about the importance of taking the course. A good relationship with student counselors across campus has resulted in dramatic increases in enrollment, particularly from the Junior Division. The reference staff's cooperation with teaching faculty in developing library assignments has encouraged and informed faculty about the formal credit course and also in the library staff's willingness to participate in the instruction process.

The two electronic classrooms planned for this next year will be a tremendous boost for the course. Students often voice their desire to have more hands-on exposure to the computer systems before assignments are given. These classrooms will allow more "in class practice" and one-on-one instruction/demonstration of the important tools such as the integrated online catalog, the LAN, LEXIS/NEXIS, and the Internet (see appendix 1).

A new textbook will be required this fall, *The Research Process: Books and Beyond*.[4] Written by one of the authors of the previous texts and a current instructor of the course, the work incorporates electronic and traditional library resources to give students an understanding of the variety and content of information stored in libraries and in computer based systems. Sample assignments and exercises are included, along with illustrations and charts to represent major concepts. By bringing the text up-to-date-electronically, the students will have printed instructions on searching all types of information. The assignments and exercises can be used by current instructors; many course handouts have been reformatted for the text, reducing the need for handouts and transparencies. The instructors are working on incorporating presentation skills packages such as PowerPoint and Compel in their lectures along with developing hands-on activities to use in the electronic classrooms for practice during class time. It is an exciting time to be an instruction librarian in an academic library!

NOTES

1. Ella Virginia Aldrich, *Books and Libraries* (Baton Rouge, LA: 1936).

2. Mary G. Hauer, et al., *Books, Libraries, and Research* (Dubuque, IA: Vendall/Hunt Publishing Co., 1979).

3. Myrtle S. Bolner, *Library Research Skills Handbook* (Dubuque, IA: Kendall/Hunt Publishing Co., 1991).

4. Myrtle S. Bolner and Gayle Poirier, *The Research Process: Books and Beyond* (Dubuque, IA: Kendall/Hunt Publishing Co., 1997).

LIS 1001
Library Research Methods and Materials
1 credit hour

Fall 1996
Instructor: Gayle Poirier
Associate Professor

Section 4 TT 9:30 - 10:30am
Section 5 TT 9:30 - 10:30pm
Section 6 W 6:30 - 8:30pm

Meet in 230-C Middleton Library
E-mail: **notgap@unix1.sncc.lsu.edu**
Phone: 388-2629 (Office, Voice Mail)
388-LOLA (Information Desk)

Office in Reference Services, Room 141J; Regular Office Hours: MTWT 10:30 - 11:30 am;
Office hours in 230-C on Wednesdays, 5:30 - 6:30 pm. Other times by appointment.

COURSE OBJECTIVES
This course serves as an introduction to the library and its resources, both traditional and nontraditional formats.

By the end of the course, you will be able to:

1)   use **basic search techniques and tools** such as LOLA, the LSU Libraries' LAN databases, printed indexes, the INTERNET, and online databases such as LEXIS/NEXIS to retrieve library information sources, including books, periodical articles, reference works, government documents and statistics;

2)   critically **select and evaluate library materials**;

3)   distinguish between **popular and scholarly works**, and between **primary and secondary sources**;

4)   **design and implement an effective library search strategy.** This will include selecting a topic, then accessing, selecting, evaluating, retrieving, and documenting a variety of appropriate sources on the topic. A typed list of sources will be prepared with a formal thesis statement.

RESERVE MATERIAL (Available at the Reserve Desk in Middleton's lobby:)
Bolner, Myrtle S., et al. *Library Research Skills Handbook.* Dubuque, Iowa: Kendall/Hunt Publishing Company, 1991.

COURSE REQUIREMENTS:	Exercises	Library Tour/E-Mail	20
		Online Catalog	30
		Online Indexes	30
		Current Events/ Internet	30
		Print & Electronic Indexes	40
	Research Project:		100
	Exams:	Midterm	50
		Comprehensive FINAL	100
			400 points

Absolutely no late assignments or makeup exams without instructor's approval!

ATTENDANCE AND CLASS PARTICIPATION:
Students are expected to participate in <u>all</u> class activities for the greatest learning experience. Exercises, assignments and handouts are intended to instruct, enhance, or reinforce class presentations. Mere attendance and notetaking are not sufficient for maximum learning.

GRADING SCALE			
	370 - 400 points	=	A
	340 - 369	=	B
	310 - 339	=	C
	280 - 309	=	D
	Below 280	=	F

IMPORTANT DATES: Last day to add:
Last day to drop without a W:
Last day to drop with a W:

1   *INTRODUCTION TO LIBRARIES*
     How libraries are organized; the variety of resources and facilities available in the LSU
     Libraries. Reviewing the course objectives in relation to research.

     Homework:
     1) Familiarize yourself with Middleton Library by completing the Library Tour Exercise.
     2) If you do not already have an Internet account, call REGGIE and get a free TIGER
        logon ID and password for access to the Internet.
     3) Send an E-mail to your Instructor by

---

2   *ORGANIZATION OF LIBRARY RESOURCES: LAYING A FOUNDATION FOR RESEARCH*
     An understanding of classification systems and call numbers. How information is
     organized and distributed. (Timeline of information distribution.)

     Homework: Complete Self-Guided Tour Exercise and E-mail.

---

3   *FINDING CATALOGED MATERIAL: ELECTRONIC SEARCH TECHNIQUES*
     Reviewing classification systems. Explanation and role of the online catalog. Subject
     ("controlled vocabulary") versus keyword" ("free text") searching. Discussion of subject
     headings, guide screens, and subheadings. Techniques used to select, broaden and
     narrow a topic.

     Homework: Begin Online Catalog Exercise.

---

4   *CONTINUE ELECTRONIC SEARCH TECHNIQUES.*   Finding and using Reference
     works, government documents, and other cataloged material.

                                        DUE: Self-Guided Tour Exercise and E-mail.

---

5   *FINDING INFORMATION IN ARTICLES: USING INDEXES ON THE ONLINE CATALOG*
     Introducing electronic periodical indexes and the retrieval process for articles. Practice
     using popular and scholarly articles. Understanding the discipline approach. Identifying
     appropriate databases. Demonstration of LOUIS indexes.

                                              DUE: Online Catalog Exercise
     Homework: Begin Online Indexes Exercise.

---

6   *USING THE INTERNET AS A RESOURCE*
     An introduction to the history, organization, and basic terminology of the Information
     Highway. Finding access tools: LSU Home Page for local resources, using search
     engines such as Alta Vista, Yahoo, Lycos, Web Crawler, or WWW Worm.

                                              DUE: Online Indexes Exercise
     Homework: Explore the LSU Virtual Library Page.

---

7   **MIDTERM EXAM**
     Review of library organization, departments, and formats, including basic access and
     retrieval of information in books, reference works, articles in magazines and journals, and
     the Internet. Understanding subject versus keyword search techniques.

---

8   *PUTTING IT ALL TOGETHER: THE RESEARCH PROCESS IN ACTION*
Criteria for selecting an appropriate topic. Finding background information and developing a thesis statement. Practice critical evaluation of thesis statements and bibliographies.

Homework: Begin Current Events Exercise, due

---

9   *FINDING CURRENT INFORMATION*
Practice using a printed national newspaper index. Retrieving online, full text access to current news through LEXIS/NEXIS. Practicing the retrieval and documentation process. Using the Internet for current news. Finding local information on the LSU Libraries' LAN.

---

10   *FINDING INFORMATION IN ARTICLES: USING PRINTED INDEXES AND ABSTRACTS*
Using online catalog skills from LOLA in retrieving information on the LSU Libraries LAN (local area network) and other sources. Using subject headings, disciplines and subheadings to find information in printed indexes.

                                    Current Events Exercise Due
Homework: Begin Printed Indexes Exercise

---

11   *FINDING STATISTICAL INFORMATION*
Introduction to basic statistical sources. Discussion of the value of using statistics in research.

---

12   *FINDING BIOGRAPHIES, BOOK REVIEWS, and LITERARY CRITICISM*
Discussion of the usefulness of these resources. Review of their access, retrieval, and documentation.

                                    DUE: Printed Indexes Exercise

---

13   *REVIEW FOR FINAL EXAM*
Evaluation of Research Projects. Question and answer period for accessing, selection and evaluation, retrieval and documentation of information sources.

---

14   **COMPREHENSIVE FINAL EXAM**

                                    DUE: Research Project

MAKING WAY FOR THE FUTURE:

DECENTRALIZING A PROGRAM THAT WORKED

Mary Pagliero Popp

The topic of this session is one that may, at first glance, seem at odds with the rest of the sessions at this conference. Most of them describe specific programs that the speakers feel are successful in teaching about information resources. This presentation, instead, describes a review of the library instruction program at the Indiana University (IU) Bloomington Libraries and the changes we made in its structure. It also provides some preliminary information about how well our changes have worked in this first year.

Particularly in large academic libraries, librarians cannot keep providing instruction in the ways we have always done so. We need to look more closely at what we do and how we do it. The changes we made in the Indiana program worked in our setting, but some of the things we did might provide suggestions or ideas that could work in your own library.

CURRENT CLIMATE OF BIBLIOGRAPHIC INSTRUCTION IN ACADEMIC LIBRARIES

I would like to begin by setting the stage. The current climate of bibliographic instruction and academic libraries includes

- an ever-more-complex information environment;

Popp is electronic services librarian, Indiana University Libraries, Bloomington, Indiana.

- an increasingly distributed computer environment in which users can access information resources from any location;

- declining budgets, and even downsizing;

- reorganization of libraries to meet new demands—Neal and Steele[1] describe some of the assumptions underlying such reorganization, including wider distribution of responsibility and authority, the need for flexibility in structure, an increasing focus on the user, and the needs for more small group collaboration and integration of routine operations. Some libraries have developed simpler versions of traditional hierarchical structures; others have implemented management structures using teams;

- changing curricula—some parts of our universities are changing, if slowly. There is more emphasis on critical thinking, lifelong learning, experiential and collaborative learning, and assessment; and

- changing user populations—our users are increasingly more diverse, with varied needs. Academic libraries are placing greater emphasis on reaching and instructing faculty and on remote users. New distance education initiatives bring new users. Finally, as Lizabeth A. Wilson[2] reminds us, our undergraduates are the first generation to have grown up in Toffler's electronic cottage.

These issues are leading many librarians to rethink the relevancy of their current instruction programs. One of the most promising concepts I have heard used to guide this thinking was first introduced at a conference on downsizing and instruction. In a speech at the "Upside of Downsizing Conference" in Santa Barbara in March 1994, Janice Simmons-Welburn introduced the concept of "post-bibliographic instruction" as a means to rethink the way we provide instructional services. Simmons-Welburn defines post-bibliographic instruction as a "pedagogy with two distinguishing characteristics. First, post-bibliographic instruction must be focused on the pragmatic concerns of the information seeker. Second, this instruction is driven and contextualized by the rapid changes in information technology." She argues that user-centered instruction should have as its goal "to promote the ability of an information seeker to move about with ease and freedom without having to learn esoteric nomenclature or memorize strict formulas for finding information."[3] Post-bibliographic instruction recognizes the differing cultures of different disciplines and different styles of learning and knowing. Simmons-Welburn reminds us that such instruction cannot be based on traditional classroom teaching styles, but must consider three approaches: collaborative, experiential group instruction in an electronic classroom; instruction at the point of need; and use of electronic information networks to teach to users at remote sites.

Embracing this concept of post-bibliographic instruction will lead us to rethink all of the parts of our instructional programs. I used it to guide my thinking as we began our instruction review process.

THE INDIANA UNIVERSITY BLOOMINGTON LIBRARIES

The climate at Indiana University in 1994 when we began our review and in 1995 when we made our recommendations is also important to this discussion. The Indiana University Bloomington Libraries system is the thirteenth largest of the ARL libraries, with more than five million volumes. A large residential campus, Bloomington is the flagship for the IU system. There are slightly more than 35,000 students, more than 26,000 undergraduates, and nearly 7,500 graduate students. We have a Main Library with an Undergraduate Library and a Research Collections. The Research Collections includes a government publications department and a separate reference department. Overseeing the collections are a number of subject and area studies librarians. We have 15 subject branch libraries, a major rare book and manuscript library, and a large residence hall library system.

At the time of the review, we had just finished a reorganization that eliminated associate dean positions for public, technical, and collections services and established 12 departments, each reporting directly to the dean. The reorganization[4] included among its goals an increasing focus on services and the user, wider distribution of authority and responsibility, integration of key activities, and the encouragement of quick and effective responses to change.

The IU Libraries were also in the midst of major technological changes within the libraries and on campus. An ever-increasing number of information resources were being made available on the library local area network and on the campus computer network. More full-text electronic resources were being added to the libraries' resources. We had recently established an electronic text reference service unit for the humanities as a joint project with University Computing Services. Within the libraries, a new team called CBRST—Computer-Based Resources and Services Team— was created to support library staff as they incorporated new electronic resources into their collections and services.

University Computing Services informed all campus units in early 1995 that our VAX campus computer network where we had comfortably provided library services for a number of years would be replaced in late May with a combination of a Unix e-mail system and the World Wide Web. In 1995 as well, the libraries began a development partnership with Ameritech Library Services to enhance the Horizon client-server integrated online information system (including the OPAC) to make it usable by large libraries and consortia.

The climate for instruction in the IUB Libraries included a fast-growing electronic resources base on top of large-print collections. There was a heavy, and growing, demand for instruction. Between 1988/89 and 1992/93, we experienced a 71 percent increase in the number of patrons receiving instruction; a 25 percent increase came in the last two years of that time period. We reached nearly 30,000 patrons in 1993/94. Our program included instruction for classes, library orientation tours, 16 sections of undergraduate credit courses in library and information skills and several graduate level courses, more than 60 printed handouts, a faculty and graduate student workshop series, and instructional visits for classes from high schools in our region.

Staff who provided library instruction services were tired and many of our instruction experts were suffering from burnout. It was evident to all of us that we were too busy to try many new approaches and that we were unable to respond adequately to new needs and priorities.

Instruction Review

Charge to the Committee

An instruction review committee representing library units from around the campus was appointed in June 1994 and charged to

- explore alternative strategies to present instruction activities and programs;

- define a new instruction program for the IUB Libraries which fit within the present resource base devoted to instructional activities; and

- detail implementation issues, particularly as they related to instructional facilities, equipment, and production.

The group was to accomplish this charge by collecting and reviewing data on the present program, receiving user input and defining user needs and instructional goals, and reviewing instructional programs at other academic libraries, as described in the literature.

Data Gathered

Members of the committee talked to undergraduate and graduate student groups, the library student advisory committee, associate instructors in large classes (English composition and speech communications) with whom we worked closely, and library staff. We talked to faculty groups, including library advisory groups for branch libraries and subject and area collections, and asked questions as part of concurrent reviews of several branch libraries. We used the results of two surveys done by the dean of the faculties office: a survey of incoming freshmen that included a chance for the students to describe their library experiences before coming to IU and a survey that included questions about faculty use of the library for assignments and their understanding of their students' library needs and preparation. We also talked to colleagues who themselves were undertaking reviews or major changes, notably those at Hunter College and Pennsylvania State University.

What the Committee Learned from Users

The most important lessons we learned from our users were the following:

- The need for instructional support, especially for electronic resources, the Internet, and full-text products is increasing.

- The human component is the most valuable part of the instruction program.

- Users want "just in time" instruction and resources that are transparent enough not to require instruction.

- Graduate students want specific library contact persons in their fields.

- Faculty believe their students learn to use the library the same way as they themselves learned (in high school, in lower level classes, and on their own).

- Instruction should be provided in a variety of ways and on a variety of electronic platforms. Computer tutorials are *not* an attractive option for most of our users. They do not have the patience to work through such tutorials.

- Hands-on instruction is the most valued type of instruction by users of all levels.

- An instructional component should be incorporated into the libraries' World Wide Web planning.

What the Committee Learned from Library Staff

Discussions with library staff at various points during the review resulted in a number of issues on which there was consensus. These included the following:

- Ninety percent of the effort in the Indiana program is centered on lower-level undergraduates. More attention needs to be paid to graduate students and faculty.

- Instruction of librarians and staff is a critical need. A strong need for help in keeping up with new technological initiatives was expressed.

- Adequate instructional facilities and equipment are a significant problem.

- Librarians need to encourage and help faculty to take an active role in information-literacy education.

CURRENT VIEW:
Users' paths to formal library instruction

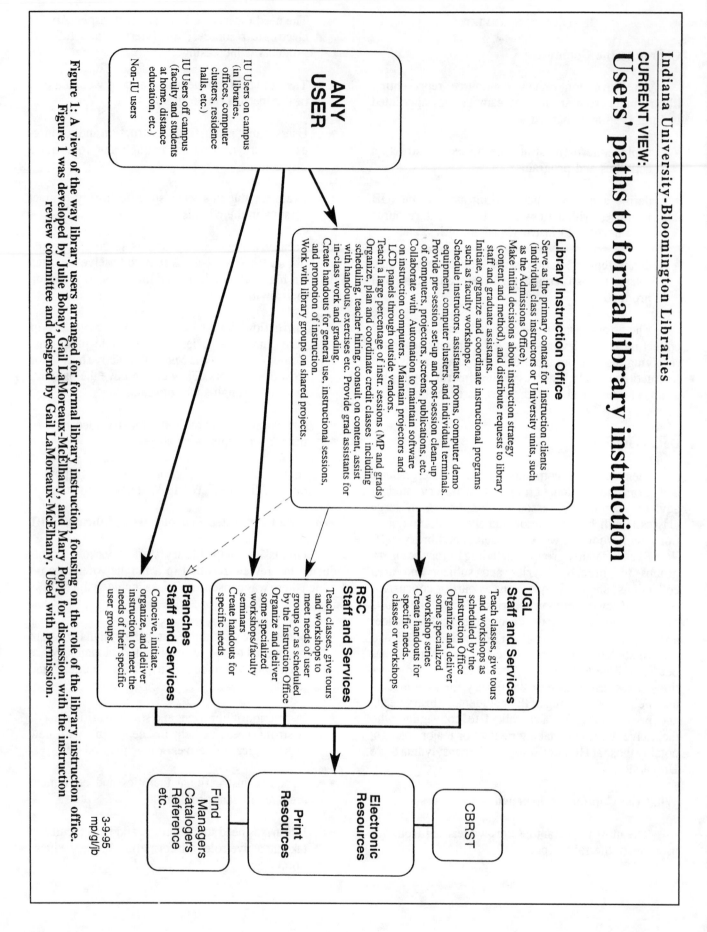

ANY USER

IU Users on campus (in libraries, offices, computer clusters, residence halls, etc.)

IU Users off campus (faculty and students at home, distance education, etc.)

Non-IU users

Library Instruction Office

Serve as the primary contact for instruction clients (individual class instructors or University units, such as the Admissions Office).

Make initial decisions about instruction strategy (content and method), and distribute requests to library staff and graduate assistants.

Initiate, organize and coordinate instructional programs such as faculty workshops.

Schedule instructors, assistants, rooms, computer demo equipment, computer clusters, and individual terminals.

Provide pre-session set-up and post-session clean-up of computers, projectors, screens, publications, etc.

Collaborate with Automation to maintain software on instruction computers. Maintain projectors and LCD panels through outside vendors.

Teach a large percentage of instr. sessions (MP and grads)

Organize, plan and coordinate credit classes including scheduling, teacher hiring, consult on content, assist with handouts, exercises etc. Provide grad assistants for in-class work and grading.

Create handouts for general use, instructional sessions.

Work with library groups on shared projects.

UGL Staff and Services

Teach classes, give tours and workshops as scheduled by the Instruction Office

Organize and deliver some specialized workshop series

Create handouts for specific needs, classes or workshops

RSC Staff and Services

Teach classes, give tours and workshops to meet needs of user groups or as scheduled by the Instruction Office

Organize and deliver some specialized workshops/faculty seminars

Create handouts for specific needs

Branches Staff and Services

Conceive, initiate, organize, and deliver instruction to meet the needs of their specific user groups.

Electronic Resources

Print Resources

Fund Managers
Catalogers
Reference
etc.

CBRST

3-9-95
mp/gl/jb

Figure 1: A view of the way library users arranged for formal library instruction, focusing on the role of the library instruction office. Figure 1 was developed by Julie Bobay, Gail LaMoreaux-McElhany, and Mary Popp for discussion with the instruction review committee and designed by Gail LaMoreaux-McElhany. Used with permission.

- A variety of approaches to instruction are important. The libraries need to develop videos, workbooks, and other approaches to augment instruction provided by librarians and to make it easier for faculty to include information-literacy skills and concepts in their teaching.

- Help with instructional design and sharing/clearinghouse functions are important to librarians who do instruction.

- Hands-on instruction is the most valuable instructional method.

- Orientation activities should be altered to provide some basic library instruction, in addition to a tour.

- New initiatives—distance education, accreditation assessment requirements—and cooperative efforts such as the CIC (Committee on Institutional Cooperation, a consortium of the Big Ten Universities and the University of Chicago) Virtual Electronic Library will have an effect on the instruction program. The libraries need to begin planning for these in advance.

A New Way of Thinking

We also tried to define, in graphical terms, the role of the instruction office. Figure 1 shows a picture of the activities of that office.

This picture make us stop and ask if a "middleman" sort of office was cost-effective in our current climate or if it served as a barrier. We decided to think about ways to organize our activities so that faculty and other users would still be able to find assistance with instructional services, but at a lower "cost" to the user and to the libraries.

Instruction Review Recommendations

One result of the review was three statements to guide the instruction program in the future: a statement of vision, a mission statement, and a list of assumptions that underlie the instructional program. The full text of these appears in appendix 1. The vision statement states simply that the library instruction program works to make the use of library resources understandable to users. The mission statement reflects that theme:

The Mission of the Library Instruction Program at Indiana University Bloomington is two-fold: 1) to serve as an advocate for the user in development of new systems and services within the Libraries; and 2) to provide library users, both those in the libraries and those accessing library resources remotely, with instructional materials in a variety of formats, at a variety of levels of sophistication, that assist them to make effective use of library resources to find the information they need.

A 1990 statement (see appendix 2) describing our instruction program for undergraduates had identified basic principles of information literacy that guided our program and determined that information literacy must be provided at two levels, the general level and the discipline level. It had wide approval and had been endorsed by the Bloomington Library faculty. We decided to realign our instruction program to ensure that we provided good quality services at both levels.

We made a commitment to put resources into innovation. One of our branch librarians described it best. He said that libraries cannot afford to put all their resources into day-to-day activities, no matter how high the demand. If we do so, there will be no resources left for innovation or just to respond to new needs. We must set some resources aside to ensure that we can be flexible and ready for change.

A complete list of the specific recommendations of the review is listed in appendix 3. The most important of these, however, relate to decentralizing the program to give each library unit responsibility for providing instruction. They are

1) Merge the present instruction office with the Computer-Based Resources and Services Team (CBRST) and expand the role of the new department. The instruction component of the new unit should focus on instruction issues that span the libraries—issues related to new technological environments, remote users, and users across disciplines, subjects, and levels.

2) Develop a new model for instruction that decentralizes responsibility for instruction planning. Each library unit will take responsibility for instruction of its own primary clientele.

A graphical depiction of this model, as shown in figure 2, is much cleaner than the earlier model. It gives users a clear path to the most appropriate unit to provide instructional services and puts into place a clear and strong support structure.

Indiana University-Bloomington Libraries

FUTURE VIEW:
Users' paths to formal library instruction

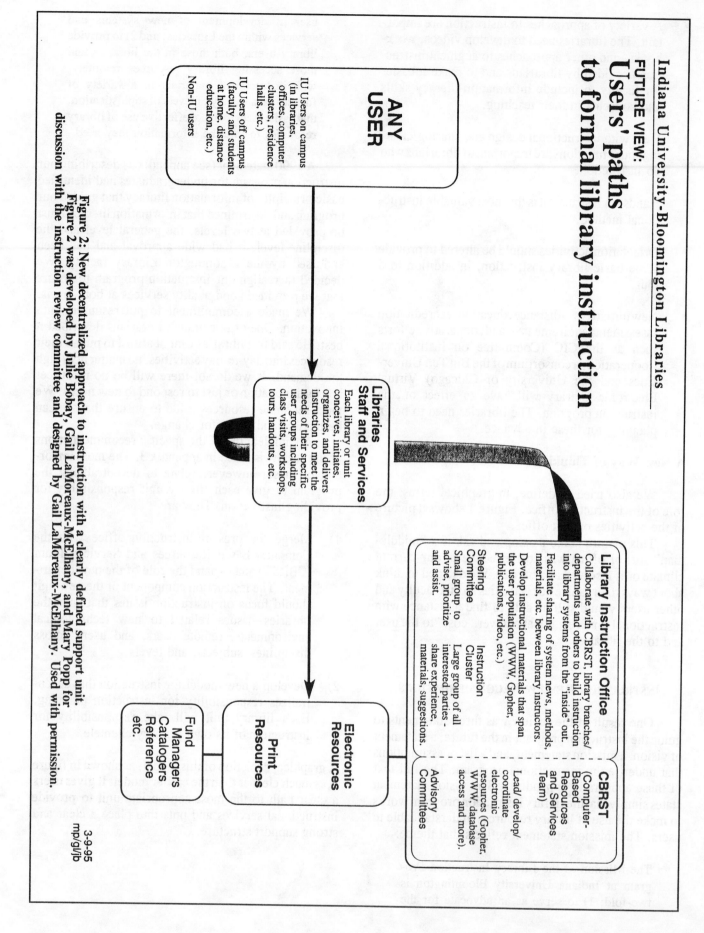

ANY USER

IU Users on campus (in libraries, offices, computer clusters, residence halls, etc.)

IU Users off campus (faculty and students at home, distance education, etc.)

Non-IU users

Libraries Staff and Services

Each library or unit conceives, initiates, organizes, and delivers instruction to meet the specific needs of their specific user groups including class visits, workshops, tours, handouts, etc.

Library Instruction Office

Collaborate with CBRST, library branches/departments and others to build instruction into library systems from the "inside" out.

Facilitate sharing of system news, methods, materials, etc. between library instructors.

Develop instructional materials that span the user population (WWW, Gopher, publications, video, etc.)

Steering Committee

Small group to advise, prioritize and assist.

Instruction Cluster

Large group of all interested parties - share experience, materials, suggestions.

CBRST

(Computer-Based Resources and Services Team)

Lead/develop/coordinate electronic resources (Gopher, WWW, database access and more).

Advisory Committees

Electronic Resources

Print Resources

Fund Managers Catalogers Reference etc.

Figure 2: New decentralized approach to instruction with a clearly defined support unit.
Figure 2 was developed by Julie Bobay, Gail LaMoreaux-McElhany, and Mary Popp for discussion with the instruction review committee and designed by Gail LaMoreaux-McElhany. Used with permission.

3-9-95
mp/gl/jb

— MARY PAGLIERO POPP —

ACTIONS RESULTING FROM THE RECOMMENDATIONS

We have taken a number of steps in the ten months since the report was finalized.

We merged the instruction and CBRST departments to form the Electronic Resources and Services Department (ERSD). The Undergraduate Library took responsibility for instruction for lower-level undergraduates (through the junior year) and for basic instruction for new international students and students in IU's high school advanced placement program. Since this is a large chunk of our instruction right now, they also took responsibility for the electronic mail and telephone calls to the central instruction number. They routinely refer calls for graduate and advanced undergraduate classes.

The reference department, as a representative of the research collections and services department, took primary responsibility for graduate students and faculty. Reference staff also routinely refer requests to the branch libraries and the Lilly Library of Rare Books, Manuscripts, and Special Collections. Branch librarians and subject and area specialists retained and increased their responsibility for classes at all levels that required resources in their disciplines.

Outside groups were divided. Those who will use the collections and need instruction stay with instruction component of the electronic resources and services department. Groups who only want a tour were taken on by the library administration, where public relations and donor relations activities reside. We no longer provide instruction for groups under high school age; we only give field trip tours given by library school students. We tried to drop such tours altogether, but the PR problems were too great. We serve a rural state that should be sending more students to college and we did not want to discourage students.

We have made a concerted effort to provide more hands-on instruction for electronic resources. In addition to the two computer clusters in the Undergraduate Library, we are putting together an electronic classroom for user education and staff training. We also received funding, as a result of the review, to renovate existing instructional space.

Control of the credit classes has moved to the School of Library and Information Science (SLIS). The Undergraduate Library staff work with SLIS administrators to plan the syllabi and to select instructors. Centrally produced publications were pared down to a core number, under 15. We are currently developing a Web site that will allow us to share handouts created by various library units. Concentrated effort has begun to develop resources on the World Wide Web as instructional tools.

An advisory committee, broadly representative of the various library units concerned with instruction of users, was appointed. It has been involved in such issues as planning for the renovation of instructional space and creation of the core list of common handouts/publications.

ELECTRONIC RESOURCES AND SERVICES DEPARTMENT

Purpose, Mission, and Components

The new department, formed by a merger of the former two-person Computer-Based Resources and Services Team (CBRST) and the library instruction office, has already begun to play a major role in library activities and is growing. CBRST was created to provide leadership for development of electronic resources and access to databases, training of staff in the use of digital information, oversight of databases offered through the library's LAN and remotely, bibliographic control of digital documents, and coordination of electronic services projects.[5] The merger added an instruction component that we believe is unique among similar departments right now.

Currently, the department includes a database specialist, a librarian with technical services background, a graphic artist, and an instruction librarian. This summer a staff training librarian and a distance education librarian will join us. Other library staff join the group for specific activities (such as oversight of our electronic text program for the humanities) or for short-term projects. All except the training librarian position reflect reallocation of resources within the IUB Libraries.

The purpose and mission of the new department is to provide the support, coordination, and leadership to enable librarians and library staff to "embrace and incorporate new tools, such as the WWW, into their everyday work of collection development, reference, instruction, and cataloging."[6] Our role is primarily to facilitate the work of the libraries: identify, articulate, coordinate. ERSD focuses on issues that cross library departments.

THE ROLE OF INSTRUCTION IN THE NEW DEPARTMENT

The instruction component of the new department was given four tasks:

1) Collaborate with other library units to build instruction into library systems from the "inside" out. Provide leadership and coordination to such efforts.

2) Participate in instruction-related partnerships with groups outside the Bloomington Libraries.

3) Provide coordination, consultation, and technical assistance to library instruction providers on the Bloomington campus. Facilitate sharing of system news, methods, materials, and so on to meet common instructional needs.

4) Develop instructional materials that span the user population.

Use of the team approach in the new department allows more staff to be concentrated on some of these demands, not just the one person who has responsibility for the activity.

HOW IS IT WORKING?

To prepare for this presentation, I interviewed my colleagues. There is agreement on two big payoffs we have derived from the decentralization of instruction:

- empowerment of individuals, leading to creativity and enthusiasm; and

- ability to refocus our time and resources on critical library resources, including assessment, the Horizon project, and the World Wide Web.

The instruction reorganization has been a great morale boost for several departments as they have begun to explore the changes in the way we "have always done things." Decentralization has allowed units to be more responsive to student needs and changes. Student needs can be better identified and incorporated into instruction immediately.

There was time to try new initiatives. Some of the activities on which we have made real progress this year include

- leadership of OPAC development—both of a Windows-based catalog and a Web catalog—in the Horizon project with Ameritech,

- development of a video on library research that faculty can use in their own classrooms and that can be used in our distance education program,

- formulation of an assessment plan for information literacy that will provide help for faculty in teaching and assessing information literacy concepts and skills,

- changes in the orientation program,

- a revitalized faculty and graduate student workshop series, one that even has waiting lists for popular programs,

- creation of a new position for staff training on electronic resources, and

- new resources available on the libraries' Web pages.

We learned also how important day-to-day practical issues are to our success. Central control of equipment and rooms is important; someone must be responsible for these. Common equipment must be made as easy to set up and use as possible.

The advisory committee has done a good job in planning for common publications. However, someone must still be responsible for reviewing these publications on a regular basis, making sure they are kept up-to-date as resources change, and designing new publications as needed.

The same decentralization that worked so well for formal instruction activities has also worked well for development of library resources on the World Wide Web. Setting parameters for the Web and allowing units/information providers to be creative has been quite effective, resulting in a high level of participation and results that are also of high quality.

Two needs that continue are for one-on-one consulting and staff training and for one person or group to play a coordinating role in providing information to all staff about new library resources.

The need for a clearinghouse function—for handouts, for information about instructional programs and about new resources available on campus or in the libraries, and for information about cooperative activities—was much greater than we had anticipated. We are still trying to determine ways to meet this need. Another problem that we had not anticipated or planned for as well as we should have was the area of general public relations for instruction. We need to review these areas and plan for a solution.

PLANS FOR THE COMING YEAR

In the coming year, we anticipate solving many of the problems listed above. We plan to better develop the clearinghouse role of the electronic resources and services department, putting copies of all handouts developed by library units up on the Web for others to adapt and use, creating a library staff listserv about new electronic resources, and developing a plan for more communication and sharing activities, such as brown bag lunches and general meetings about topics of shared interest. We plan to finish setting up our electronic classroom/training room and renovating instructional space. With the new training coordinator and distance education coordinators in place, we will develop plans in those areas. The advisory committee will have two new tasks: to review the publications policies and procedures and develop plans for a regular review of core publications; and to review areas where central coordination and general public relations for instruction are needed.

CONCLUSION

As I said when we began, what we did at Indiana University Bloomington is not for everyone. It fit well into our organizational climate and allowed us to meet the challenges we faced as a library. If you ask me, though, whether it has been successful, I will say a resounding *yes*. Without the decentralization and reorganization that resulted from the review, we would have accomplished few of the new initiatives we attempted this year.

NOTES

1.   James G. Neal and Patricia A. Steele, "Empowerment, Organization and Structure: The Experience of the Indiana University Libraries," *Journal of Library Administration* 19:3/4 (1993): 82-86.

2.   Lizabeth A. Wilson, "Changing Users: Bibliographic Instruction for Whom?," in *The Evolving Educational Mission of the Library*, ed. by Betsy Baker and Mary Ellen Litzinger (Chicago: American Library Association, 1992), 49.

3.   Janice Simmons-Welburn, "Alternative Models for Instruction in the Academic Library: Another View of the Upside of Downsizing," in *The Upside of Downsizing: Using Library Instruction to Cope*, ed. by Cheryl LaGuardia, Stella Bentley, and Janet Martorana (New York: Neal-Schuman, 1995), 17-18.

4.   Neal and Steele, 88.

5.   Julie Bobay, "An Organizational Model for Library Faculty and Staff Involvement in the Development of New Electronic Services." Paper presented at "Harvard Conference on Finding Common Ground: Creating the Library of the Future Without Diminishing the Library of the Past," Harvard University, 30-31 March 1996.

6.   Bobay.

APPENDIX 1: INDIANA UNIVERSITY BLOOMINGTON LIBRARIES INSTRUCTION PROGRAM

Vision

We envision the library instruction program as a campuswide program that meets the information literacy needs of users at all levels and in all disciplines, including users who come to a library and those who access the library's resources remotely. It provides instructional materials and opportunities which accommodate the varying learning styles and learning strategies of users (print, electronic, media and multimedia, one-on-one, workshops, course-integrated instruction). The program gives users information covering 1) what resources are available to them, 2) how to access resources via varied technologies, and 3) specific resources and how to use them. The library instruction program works to ensure that the needs of users are a central concern in planning for new electronic resources and services and in evaluating currently available resources and services. It works to make the use of library resources understandable to users.

Mission

The Mission of the Library Instruction Program at Indiana University Bloomington is two-fold: 1) to serve as an advocate for the user in development of new systems and services within the libraries; and 2) to provide library users, both those in the libraries and those accessing library resources remotely, with instructional materials in a variety of formats, at a variety of levels of sophistication, that assist them to make effective use of library resources to find the information they need.

Assumptions

1) The IUB Libraries will continue to be a leader in the development of electronic library and information services.

2) The electronic environment will continue to become richer and more complex.

3) Platforms for electronic resources and the platforms used by members of the IUB community will become more diverse and customized.

4) The need for traditional library resources will continue to be important.

5) The instruction program is campuswide.

6) The library instruction component of the electronic resources and services department has responsibility for development of general instructional services and resources (print, nonprint, and electronic) that span the user population, subject disciplines, and the campus.

7) Each individual unit includes in its mission a responsibility to instruct its constituent body to use the resources important to their success in finding information.

8) The August 1990 statement on "Information Literacy and Undergraduate Education" continues to be a valid description of the goals of the undergraduate information literacy program.

9) Library instruction is a part of many job descriptions at all levels.

APPENDIX 2: INFORMATION LITERACY AND UNDERGRADUATE EDUCATION: A REPORT FROM THE IUB LIBRARIES' AD HOC INFORMATION LITERACY COMMITTEE

David Fenske, Lou Malcomb, Mary Popp, and Pat Steele

"To be information literate, a person must be able to recognize when information is needed and have the ability to locate, evaluate, and use effectively the needed information. Producing such a citizenry will require that schools and colleges appreciate and integrate the concept of information literacy into their learning programs and that they play a leadership role in equipping individuals and institutions to take advantage of the opportunities inherent within the information society. Ultimately, information literate people are those who have learned how to learn. They know how to learn because they know how knowledge is organized, how to find information, and how to use information in such a way that others can learn from them." (American Library Association, January 1989)

Rapidly expanding technologies have transferred our world. Computers represent one part of an array of electronic technologies which have helped create the networks and sources which mark the Information Age. The Report of the Committee on Computers in Undergraduate Education addresses the ways in which the university should promote computer proficiency. That proficiency is part of a broader literacy which students at Indiana University must achieve—information literacy.

Within the context of this statement, information is defined as the raw material of knowledge encompassing print, image, sound, numeric, and, indeed, data sources as yet unknown. This era of unprecedented information expansion challenges educators to develop new models of learning which are based on active, integrated use of information resources available to students. These new models will result in students who understand how knowledge is organized, stored, and transmitted allowing them to pursue lifelong learning and problem solving based on information resources. They will have critical thinking skills and will be empowered to perform effectively in their professional and civic lives.

Students should know about information retrieval systems. They should have opportunities in core courses to develop an understanding of the organization in our society and beyond: locating information, evaluating information, managing stored information at the personal level, and understanding the surrounding ethical issues.

The student needs first to acquire a broad understanding of the structure and usage of published information at both the general (cultural) and specific (discipline) levels, and to be familiar with the resources available for locating information. Students need to be able to evaluate the differences in these resources, select those appropriate to a particular need, and access them efficiently. For example, students must understand the difference between an online catalog and a CD-ROM bibliographic database. They should be able to search using Boolean statements, keywords, and hierarchical information trees as necessary. In this example, the student must also be able to distinguish between the appropriate use of electronic and printed sources of information.

To evaluate information, students must be able to determine the quality of information in terms of relevance, accuracy, and significance. They need the reliability of an information source, to understand how the technology itself may shape the information carried, and to be aware of the economic and political forces which affect information.

To manage information effectively students must be able to transfer information into their own databases, through networks, into word processing, or whatever electronic tools necessary to facilitate personal and collaborative work.

To achieve ethical awareness, students must appreciate academic and scholarly standards for the attribution of ideas, for handling of quoted materials, and for the presentation of balanced perspectives. They must also recognize the breadth and diversity of items protected by copyright law and the importance of that law to the creative and publication processes.

Information literacy often is most readily learned in the context of course-related subject material. Library faculty understand aspects of the organization, storage, and transmission of knowledge in ways often different from those of teaching faculty: understandings which better appreciate the structure of information systems. A partnership for this effort is clearly required. Specific goals for implementation include the following:

1) Academic unit curriculum committees need to identify core courses where the concepts of information literacy would be or are best presented.

2) The IUB Libraries must identify library faculty members with the appropriate course subject knowledge and pedagogical experience.

3) Teaching and library faculty would review the present information literacy goals of the selected courses and recommend any appropriate changes.

4) Library faculty members should be available for consulting with teaching faculty, for individual lectures, and for planning library-related assignments.

Information literacy may be taught using multiple media in existing courses by involving library faculty in relevant aspects or as stand-alone courses. Where course integration is the most appropriate solution, library faculty must participate with teaching faculty in a partnership arrangement. Where separate courses are the most appropriate solution, these classes should be taught by library faculty, when such individuals with the appropriate subject expertise are available, and when such courses can be coordinated closely within the curriculum of the department or school sponsoring the course.

The activities described above are already underway in many departments, particularly at the basic level. These recommendations would expand student access to educational opportunities which foster information literacy and ensure that Indiana University graduates are prepared to meet the challenges of life and work in an environment in which information is power.

APPENDIX 3: INDIANA UNIVERSITY LIBRARIES RECOMMENDATIONS OF THE INSTRUCTION REVIEW, 1995

1) Merge the present instruction office with the Computer Based Resources and Services Team and expand the role of the new unit. The instruction component of the new unit will focus on instruction issues that span the libraries—issues related to new technological environments, remote users, and users across disciplines, subjects, and levels.

2) Develop a new model for instruction which decentralizes responsibility for instruction planning. Each library unit will take responsibility for instruction of its own primary clientele. Shift hourly funding and other resources.

3) Establish an advisory/steering committee.

4) Review policies and procedures for providing instruction to outside groups.

5) Change the library's orientation program to make it more instruction-focused.

6) Develop strategies to communicate effectively with faculty and associate instructors about instructional issues.

7) Initiate negotiations with the School of Library and Information Science to take responsibility for the courses they now offer using the libraries' resources. Eliminate the cross-listed sections of the general library skills course offered through the College of Arts and Sciences.

8) Examine library publications to reduce the printing budget. Explore ways to support unit-level customization and the use of the Web to provide instruction.

9) Form an assessment committee to develop an assessment plan for information literacy.

— MARY PAGLIERO POPP —

A Student Training Program that Works

Beverly J. Stearns and Anne M. Tracy

BACKGROUND

Each area in the library hires and trains student employees. Without doubt, there is a wide variety of and uniqueness to duties that student employees perform in their units. However, there are also duties, policies, and philosophies that are common to all units. Hence, duplication of training efforts and inconsistency in training often occurs in the library.

How was librarywide training administered in the olden days before this new student employee training program? The student employment liaison for the library conducted a two-hour orientation/reception at the start of each academic year. Supervisors gave five-minute verbal "snapshot" tours of their units, and issues such as preservation, safety, and security were covered. A problem we encountered with this type of orientation was low attendance since the session was scheduled only once during the day, when many students were in class. Because student employees are hired throughout the year, those who began employment after the initial thrust of hiring in the fall missed the orientation. Another problem was using the lecture format, with no hands-on component. Even cookies and other enticements could not prevent much of the content from falling on deaf ears. A change was in order.

A group of library supervisors met informally to examine ways to insure that every new student employee be uniformly trained in the workings, procedures,

Stearns is assistant to the dean, Libraries and Learning Resources, and *Tracy* is library associate, Music Library, Bowling Green State University, Bowling Green, Ohio.

and philosophies common to all library departments. They believed that this would translate to money saved—in other words, more bang for your buck! In no way was the intent to preclude the unique training that individual departments conduct.

PROGRAM DEVELOPMENT

Process

This group of supervisors drafted a proposal to develop a training program for newly hired student employees and presented it to the library's administrative council. Following the council's endorsement, the dean appointed a task force of student supervisors from each library department to design a curriculum, develop appropriate training modules, and coordinate the initial training for all student supervisors. The dean issued the charge in March 1994, and the training program was to be in place by the beginning of the fall semester—only six short months away. (No easy task!)

Design

Members of the task force researched the literature on the topic of student training and orientation programs and provided the rest of the group with articles for review before the initial task force meeting. We discovered a dearth of current resources on the topic. The literature argues that structured training programs convey to student employees that their work is valued. Training outcomes include 1) a strengthened commitment to assigned work, and 2) increased knowledge of library operations.[1]

The task force used the endorsed proposal as a springboard for identifying common areas of training to include in the program. We had lots of ideas, but because of the tight timeframe, we had to scale down our list to what we thought would be a manageable undertaking. We excluded areas unique to individual departments, such as understanding local call number configurations, and decided that important university policies such as the racial and sexual harassment policies be addressed by individual supervisors and supplemented with inserts in the training folder.

Issues we considered included 1) how much of the student's time the program should involve, 2) whether students should be paid while training, and 3) to what degree training should be self-directed and/or moderated by the supervisor. We decided that the training program should take no more than three to four hours to complete and should be modular so that it could be broken down into manageable segments of time. Because training is integral to one's job, we all agreed that students should be paid to train. Our discussion of how the program works will explain how we solved the third issue.

We consolidated our ideas and produced a program containing four main training modules: the library tour, the collection development process (which traces materials from the point of order to shelf status), public service, and BGLink system training. BGLink is the computerized library and information network of Bowling Green State University Libraries and Learning Resources. BGLink is made up of the BGSU Libraries Catalog, the OhioLINK Statewide Catalog, which allows users to request books from member libraries, research databases, and a gateway to the Internet through the OhioLINK gopher and the World Wide Web. The task force divided into four subgroups. Each was assigned a module and given the responsibility for selecting the media format for their module.

Assessment

Did we encounter problems along the way? Of course we did! We did not realistically estimate the amount of lead time necessary for the production of the tapes and videos by our instructional media services (the media specialists within Libraries and Learning Resources). Choosing the background music, identifying inhouse experts for dubbing voice-overs, and videotaping were time-consuming activities. Balancing the advantages of using staff and student employees with the potential for producing one of "America's Funniest Home Videos" became a sensitive issue. We

wanted our viewers to focus on the content of our product rather than on the quality of the performance.

Did we encounter successes? You bet! Students reported via their evaluations of the program that they gained the added value of enhancing their research skills especially through the BGLink component. The program proved to give our student employees an overview of the library's facilities and how their areas of employment contribute to the organization as a whole—the big picture. We also found that the program addressed the administration's expectation that employees be knowledgeable about the library's products and services.

Training Program Components

The program includes 1) a welcome letter from the dean, which is sent directly to each newly hired student employee, 2) a training folder, which contains information about the program as well as policy guides, and more, 3) two videos, made inhouse, and 4) a series of BGLink system training cassettes and accompanying worksheets.

The Welcome Letter

Soon after being hired, the new student employee receives a welcome letter from the dean. In addition to welcoming the student to Libraries and Learning Resources, the letter serves as the first step in accountability for supervisors and students. Initially, the letter was part of the training folder, but after the first year it was apparent that some supervisors opted not to have their students participate in the program. The welcome letter explains to the new employees that their supervisors will contact them about participation in the program.

Training Folder

Each student receives from his or her supervisor a training folder consisting of the following:

- Training Program Overview,

- Program Completion Form,

- Evaluation Questionnaire,

- Student Employee Information Guide—covers library policies such as dress, attendance, and so on),

- Universitywide policy guides such as BGSU Racial/Sexual Harassment Policy, BGSU Sexual

Harassment Policy, and BGSU Drug and Alcohol Policy,

- Subtle Discrimination Awareness Guide—identifies subtle behaviors that are discriminatory),

- Helpful Hints for Effective Communication—directed primarily at students working in public service areas),

- Safety and Security Procedures,

- Fire Emergency Procedures, and

- Introduction to the BGLink System Training.

Folders for supervisors also contain a checksheet for monitoring students' progress in the program and an answer key for the BGLink training worksheets.

Videos

Currently, the training program utilizes two videos. The first is a library tour, which, in addition to an introduction to the main collection, includes a visit to branch libraries and remote departments. The other describes the collection development process; that is, tracing materials from the time of order to arrival, cataloging, linking in the system, and finally shelf status. We discontinued using a third video on the subject of customer service after it received poor evaluations, and are searching for a professionally-made replacement.

Members of the video subgroups wrote the scripts, which were revised by co-chairs. Writers made arrangements with instructional media services, which did the actual taping.

BGLink Materials

It is the administration's philosophy that all employees be knowledgeable in the services and products provided by the library, and this includes having facility with our online catalog, BGLink. Additionally, it is our experience that student staff are frequently asked questions about the library and its online catalog; perhaps they appear more approachable to student patrons. For these reasons, library instruction and orientation should extend to student employees in the library as well as to permanent staff. Scheduling multiple hands-on training sessions is impossible because of the large numbers of students hired each fall, and because hiring occurs throughout the year. So, we needed something the students could work on independently. We decided to record the presentations onto cassette tape and develop accompanying worksheets.

BGLink training is divided somewhat arbitrarily into four modules. Module 1 (The Basics) covers searching by author, title, keyword, and subject, as well as searching for periodicals and interpreting checkin records. The second module (Advanced Online Catalog) introduces the jump and limit features, as well as uploading searches to the OhioLINK statewide catalog. Module 3 covers research databases; of the over 40 available on BGLink, the students search two: Periodicals Abstracts and PAIS. Finally, we have Internet Resources—the OhioLINK gopher. This module is in constant need of revision as many gopher sites are no longer maintained. Also, the World Wide Web (WWW) is now a choice on our welcome menu and therefore should be covered in the training.

Scripts for the system training were written by members of the subcommittee and tested by other task force members, as well as by some student assistants. The writers scheduled the taping, found willing and able readers from the ranks of the library staff, and supervised the actual recording. Because the online catalog is ever-changing, we were careful to choose examples that were likely to remain constant for a semester or two. In spite of this, we knew that the tapes would need to be revised from time to time.

In anticipation of system-related problems, the opening remarks on each tape instruct the student assistants to turn off the tape if the system slows down. This is especially important while working on the database and Internet modules. At various intervals, the listener is specifically instructed to turn the tape off and answer a question on a worksheet.

HOW IT WORKS

How does this training program work? Once the dean sends the welcome letter to the student employee, the supervisor issues the training folder. The student employee receives time on the clock to read all of the handouts.

The videos, system training cassette tapes and cassette players are housed in the library's reserve room and in remote departments, so student employees may check them out for use inhouse. The new hirees watch the videos, listen to the tapes, and complete the worksheets during regularly scheduled hours, or during additionally scheduled times, which are arranged with supervisors. It is the responsibility of supervisors to monitor students' progress, to check completed worksheets, and to answer any questions students have regarding any of the modules.

When a student employee completes all modules, they fill the Evaluation Questionnaire and sign the Program Completion Form, and send both to the program coordinator in the dean's office. Receipt of the completion form generates a certificate of completion for the student and a note of congratulations for both the student and the supervisor in the dean's weekly e-mail message to all staff.

SUPERVISOR ORIENTATION

Enthusiasm for participation in the training has to originate with the supervisor; therefore, after all components were written, filmed, and taped, an orientation session for supervisors was scheduled. To effectively administer the training, supervisors must be knowledgeable about all aspects of the program. During this session, we not only outlined the "how-tos" but also tried to motivate enthusiasm for the project. The final question on the Evaluation Questionnaire seeks to measure the supervisor's enthusiasm by asking the new employees if their supervisors were enthusiastic about their participation. Most responded affirmatively.

PROGRAM EVALUATION

In order to get necessary feedback about what works and what doesn't work, the task force developed a two-pronged evaluation system. The two-pronged evaluation system includes student employees completing the Evaluation Questionnaire and supervisors assessing the program on an annual basis—usually at the end of the academic year.

In the 1995/1996 academic year, an impressive 87 percent of the new library student employees who participated in the training program returned their evaluation questionnaires: 97 percent of the respondents believed that they gained appropriate information about the library with only one respondent indicating to the contrary; 83 percent felt the program was worthwhile and were glad they participated, with only five respondents indicating otherwise.

In Spring 1995, supervisors revealed in their assessments of the program that they could effectively administer the training program. Furthermore, they believed that the material covered was appropriate for their needs and complemented the unique training they provided in their units.

RECOMMENDATIONS

Our program is not perfect. Each year we expect to improve and perhaps add new modules to the program. The following are recommendations for improving the program made by supervisors and student employees:

1) Discontinue using the customer service video and purchase a professionally made replacement. (implemented)

2) Change procedures for students to report completion of the program. This process was streamlined from students submitting slips to their supervisors each time they completed a module, to filling out one completion form, which is sent to the program coordinator in the dean's office. The supervisors develop individual means for monitoring progress. (implemented)

3) Identify a program coordinator. (implemented)

4) Address supervisor accountability. Initial steps have been taken by removing the dean's welcome letter from the folder and directly mailing it to the new student employee. This sets the students' expectation that their supervisors will initiate training and prompts the supervisor to follow up in a timely manner. The dean's weekly message to all library staff not only recognizes the students and their supervisors who complete the program, but recognizes by omission the supervisors whose names do not appear regularly in the message. This serves as a vehicle for the program coordinator to follow up with the supervisors. What we have not yet resolved is an appropriate means for evaluating supervisors on their commitment to and participation in the training program. One question on the student Evaluation Questionnaire was originally designed to do just that. We face logistical problems incorporating this element into the university's various evaluation systems. (implemented in part)

5) Annually revise BGLink system training audio cassette tapes. (implemented)

6) Address the importance of confidentiality in offices as well as in public service areas with a folder insert or video. (to be implemented)

7) Supplement the video tour of the library with an organizational chart inserted in the folder. This would enhance the student employees' understand-

ing of where their units fit in the organization. (to be implemented)

8) Possible creation of a module on the subject of security of the collections. (to be implemented)

NOTE

1. Morell D. Boone, et al. *Training Student Library Assistants* (Chicago: American Library Association, 1991).

FURTHER RESOURCES

Burrows, Janice H. "Training Student Workers in Academic Libraries: How and Why?" *Journal of Library Administration* 21 (1995): 77-86.

Wesley, Threasa L. "Beyond Job Training: An Orientation Program for Library Student Assistants." *Catholic Library World* 61 (March-April 1990): 215-217.

White, Emilie C. "Student Assistants in Academic Libraries: From Reluctance to Reliance." *Journal of Academic Librarianship* 11 (May 1985): 93-97.

INFORMATION LITERACY IN THE

COMMUNITY COLLEGE

John Walker and Winnie Tseng

During the 1995-96 academic year, the Sinclair Community College (SCC) Learning Resources Center (LRC) initiated a new information-literacy program as its primary method of delivering library instruction. This new instructional effort became necessary for a variety of reasons. Essentially, Sinclair's inclusion in the OhioLINK electronic library effort, as well as the introduction of new electronic informational resources such as CD-ROM packages and the Internet within the LRC, presented our library users with a host of new electronic research options. Also, the library's traditional bibliographic instruction efforts, although extensive and commendable, appeared to be failing in giving students and faculty proper skills in the use of these new electronic informational resources. Our presentation describes the information literacy program that the librarians and English faculty have developed to meet the increasingly complex research possibilities presented to Sinclair students.

Background Information

The Sinclair Community College Learning Resources Center is designed to meet the print and non-print informational needs of users, both attending and working within a large, comprehensive, urban community college. In 1994, the college reached the 20,000 student level. Academic programs at Sinclair encompass remedial education, two-year college transfer courses, and a host of occupational training programs. Students

Walker and *Tseng* are reference librarians at Sinclair Community College, Dayton, Ohio.

attending the college are typical of those attending most community colleges. That is, they are generally older, they are typically working at jobs while attending college, and they bring a sense of seriousness to their academic work (including researching for library information).

The Learning Resources Center at Sinclair is quite large and complex, as community college LRCs go. About 135,000 books grace the shelves. Since the LRC was extensively damaged in a flood in 1983, the book collection has been reconstructed over the last decade, and consequently, remains both current and closely tied to the actual requirements of the curriculum. There are 650 titles maintained in the periodical collection. Of course, no library has enough periodicals within its collection. Considering the typical budgetary constraints of collection development, the LRC's periodical collection seems adequate. Also, the media services area of the LRC gives SCC students access to thousands of video tapes and other typical audiovisual resources.

Bibliographic instruction has long been a major activity of the reference staff (composed of 4.5 librarians). More than 300 instructional sessions a year were delivered year after year. Most of the typical bibliographic instruction approaches were tried at some time during the last two decades. These approaches included the use of pathfinders, tours, homemade slide presentations, videotapes, special exercises, handouts, handbooks, and the like. The cooperation and interaction between the Sinclair faculty and the reference staff in regards to library instruction has been spectacular. In fact, this wonderful interaction became something of a curse in the 1990s. So many customized instructional presentations were devised as part of the LRC's bibliographic instruction efforts that no one could keep up with them. Special guides for each instructor proliferated. Despite the tremendous time and effort put forth by the reference staff, the entire bibliographic instruction program was a confusing and jumbled maze.

In recent years, the Sinclair LRC has made rapid strides in the introduction of electronic information technologies. For a number of years, the LRC has maintained an electronic catalog. Online searching of databases on DIALOG by reference librarians has given way to the use of full-text CD-ROM databases, searched directly by students. In 1994, Sinclair joined the OhioLINK system, giving users access to major online catalogs of Ohio universities and colleges, numerous periodical databases, and the Internet. Bibliographic instruction has also evolved a technological base with the use of computer-networked demonstrations, along with a small, networked, microcomputer-training facility with 14 computer workstations. In short, the confluence of information technology within the last five years, both in electronic research by users and in library instruction, has provided the LRC reference staff with an opportunity to refocus its instructional efforts towards an information-literacy concept.

Training Design at Sinclair

The first phase in the creation of an information-literacy program at Sinclair involved a general analysis of the instructional needs of Sinclair classes and students. Essentially, three groups of library users were identified as needing some type of focused information-literacy training. The first group were the thousands of students writing typical bread-and-butter research papers within the English curriculum. The second group were students in occupational or subject-based classes (such as nursing, marketing, speech, and respiratory therapy) who had increasingly complex library research needs within their courses. (Sinclair as a college had jumped on the "writing across the curriculum" bandwagon in the 1980s so this group was quite substantial.) Finally, a third group of students needing specific information-literacy instruction were those who just fell between the cracks, in a sense—older students returning to college and facing online databases and CD-ROM packages for the first time, or those who just wanted to get on the Internet in order to surf the World Wide Web or send e-mail to friends. All three groups posed substantial problems concerning library instruction design.

The training sessions we devised at Sinclair to help prepare students for information literacy focused on these three groups of students: research process

instruction for the numerous English department classes, subject-focused training for occupational courses, and LRC-sponsored, one-hour sessions on specific informational topics.

Research Process—English Department

Sinclair's English curriculum has always included a research paper component. Historically, much of the LRC's bibliographic instruction efforts have been directed at helping these students locate the information they needed for their papers. Teaching how to manipulate the increasing complexity of electronic research choices confronted by the average student was difficult to handle in the typical one-hour library instruction session. In 1995, a five-person librarian-English faculty information literacy team met to devise a new approach to instruction for the research process. What resulted from this collaboration was an innovative approach that combined a one-hour computerized demonstration with at least another hour of hands-on training in the LRC's microcomputer lab for each student. Students are required to complete a library exercise that directs them to locate citations and information on their topics using the OhioLINK system and various other CD-ROM databases. Faculty were required to create at least two library sessions within their curriculum. In fact, the program devised by the information literacy team suggested that at least three sessions be allotted for direct library instruction. Faculty are encouraged to set up a third session so that students have one additional hour of hands-on experience. In the 1995-96 academic year, over 100 of these two-part or three-part hands-on information literacy sessions for English students were conducted.

An evaluation of this new approach for information-literacy training was conducted in the Winter 1996 academic term. A total of 333 surveys were collected from English research paper writing students. The survey instrument was designed to get the students' impressions of the entire process—from computer demonstration, through hands-on training, to the actual collection of pertinent and useful information of their topics. We discovered that the students overwhelmingly (80 percent) endorsed our approach that combined both a computer demonstration and hands-on experience. Nearly the same number felt the handouts and exercises used in these sessions were very helpful. Perhaps most important, the English faculty members found this approach to be very productive, even though the approach asked them to give up precious class time for hands-on library training.

Subject-Based Training

During the 1995-96 academic year, the LRC conducted over 150 subject-based training sessions. These sessions covered such topics as marketing, nursing, dental hygiene, travel and tourism, psychology, electronic engineering, and culinary arts. Every class received an informational guide on the electronic (databases and World Wide Web as well as print resources in the LRC on their subject. Faculty members in these disciplines and the reference librarians designed the content coverage of each session. Consequently, these instructional sessions varied greatly in the mode in which each was conducted. Some sessions involved just a lecture and computer demonstration of electronic resources in the subject. Other sessions involved hands-on training of electronic resources and World Wide Web sites. In truth, however, the complexity of offering so many custom-tailored instructional sessions that included guides, exercises (in some cases), and hands-on training proved to be quite difficult. Some of the reference librarians became quite uneasy about the increased workload that resulted from the preparation and presentation of so many different subject-based sessions.

LRC-Sponsored Sessions

A final group of sessions developed as part of the LRC's information literacy program entailed a number of special sessions sponsored and promoted by the LRC. These sessions, about 50 altogether during the academic year, consisted of one-hour instructional programs offered on a first-come-first-serve basis. Essentially, the LRC offered sessions on such topics as using the online catalog, using OhioLINK databases, understanding e-mail, and using Netscape for access to the World Wide Web. The LRC promoted the sessions to students and faculty with flyers and brochures, articles in the campus newspaper, and word-of-mouth. Students and others who wanted to attend one of the LRC's special instructional sessions could sign up for one at the LRC's reference desk.

In truth, these sessions enjoyed mixed success. As most know who have worked in a community college setting, it is difficult to get students to attend out-of-classroom events, be they special programs, concerts, plays, or whatever. Most community college students are chronologically older, and nearly always

have outside job or family obligations along with their educational endeavors. Consequently, most of these special sessions had only five or six students in attendance. On the other hand, the librarians who conducted these programs almost universally thought their sessions were particularly successful and useful for those students who attended.

Problems and Concerns

A number of serious problems jumped up during the year in regards to this information-literacy initiative. Certainly the most serious problem concerned an increased workload for reference librarians. The preparations of guides, exercises, and handouts, in addition to developing and conducting computer demonstrations of different disciplines and handling all the little snafus that come with hands-on training with multiple computers, all taxed the patience and imagination of the LRC's reference librarians. Generally speaking, the low turnout of student interest in LRC's sponsored instructional sessions was dismaying. We plan on increasing the promotion of these sessions in the 1996-97 academic year. Also, the LRC conducted some evaluation of the research process program designed in collaboration with the English department. During the coming year, we plan on developing some type of evaluation of the numerous subject-based sessions conducted each year.

New Developments

Because information-literacy training is rooted in the rapidly changing electronic information technology, our program as it was developed for 1995-96 will certainly be significantly altered in 1996-97 and beyond. We are developing a strategy to utilize both the information kiosks on Sinclair's campus and the LRC's home page for the dissemination of library research information. Like many colleges, Sinclair is launching into the burgeoning area of distance education. How we as Sinclair librarians support the information literacy needs of students taking Sinclair classes from virtually anywhere in the world has not been thought out clearly. What does seem certain is that we as Sinclair librarians have no choice but to actively pursue information literacy for our students. The days of simple bibliographic instruction tours of the library resources seem almost a distant memory.

THE FRESHMAN YEAR EXPERIENCE:
A LIBRARY COMPONENT THAT WORKS

Emily Werrell

The library instruction program at Northern Kentucky University (NKU) consists primarily of course-related rather than curriculum-integrated sessions. One component in particular, however, has become quite well integrated into our extended orientation course for freshmen, University 101. My presentation today centers on this component, how it has evolved over the past ten years, and what changes we have made in order to transform the course's library exercise from a peripheral skills unit into a much better integrated component that meshes well with the course content and seems to "work" for everyone involved.

University 101 is modeled after the course of the same name developed 24 years ago at the University of South Carolina, home of the National Resource Center for the Freshman Year Experience. Theirs is one of the best-known and most widely replicated orientation programs for college freshmen, although versions of their model course vary in style, nomenclature (e.g., student success course, freshman seminar), and content. As colleges fight to improve retention rates and help freshmen succeed, such full-fledged orientation courses have become popular across the country; they're now offered on about two-thirds of college campuses. Except for the "freshman seminar," which generally has a more pronounced academic focus, most of these courses have in common some essential goals, which include not just orienting new students to campus, but preparing them for the demands and expectations—both social and academic—of contem-

Werrell is coordinator of instructional services, Northern Kentucky University, Highland Heights, Kentucky.

porary college life. Orientation courses have been shown to improve retention and graduation rates, have a positive impact on student persistence, and generally help freshmen become more informed, more comfortable, and more academically integrated.[1]

Ten years ago, Northern Kentucky University implemented a pilot program with ten sections of UNV 101. This past fall (1995) we offered 47 sections, all of which were filled, and the course now reaches about half of our freshman class (or approximately 1,000 students each year). It covers a fairly typical mix of personal survival skills and an introduction to campus resources including the writing lab, tutoring services, career development center, and counseling. Academic advising is heavily emphasized.

Where does the library fit in? Well, in the grand scheme of freshman success in college, learning to use the library does not come in at the top of the list as far as most program designers are concerned. In terms of retention and even academic success in the freshman year, information literacy just can't compete, as a make-it-or-break-it factor, with alcohol abuse, loneliness, preventing pregnancy, or juggling a full course load and two part-time jobs. In a national survey of freshman seminar programs, "using the library" did make the list as one of the topics covered in the course, but on a national scale it ranked well below basic study skills, time management, relationship issues, campus rules and regulations, goal setting, and wellness. Of those who described their courses as "extended orientation" types, like Northern Kentucky University's, only 47 of 494 or so colleges listed "using the library" as a frequently covered topic. It ranked next to last, in fact, beating out only "history and mission of the institution."[2] However, NKU planners did include a library component, so we count ourselves fortunate.

PROBLEMS

From the beginning, however, library instruction for this program was problematic. We were glad to learn, that first year, that there was more to the library component than a simple orientation to the building. Unfortunately, the library research assignment that most of the instructors were using presented difficulties. An additional hurdle, which we did not at first anticipate, was the need for the library to do special training for UNV 101 instructors. I'll take these two issues—the assignment and the instructors—one at a time and discuss them in some detail, because they are the two most important aspects of our library component's ultimate success.

The Assignment

The library exercise our instructors were using in the early years came from the textbook in use on our campus. This textbook was written by two of the directors of the UNV 101 program at the University of South Carolina, A. Jerome Jewler and John N. Gardner.[3] The library chapter was written by a professor of library science at the same institution, Charles C. Curran. The textbook exercise consists of a narrative portion, which explains the exercise and a strategy to be used in the library research process, and a workbook section to be filled in by the student, the intended final product being a group presentation in class. The narrative portion begins by saying some very good things about the importance of information literacy, and promises that "the skills you are about to practice won't solve all your problems, but they will help you address every college assignment that involves some need for information."[4] The framework then laid out for the assignment consists of "1) a topic to be researched, 2) some information to be retrieved, interpreted, and organized, and 3) a five-minute oral presentation to your class." Suggested topics include AIDS, hypnosis, the Ku Klux Klan, values, the Mafia, the Reformation, and love. An outline is suggested for this oral presentation: Definition: What is the topic about? Importance: Why is this topic important? Effect: How has the research influenced my thinking? What is there about this information that contributes to my understanding of the topic? Reaction: What do I want to tell others? How does this information make me feel?[5]

Jewler has written elsewhere about this library exercise, describing it as a "structured research assignment in the college library, in which a student learns *the proper method for conducting research on any topic* [emphasis added]....Far from being a 'scavenger hunt,' in which the student might be asked to locate specific books and periodicals, our exercise asks the student to conduct research on a topic of his or her choosing and provides step-by-step instructions on how to do it."[6]

The prescribed search strategy requires students to proceed systematically through general and subject encyclopedias, general and subject periodical indexes, the LC list, the book catalog, and Editorials on File, filling worksheets with citations throughout the process. While the text explains that one moves logically from one step to the next, there is little explanation *why* one would want to move from periodicals to books to opinion pieces, or when one might want to select, for example, articles rather than books, or editorials rather than news reports. Jewler claims that this exercise guides students in a "logical order" through reference tools "that will help the novice researcher exhaust as many resources as possible."[7] Well, not only did the assignment exhaust as many sources as possible; unfortunately it exhausted our students as well!

Let me enumerate the problems we had with this assignment. First of all, students didn't like it. Now, I know freshmen, as a rule, don't like library exercises—we'll talk a little about that later. But this particular exercise *was* tedious. The students complained, interestingly, that it was both "too hard" and "busy work" at the same time. Not only did they find it tedious, they often skipped over the first 12 to 13 pages which explain the assignment, and went directly to the fill-in-the-blanks section so they could get it done as quickly as possible. As a consequence, when they got to the workbook page requiring them to "ask a librarian for the name of the subject authority list in your library because it might not be the LC list," and then to write down the "legal" terms for their topics, you can imagine how confused they were...despite a 50-minute library instruction session.

Second, instructors didn't like it, I think primarily because they had to listen to so much whining over it (just kidding), but truly because, for one thing, they could see that the assignment wasn't necessarily helping their students to understand how the library really works, and, moreover, many of the instructors did not feel comfortable teaching this unit. Later in my talk, I will provide more detail about how instructors' concerns factored into our solutions.

Third, the reference librarians disliked it, to put it mildly, for a number of reasons. Foremost among our objections was that it did not mesh at all with the direction in which our instruction program was moving. At the time we were first experiencing UNV 101, we were reading about and beginning to experiment with the exciting new ideas emerging from writing teachers and librarians who were applying learning theory, especially constructivist theory, to writing and library research instruction. Constructivist theory holds that new knowledge is not imparted from the "sage on the stage" or the textbook and then absorbed by the student, but is created by individuals through their experiences, and assimilated best when it is directly related to something they already know. It follows that library research skills should not be taught in isolation, but in the broader context of the intellectual search, in which information is sought for a real need, and related to the subject matter being covered in the course. We were influenced especially by Carol Kuhlthau[8] and Barbara Fister,[9] who were making strong cases for revamping our entire approach to instruction from the one-size-fits-all search-strategy approach we had been employing to a more natural, more meaningful, and possibly more effective process approach. "Library instruction that guides students through the levels of information needs, to solve a problem or shape a topic, enables them to use information for learning. Instruction that helps them develop a realistic perception of an information system prepares them to be more successful searchers."[10] As long ago as 1984, Cerise Oberman was claiming that the shift from a "fixed, static search strategy to the dynamic search strategy reinforces the reality of research, which is flexible, malleable and distinct."[11]

We were also convinced by the related material on critical thinking, and were moving away from tool-based instruction and in the direction of conceptual skills, believing that the tool-based approach did not provide for the transfer of skills to new situations, and that its rigid emphasis on learning specific tools prevented students from developing their own realistic strategies based on a more holistic understanding of information systems. Phyllis Reich wrote in 1986, "Library instruction should make the tools of library research as unobtrusive as possible, much like a piece of laboratory equipment whose operation requires some special skills and knowledge, but is incidental to the main purpose."[12]

So, our major complaint about the UNV 101 library exercise had to do with issues far more problematic than the library jargon it employed or its unmanageable research topics (ever tried to look up "Love" in Editorials on File?). In brief, it fell short of what we considered to be the emerging, but valid, educational goals of our instruction program. Our reading and thinking had been leading us in a direction *away* from "choose a topic and research it," and *toward* the development of questions and an individual strategy that arises from the student's particular research problem. We knew it was important to emphasize the early stages of the research process, in which students define what kind of information they need, and articulate these needs, *before* they come to the library, and we had begun working on this with instructors of English composition. Both Carol Kuhlthau and Carmen Schmersahl, a writing instructor, present guidelines for library research projects using the process approach, and one factor of primary importance according to both these authors is that the topics need to arise from and be directly related to the curriculum.[13] Students should be seeking information in order to complete an "authentic" task, and "because the research is intended to support and challenge their own ideas, students venture into the library only after they have begun working on their analysis and have formulated some preliminary ideas."[14] In a nutshell, our philosophical objections to the UNV 101 textbook exercise were that it imposed artificial topics and procedures, it lacked authenticity as a task, and it lacked relevance to the rest of what was going on in the course.

So the question was, then, what to do with our dissatisfaction? The first year or two, we simply muttered under our breath at the reference desk and grew frustrated in the classroom, trying to teach to this assignment. Some of us tried valiantly in instruction sessions to place the exercise in a larger context, and *lectured freshmen*, if you can imagine, about how important library research was going to be in their academic careers, how it would help them to make connections among the topics they were studying, help them make decisions and bolster arguments....Of course you can imagine the blank stares. When some of us tried making the sessions more active, and related the presentation directly to specific information they would need to finish the assignment, the response was a little better, but still unsatisfactory.

So, we devoted ourselves to "improving" the exercise. First, we lobbied for more time during the annual UNV 101 workshops to explain our concerns to instructors. We thought that all we needed to do was explain to the faculty what was wrong with the library exercise, and suggest that they create their own, more relevant, and better designed assignments instead. We did offer assistance and a long list of guidelines, and went over these in our workshop session in some detail. The instructors responded positively at the time, but when fall came, they fell back on the textbook assignment, and it became apparent that we had succeeded only in making them feel guilty for using it. We received plenty of apologies along with their legitimate claims of a lack of time to develop new assignments.

The following year, resigned that they would probably continue to use the text assignment, we made concrete suggestions for helping students get the most out of it: create a schedule for completing the assignment (giving it four to five weeks, instead of one); go over the requirements of the assignment in class; allow time for brainstorming and other activities to help create focused questions from the vague topics; make sure there is an end product, so that using the library is not an end in itself (some students were required to do no more than fill out the worksheets); eliminate the requirements that students use a prescribed group of research tools; and substitute a list of topics related to the class units. Still, although a few of the instructors did come up with their own projects, most people used the textbook assignment as it was, with apologies once again, and I think we drove others away, because there were some who never called that year to schedule sessions in the library.

Dejected, we gave up for a time. I concentrated on "correcting" the textbook chapter, a minor improvement in my mind. They could simply substitute my corrected version, which included local information, placed more emphasis on critical evaluation of sources, and did a better job of explaining the value of subject encyclopedias and periodical indexes. But it still used a generic search strategy, the topics were still not generated from the curriculum, and it wasn't much of an improvement from the students' point of view, especially as my "enhancements" added a lot more text to the workbook portion and a lot less nice white space.

What struck me, though, was the response from the instructors. They all used my revised version of the textbook exercise! It was clear that this was what they really wanted—a ready-made assignment that met with the library's approval, that they could plug in at the appropriate place in their syllabus. It was at this point that we began to pay attention to what these instructors expected from the library component, and to realize the large difference between *our* perception and *their* perceptions of the purposes of library research assignments. This was a turning point for us, because it motivated us to concentrate as much on the instructors as we had on the library assignment.

The Instructors

In our course-related program, the librarians were accustomed to putting together library instruction sessions in support of a course of academic study, almost like an extension of reference desk work, in which classes had specific information needs. Faculty in academic departments, for their part, were accustomed to taking responsibility for library research assignments. It finally dawned on us that the University 101 instructors were as a group completely different from our usual "clients." First of all, because of the nature of the course, there was no real academic

content—UNV 101 is a series of units, more or less, with field trips and guest speakers, with the unifying theme being not U.S. history or sociology but surviving in college. They go to the computer lab, they have a visit from the campus nurse, they see skits about race relations. So the library assignment was not tied to learning about a "subject," and was perceived by the instructors as one more "unit" that they should be able to just take care of with a guest speaker from the library and a one-day exercise. They didn't understand at all why we were making such a big deal over the quality of the library research assignments, and why we couldn't just come up with a little tour and hands-on practice session and be done with it.

But the major revelation for us was that few of our University 101 instructors are members of the teaching faculty. My impression is that this is also true on other campuses where the freshman seminar is not necessarily tied to an academic subject. Over 80 percent of our UNV 101 instructors are "staff" whose "day jobs" normally don't take them into the classroom: coaches, secretaries, administrators, and counselors.

This explained much of our difficulty. Regular teaching faculty, as a rule, stay current with research methods and tools in their own disciplines, and most can confidently lead undergraduates through the intellectual process of conducting research for a paper. The staff and administrators teaching UNV 101 are excellent choices to teach the course. They are often the people on our campus best able to motivate, support, and assist freshmen, as they are familiar with most university services and procedures, and they are popular teachers in the program. But the library was almost as alien a place to many of them as it was to their students. When we understood better that they did care about the library, but were uncomfortable teaching it, their behavior made more sense. This explained why they would neglect to mention the library exercise to the class until the day they came for library instruction, why they would drop their students off at the library and go back to their offices, why they didn't bring their classes back for any working group sessions, and why they frequently eliminated the requirement that the students actually present any kind of final product based on the research that they did. They didn't make the connection between the students' complaints about busy work and their own attitudes and practices in presenting library research. We realized that although we might never get the instructors to completely buy into the library's goals and philosophy, we still had to come up with a way to help them feel familiar and comfortable helping their students in the library, to bring them back for working sessions during class time, and to take some personal responsibility for this portion of the course. As far as the library exercise itself was concerned, we determined that we would have to develop something ourselves.

SOLUTIONS

Over the summer of 1993, we changed the component in two important ways: we wrote a variety of assignments ourselves, for instructors to choose from, and we began a training workshop for instructors, separate from the annual UNV 101 training all instructors attend in May, that combined hands-on library work and guidance in how to handle the library portion of the course.

In designing the assignments, we had to take into consideration both the goals of the UNV 101 program and the library's goals for freshman-level instruction. Developing a feeling of belonging is a crucial aspect of UNV 101. According to the national Freshman Year Experience survey I cited earlier, the development of a community and active involvement in the life of the institution are central factors in the success of freshmen.[15] One goal of our program is to provide students with a supportive community of peers who will assist them in their transition to college. Therefore, group work is important in this course, and continues outside of class time—the class goes together to the theater, a basketball game, and for pizza. In the spirit of social support, we designed most of the assignments so that group work was built into the research process, partly for the "community" goals, and partly because we knew that freshmen feel safety in numbers when in unfamiliar territory like a college library. We also made sure that the library assignments each incorporated an instruction session with a librarian, as well as numerous one-on-one contacts at the reference desk and working sessions for the whole class to spend time together in the library. This was not only to provide an opportunity for freshmen to experience our support, but also because according to those who study the social and cognitive aspect of the process of writing, the *modeling* of the research process by experts, but in a collaborative rather than an instructive way—in this case the experts are the librarians and sometimes the instructors, and even some savvy classmates—helps the students to eventually internalize a model of the research process that works.[16]

The *library's* goals for this component developed partly from our general goals for freshman instruction, which we had been developing at about the same time. The basic abilities we want freshmen to learn (ideally) include, first of all, orientation—navigating our library, understanding the differences between public and academic libraries, and understanding the role of the reference librarian; but also the ability to use basic tools for locating books and periodicals, formulate research questions, determine information needs, select tools appropriate to the scope and complexity of the research question, understand the concepts of controlled vocabulary, keyword, and BASIC Boolean searching, interpret citations, and evaluate on a basic level—in other words, be aware that not all information is of equal value for a given information need.

In designing our assignments we also took into consideration Carol Kuhlthau's guidelines regarding implementing a process approach in library research and writing instruction. She suggests that groundwork for research should be laid by introducing issues and concepts worthy of further investigation, preferably by using something attention-grabbing like a video, debate, or thought-provoking reading. She recommends brainstorming to generate, clarify, and share research ideas, which encourages collaborative learning. An audience beyond the teacher should be established from the start, and mechanics are stated directly but in no way overshadow the central task of gaining a deeper understanding of a particular problem, issues, or topic.[17]

Carmen Schmersahl echoes a number of these guidelines and states furthermore that "just as beginning writers should not be asked to do research in isolation of a real writing-engendered need, they should not be expected to assimilate all the mechanics of researching at once."[18] We took this to heart and decided that it was all right if our assignments required them to use only one or two types of tools—the important thing would be the appropriateness of the tools for their particular information needs. As a result, for some of our assignments, there is no need to use any type of tool beyond a periodical index.

In the assignments presented in the appendixes you will see a few examples of how we implemented these various goals. At any one time there are six or seven assignments for instructors to choose from; the three reproduced here are representative. They are ready to be photocopied as they are, with a place in most of them for the instructor to fill in the blanks for dates. The assignments are all available to instructors in a UNV 101 resource book, and they are free to either pick one of ours or write one of their own using our guidelines. The first year we did this, 1993, we had assignments that covered a wider variety of topics, including nontraditional students in college, controversial issues in health and fitness (like steroid use, liquid diets, tanning parlors, dietary supplements), and sexual harassment. In 1994, the UNV 101 director decided that there were some particular issues that needed to be stressed more in the course, and she asked the instructors to concentrate on cultural diversity issues, especially racism, sexism, and homophobia, drug and alcohol abuse, and relationship and sexuality issues, especially date rape, sexually transmitted diseases, and AIDS. Our challenge was to come up with library research assignments—with a purpose—that would relate to these topics and meet most of our other goals as well.

The Assignments

The "Forum on Gay Rights" (see appendix 1) we used in 1994, but not this last year, as the public furor over this issue in the Cincinnati area had momentarily died down. Notice that the topics, or questions, are already formulated for the students. This was a conscious decision that we made to get them past the difficult process of topic formulation, knowing the limited time UNV 101 devoted to the library component. We expected these same students to gain more research experience in other classes taken the first year. Providing the research questions already formulated permitted a kind of shortcut, although we still spend time on question analysis in instruction sessions. The gay rights assignment meets most of our other goals: it has the students working in groups, it discusses a current issue related to the course content and of keen interest to many of them, it allows them to decide for themselves what kind of information is needed, gives them some leeway, with guidance, in choosing appropriate sources, but is not laid so wide open that *any* old article will do. One group will find they have to use local newspaper information, another will find books and reference materials most useful for background and history, and another group will want to look for current periodical articles on civil rights for homosexuals. The group working on comparing the local ordinance to affirmative action will probably need to use a combination of sources, including reference books. The project culminates in an oral presentation to the class.

The assignment in appendix 2 is based on an instructor's assignment from a few years ago. We worked on it together and modified the subject content to match the new course emphasis on drug and alcohol issues. Again, this involves group work, the students define their information needs, and this particular one directly addresses the need to select and evaluate sources, because each student in a group does independent research and then shares the *best* articles with his or her group before they create an presentation. Also, again, this assignment requires a variety of sources, but still all are easily accessible in our library.

The one labeled Library Research Project (see appendix 3) has them visit the issue of discrimination and homophobia. Students are asked to imagine they are giving advice to a friend who has been diagnosed

as HIV positive. Again, it involves group work and requires sharing with the class at the end. The questions are once again specific enough that certain types of sources make the most sense, but the assignment does not dictate which tools to use. We've tried to do this with all the assignments so that the instructional support is there in a stronger sense than it is when they're just assigned a topic and left to their own devices, but is not so artificially structured that they feel they are doing a busy-work exercise. This is still far from student-generated research problems, but it gives them a little bit of responsibility for choosing tools.

Other assignments currently in use I will describe briefly. We have a biography assignment, which results in an individual paper, not a group project, and it addresses the cultural diversity issue in a less direct and certainly less threatening way than a class forum on gay rights. It has them choose from a list a member of an ethnic minority who has made significant contributions to American life. Right now this list includes astronauts, entrepreneurs, politicians, writers, artists, and activists. They are to write essays discussing their subjects' most important accomplishments and contributions. This assignments satisfies the instructors who don't feel their particular class is ready to handle the more controversial topics in a class discussion. A second fairly innocuous assignment is our straightforward career exploration.

We also have an assignment in which groups prepare informative presentations to the class on various issues. The twist here is that for each group, the class plays the imaginary role of a different type of audience. For example, one group has to make a presentation on alcohol abuse on college campuses, but the audience is Oprah Winfrey's television studio audience. Another topic is HIV testing for all NKU students, and the audience is the university president and administrators who have expressed concern about preventing the spread of AIDS on campus. A third group makes a presentation about the spread of AIDS among heterosexuals, and the audience is fraternity and sorority members and pledges at NKU. One purpose here is to promote the goals of entering into others' frames of reference and writing with an audience in mind.

These assignments are regularly updated by the library, and new ones are written periodically according to changes in the curriculum. Some instructors use them as they are, some modify them, and some create new ones. One instructor developed a successful assignment she calls "Diversity Research Project." She has each student start out by finding just one article from a magazine about a diversity topic that interests him or her. She makes it a point that it should be a personal narrative, if possible, a "this is my story" article. She gives them a wide range of possible topics: overweight in a "thin is in" world; homeless or low income persons, fathers with custody of their children, stereotypical images of stepparents, persons with disabilities trying to get jobs, go to school, attend plays. They are to copy their articles, underline possible ideas for research, look up and define unfamiliar terms, and then spend time with a process she calls "clustering." They group the topics they've underlined according to categories—social, political, economic, ethical, medical. The next step is to ask questions about the issues brought up in the article. Finally, they determine topics for further research. What I like best about this assignment is that all of this work takes place before they come to the library for a formal instruction session. They have already used indexes to find articles, they have gone through the process of using a microfiche readers, probably, and they have found their way around the building. Not only that, but they have spent a good deal of time focusing on specific questions for their research. Their preparation is evident in the kinds of questions they ask during their library instruction session.

The Workshops

The second major aspect of our new component is training. By training I mean that we are no longer simply suggesting what kind of assignments work in the library, but because of our new understanding of the instructors, we are guiding them in this endeavor by giving them enough information so that they understand the library's educational goals and can perhaps buy into them, and we are also providing library instruction for them. In the summer, usually July, when most instructors are just beginning to think in earnest about their fall syllabi, we hold a two- to three-hour workshop for UNV 101 instructors. The workshop has been modified over time, but the idea is to do two things: help the instructors feel more comfortable in the library by giving them some hands-on time, and help them understand what makes an effective library research assignment for freshmen. In appendix 4 you will find a brief outline of what we generally cover, although the content of the workshop evolves as new participants become involved and the needs of the program change. Generally, we share the assignments that are being used in that year's resource book, and go over each one. We take the time as we're discussing these to delve into the ideas that guided their development. Then, we have the instructors take about 45 minutes to do an exercise themselves. Last year, they picked a specific question from one of these assignments, and had to find a book or article related to that question that might make a good reading for their class. (This part of the workshop would be modified for more experienced library users—i.e., teaching faculty. Instructors who were truly in need of an introduction to a modern university library, or at least a refresher course, expressed relief that we gave them a chance to practice some of these skills.) We then had them return to the classroom for a "debriefing." They shared with the group how they went about the research process, what kinds of problems and pitfalls they encountered, what strategies worked successfully, and what kinds of decisions they had to make along the way.

This discussion paves the way for the librarian facilitating the workshop to wrap up by suggesting what areas instructors should concentrate on in teaching library research, such as numerous opportunities for practice, feedback and reflection, and developing individual or group strategies that are unique to a given information need. We tell the instructors that the assignments should be closely related to what's happening in class, they should be assigned for a reason beyond "it's good to learn to use the library," they should involve a certain amount of metacognitive activity, and they should bring students back to the library as a group as often as possible, so that students will eventually feel so comfortable with the mechanics of the process that they can finally concentrate on what's really important.

We include in the Resource Book a copy of our guidelines for assignments (see appendix 5). This includes some practical information; for example, we urge them to require students to take the library's self-guided tour on audiotape before they come to the instruction session. Since we incorporated the summer workshop and the guidelines into the UNV 101 training, we have seen major improvements in attitudes, more requests for consultations, and more involvement on the part of the instructors in the library component of the course. We have also seen more positive responses to the whole program among the librarians who do instruction.

An added benefit for us, and one that I did not anticipate, is that the librarians who do instruction now have a much better understanding of freshmen and their needs, as well as why they behave the way they do. This is a direct positive result of our close contact with the coordinator of the University 101 program on our campus. We complained to her frequently about how difficult it is to motivate freshmen in a library instruction session, and she was able to educate us about what she called the "freshman effect" (too cool to be interested in the library), what's really behind it (sheer terror and lots of distractions), and some strategies for combatting it in the classroom.

Conclusion

In conclusion, we have created a course component that seems to work. We solved some practical problems, eliminated a lot of negative feelings surrounding the library exercise, opened up new lines of communication, and came up with something that is flexible, manageable, seems to be enjoyed—or at least well tolerated—by students, and makes sense to the librarians. Does it accomplish every one of our goals for freshmen? No. It falls short in that there are skills left out of the equation, in some assignments more than in others, depending on what types of tools and what methods of searching are used. Some of our UNV 101 students are learning the difference between keyword and subject searching, and some are not; some are learning to decipher book or documents citations and some only periodicals or newspapers. So, it does not make an easy building block for successive courses. However, UNV 101 is not a required course, and so it would be impossible to assume we could build on it in the same way we can build on a course like English composition.

It falls short of our goals in the area of connecting library research to the intellectual process of writing because it gives such short shrift to topic formulation and less attention to question analysis than I would like. But it certainly satisfies the intentions I am assuming the course's developers had in mind for learning to use the library: orientation, alleviating library anxiety, and learning about some basic tools and strategies. If freshmen begin to see library research as a process requiring forethought, flexibility, reasoning, judgment, and analysis; if this experience helps them learn the value of phrasing topics in the form of questions; if it helps them understand that the library faculty are partners with classroom faculty in their education, then I think we have started in the right direction.

NOTES

1. Betsy O. Barefoot and John N. Gardner, "The Freshman Orientation Seminar: Extending the Benefits of Traditional Orientation," in *Designing Successful Transitions: A Guide for Orienting Students to College*, National Orientation Directors Association Monograph Series, no. 13, ed. by M. Lee Upcraft, (Columbia, SC: National Resource Center for the Freshman Year Experience, University of South Carolina, 1993), 14.

2. Betsy O. Barefoot and Paul P. Fidler, *National Survey of Freshman Seminar Programming, 1991: Helping First Year College Students Climb the Academic Ladder*. The Freshman Year Experience Monograph Series, no. 10

(Columbia, SC: National Resource Center for the Freshman Year Experience, University of South Carolina, 1992), 16. EDRS #ED354842, microfiche.

3. A. Jerome Jewler and John N. Gardner, eds., *Your College Experience: Strategies for Success,* concise ed. (Belmont, CA: Wadsworth Publishing Co., 1993).

4. Jewler and Gardner, 130.

5. Jewler and Gardner, 131.

6. A. Jerome Jewler, "Elements of the Effective Seminar: The University 101 Program," in *The Freshman Year Experience: Helping Students Survive and Succeed in College*, ed. by M. Lee Upcraft, John N. Gardner and Associates (San Francisco: Jossey-Bass, 1989), 204.

7. Jewler, 204.

8. Carol C. Kuhlthau, "An Emerging Theory of Library Instruction," *School Library Media Quarterly* 16 (Fall 1987): 23-28; and Carol C. Kuhlthau, "Inside the Search Process: Information Seeking from the User's Perspective," *Journal of the American Society for Information Science* 42:5 (1991): 361-371.

9. Barbara Fister, "The Research Processes of Undergraduate Students," *Journal of Academic Librarianship* 18:3 (1992): 163-169.

10. Kuhlthau, "Emerging," 26.

11. Cerise Oberman, "Patterns for Research," in *Increasing the Teaching Role of Academic Libraries*, ed. by Tom Kirk, (San Francisco: Jossey-Bass, 1984), 42.

12. Phyllis Reich, "Choosing a Topic in a Research Methods-Oriented Library Instructional Program," *Research Strategies* 4 (Fall 1986): 186.

13. Carol C. Kuhlthau, "Implementing a Process Approach to Information Skills: A Study Identifying Indicators of Success in Library Media Programs," *School Library Media Quarterly* 22 (Fall 1993): 11-18; Carmen B. Schmersahl, "Teaching Library Research: Process, Not Product," *Journal of Teaching and Writing* 6:2 (1987): 231-238.

14. Schmersahl, 235.

15. Barefoot and Fidler, 16.

16. Glynda Ann Hull, "Research on Writing: Building a Cognitive and Social Understanding of Composing," in *Toward the Thinking Curriculum: Current Cognitive Re-*

search, 1989 Yearbook of the Association for Supervision and Curriculum Development, Lauren B. Resnik and Leopold E. Klopfer (Pittsburgh: Association for Supervision and Curriculum Development, 1989), 121.

17. Kuhlthau, "Implementing," 12.

18. Schmersahl, 233.

APPENDIX 1: FORUM ON GAY RIGHTS

In November 1992, Cincinnati City Council passed a new human rights ordinance which prohibits discrimination against homosexuals in employment, housing, and public accommodations. This was (and still is) a very controversial law. Opponents who fought the ordinance's passage last year are now petitioning the city to reconsider. Supporters insist that it is necessary.

We are going to inform ourselves about this issue and hold a forum in class in which we present what we've learned. The class will be divided into four groups, each with a specific question to answer.

GROUP #1:
What other city or state governments have adopted similar laws? Have any been successfully challenged?

GROUP #2:
What are the arguments made by both supporters and opponents, either here or in other cities, about whether homosexuals need special civil rights protection?

GROUP #3:
How long has the gay rights movement been around? Has it been successful? What kinds of rights are at issue now?

GROUP #4:
Some opponents argue that this ordinance is like an affirmative-action law for homosexuals. How does it really compare to affirmative-action?

YOU ARE IN GROUP #_____.

You will use the library to help you discover answers to your question, but you are not limited to the library. You may also use interviews, phone calls, etc. We will meet with a reference librarian on _____ . The librarian knows about this project and is prepared to give you specific helpful hints for finding information about your assigned questions.

In your group, use the suggested library sources and any others you like to help you answer your question. KEEP TRACK OF WHAT YOU USE, and which library sources seem to be most helpful. You will need this information later. HELP EACH OTHER throughout the research process. Meet as a group on _____ to discuss what you've found. Come to class on _____ prepared to inform the rest of the class about the information you've uncovered. Remember, your goal is to inform, not to argue or persuade. Individually, turn in a journal entry in which you discuss the library research process. What were the most useful reference sources you used? Why were they the best ones? What were some of the problems you encountered in the process?

APPENDIX 2: LIBRARY ASSIGNMENT
UNV 101

Choose one of the following topics:

1. Alcohol or drug addiction: What does addiction mean? How much drug/alcohol use is too much?

2. Alcohol/drug use and college students: Is it a widespread problem? Has it gotten worse? What are colleges doing about it?

3. What is the relationship between drinking and sexual assault/date rape? Is this a particular problem on college campuses?

4. What is the relationship between drinking/drug use and physical health? To what extent are injuries, accidents, mental and physical impairment, illnesses, and deaths connected to alcohol or drug use?

5. To what extent does peer pressure influence college students in their decisions about using drugs or alcohol?

6. What are the laws in Kentucky relating to alcohol use? What penalties are used in DUI convictions in KY? What future problems might the DUI offender experience?

Directions:

1. Students choose a topic and divide into groups of four.
2. Students work in the library in groups to find materials on the topic. **Follow the attached directions.**
3. After students have done the research, groups make a five- to seven-minute presentation to the class. See the schedule for dates due.

Goals of the assignment:

1. To experience group academic work: to learn to work cooperatively in the library; to plan together an oral presentation.
2. To introduce the idea of "library research" and its role in academic life.
3. To use some of the most important research tools in the library.
4. To learn to make judgements about diverse information sources.
5. To learn information about a topic which impacts on college students.

[Linda, Is this part of appendix 2?]

LIBRARY ASSIGNMENT/2

Directions for work in the library

Your name _____   Group number _____
Other group members:

TOPIC:
Problems or questions you want to find out about in your research (the group should decide on a problem or question to work on together):

_____

_____

STEP 1: Discuss the question you've chosen in your group so that everyone has the same understanding of the question. **Decide what kind of information would help you answer your question:** statistics? an expert's opinion? an individual's personal story? a news article? Make a list of the information you think would be useful (this may change as you go through the process):

_____

_____

_____

_____

_____

STEP 2: Retrieve useful information on your topic from the library.
- A reference librarian will meet with our class on _____ to explain the various tools you can use to find material for your presentation. You will learn about periodical indexes, newspaper indexes, the online catalog (NKUIRE), and other reference tools, but some will be more useful to your group than others, depending on your question and the kind of information you want. **Use this opportunity to ask questions** of the reference librarian based on your group's particular interests.
- **Locate** books, articles, or other sources of information on your topic.

_____

_____

LIBRARY ASSIGNMENT/3

_____

_____

_____

_____

_____

_____

STEP 3: Read the books or articles to decide whether they are useful to the group (do they help the group answer their question?) **Select the best articles** (or sections of books, or other pieces of information) and make copies for all members of the group.

Remember that at the end of this assignment, your group must make a brief oral presentation on this topic. The group should decide who should talk about what. In this presentation you will want to tell us any important background information on your topic as well as the specific information that answers your question. In the library you will collect information to use in the presentation. Keep this in mind as you work.

— EMILY WERRELL —

Information seeking is a very important skill for you to develop during your college career. The ability to find evidence, a variety of opinions, tested solutions, etc. will be necessary to success as you make decisions in both your personal life and work life. In this assignment, you will see one example of the value of being able to find pertinent information when making personal decisions.

A friend of yours has just learned that s/he is HIV positive. You will work with a group of your classmates to find information for this individual as s/he tries to answer the following questions.

-How likely is s/he actually to develop full-blown AIDS?*
-What medical treatments for AIDS are available?
-How effective are they?
-What are the side effects?
-Are there any preventive measures s/he can use to avoid getting AIDS?

A librarian will work with our class on _____. During this class session we will plan our strategy for finding information in the Library, so ask the librarian as many specific questions as you can so that you will be able to uncover useful facts and guidance for this friend.

After working in the Library individually, bring the results of your research to class on _____. Share with your group the information you have discovered. Discuss as a group how you would advise this person after seeing this research. Write below your summary of that advice.

*NOTE: Three other groups are given the same assignment but with different sets of questions. Group #2 is asked to find out if people with the HIV virus have suffered employment discrimination, and what their remedies might be. Group #3 is asked to find out about infection and spread of the virus, and what sexual partners should be told. Group #4 must find out about the financial costs of AIDS treatment and whether insurance companies are responding.

APPENDIX 4: OUTLINE: SUMMER WORKSHOP FOR UNV 101 INSTRUCTORS

I.   Introductions; pass out new assignments

II.   Discuss each assignment in light of issues we covered in May workshop (15 minutes)
   A.   Topics aligned with curriculum; in form of "questions" rather than "topics"
   B.   Why we model topic formulation rather than asking them to do this step themselves
   C.   Most require group work
   D.   Authentic purpose/end product; info must be evaluated and selected
   E.   Process more important than specific tools
   F.   Library research should not be limited to this one assignment—send them back frequently on smaller errands—to increase familiarity

III. Library activity (45 minutes)
   A.   Divide into small groups of 2 or 3
      1.   Choose an assignment and pick a research question to work on
         a.   Find a book or article that would make a good reading for class
            1)   Use tools you're not familiar with; help each other
            3)   Each group will have a librarian assigned to help you

IV.   Return to classroom for "debriefing" (45 minutes)
   A.   Discuss steps needed to find item: what did you have to do in order to find it?
      1.   Looking at the question to determine what kind of info. is needed
      2.   Breaking the question into manageable parts
      3.   Choosing an appropriate finding tool
      4.   Choosing a source (article, book) from index or catalog
      5.   Navigating the building and the machines

   B.   Other than "navigation," all are intellectual/decision-making processes
      1.   These intellectual skills are intuitive for us—we have internalized criteria for appropriateness/usefulness, based on discipline, audience, readability etc.; much harder for freshmen
      2.   Keep in mind the "navigation" skills are best learned by doing, not by being lectured to by a librarian; also, tools are changing too rapidly for instruction in the mechanics of searching to be useful—this is why librarians will concentrate in instruction sessions on strategy rather than specific tools.
      3.   Important to incorporate time for feedback, reflection and discussion during research process—so students can be conscious of their own decision-making processes.

V.   Practical considerations and wrap-up (15 minutes)
   A.   Scheduling and timing of library assignments and instructional sessions—important
   B.   Self-guided tour on audiotape available at reserve desk; assign before research begins

Appendix 5: GUIDELINES FOR USING LIBRARY ASSIGNMENTS IN UNV 101—1996/97

Any of these assignments could be used to introduce your students to the library. They have been written in such a way that you can reproduce them as they are; however, feel free to modify them in any way that would make them more applicable to your own course's focus. Of course, I would also be happy to consult with you in developing assignments of your own. Either way, I hope you'll keep in mind the following guidelines:

- **Learning to use the library should not be an end in itself.** The experience will be more meaningful, and they will retain more, if students use the information they find for an authentic task related to the subjects you are studying in the course. Library assignments which take students through the procedural steps of using the library, without asking them to read, analyze, and apply the information, fall short of academic goals for library use.

- **Take time in class, before you visit the library, to go over the library assignment.** This will help the students to understand what kind of information they'll be looking for when they come to the library, and they'll know what to listen for during the librarian's presentation (and WHY they need to listen!). They may even be motivated to ask some questions, which would be wonderful.

- **Allow students opportunities to reflect on the research process.** By incorporating opportunities for feedback and review of successes and problems, you will enhance your students' ability to transfer what they learn to new tasks.

- **Bring them back as often as you can.** We would like students to see library research as a natural way to learn about a subject. Just as they read their textbooks and participate in class discussions, they should expect to learn independently by searching for information in the library's collection. Perhaps the most realistic way to model this in your class would be to include small, incremental library assignments throughout the course rather than focusing on one major research project.

- **Remember that you can't teach all the skills of library research in one course.** Library research skills, like other learning skills, are developed over a long period of time. What is important in UNV 101 is that students understand the role and significance of information-gathering in their academic careers.

- **Schedule a library instruction session for your class.** We will gear the session to the particular assignment you're using. We can make flexible arrangements that will fit in with your course plans, whether we're meeting with your class just once or providing support throughout the semester. Please call me (x6523) **by September 20** to schedule for Fall 1996. Our Spring deadline is February 10, 1997.

- **Have your students take the self-guided tour of the library** *before* **your scheduled session with a librarian.** The tapes, players, "walkman" headphones, and maps are available at the reserve desk. It takes 20 to 30 minutes, shows them the building, introduces important services and collections, and even has them do a little hands-on work. We believe that this orientation allays some of their anxiety and allows them to concentrate, during the librarian's session, on their research tasks.

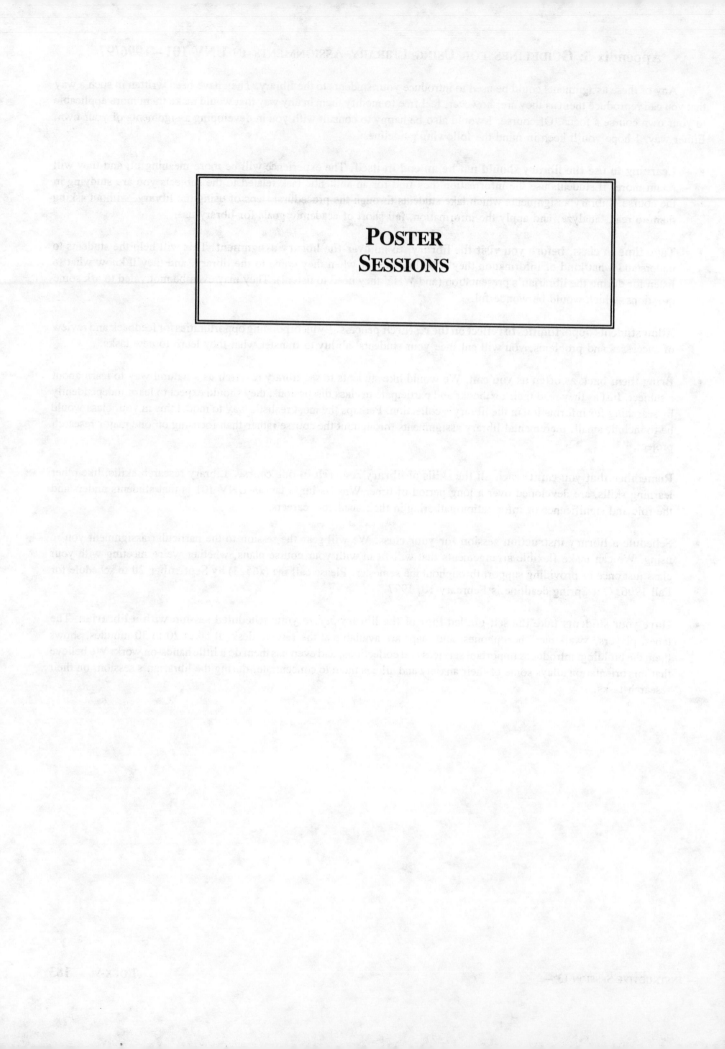

POSTER
SESSIONS

PROGRAMS THAT WORK

IDS 110 and The Making of a Library Video Tour

Abstract During the Spring 1994 Semester, Southwest Missouri State University decided that all incoming freshman would take a new 1 credit hour course, IDS 110: An Introduction to University Life. This course would be optional for the 1994–1995 year. It will be mandatory beginning with the Fall Semester of 1995. This new course is modeled after the Freshman Year Experience Program at the University of South Carolina.

Meyer Library at Southwest Missouri State University faced a big problem. The Fall 1994 semester had some 20 sections of this new course. With the cooperation of other areas of the Library, these twenty sections were able to tour the library within a two week period early in the semester. The Spring 1995 Semester was no problem with only ten sections of this course being offered. In planning for the Fall 1995 Semester, the problem arose. Librarians were facing the prospect of 125 sections of this new course. Other methods of imparting this information in a consistent manner were explored. A video tour was decided upon as the most feasible method of accomplishing this goal.

Prepared by:
Edward J. DeLong
Assistant Professor of Library Science
Meyer Library
Southwest Missouri State University
901 South National Avenue
Springfield, MO 65804-0095

(417) 836-4551 (Voice)
(417) 836-4538 (Fax)

EJD449F@VMA.SMSU.EDU

Poster session 1 (DeLong): Part 1 - IDS 110 and the Making of a Library Video Tour

The Problem

Interdisciplinary Studies 110, potentially 125 sections of a new, required course for freshmen, would impact the ability of a small Reference faculty (5) and Library Science faculty (18) to give effective tours. Even the addition of some of the staff, potentially 30 additional people, would not give us enough bodies to cover the mandatory library unit in this course. The Library Awareness Committee knew that something had to be done.

Analysis of the options included discussions on using computerized, hyperstack tours, additional walking tours, a tape-slide show, an audio guided tour or a complete video tape production. With the University using locally produced video productions for other segments of the course, it was decided that the video production would be explored. A budget figure of $1,000.00 was given by Television Services. In early December, 1994, a sub-committee of the Library Awareness Committee was appointed to draft the treatment of the script. One proposal came in. (See Script Ideas.) The Library Awareness Committee accepted the proposal with the idea that the flow may be improved by traveling from the second floor, down to the first floor, and then up to the third floor.

Poster session 1 (DeLong): Part 2 - The Problem

The Script

The script assignment was given to the author of the winning script idea treatment with the understanding that all areas of the library would contribute with facts needed to fill in details. In consultation with Television Services, the script deadline for the first draft was set at January 31, 1995. Fine tuning the script took 12 (or more) drafts. Final script completed by March 31, 1996.

Problems

- What to cover.
- Format of script.
- Opening.
- Talent .
- Writing problems.
- What not to cover.

- Many draft copies.

- Time schedule.

- Author's qualifications.

- Controversy over opening.

Solutions

- Focus on incoming freshman.
- Two column (action/script).
- Snazzy, light, fun, different.
- Selected by TV Services.
- Committee edited final versions.
- Parts of Library not relevant to freshman.
- Use word processor and colored paper to keep separate.
- Plan ahead. From inception to completion took 11 months.
- Knows Library. Knows tours of Library. Knows theatre and media and how this needs to flow effectively together.
- Discuss with Director. Make feelings known. Trust him. And let him tape it with his artistic vision.

Poster session 1 (DeLong): Part 3 - The Script

The Production

Taping was scheduled for the last weekend of the Spring 1995 semester. Two all day marathon sessions were scheduled and needed. Some pre-production shooting of materials was taped in advance in the Library's television studio. Some final shots were taped in late June. Production deadline called for first screening by the first day of classes for Fall 1995 Semester. Deadline was met with one week to spare.

Problems

- Noise in Library.

- Talent not familiar with Library.

- Rigid scheduling and many takes of the same scene.

- Language of script.

- Tired talent and crew.

- Background extras.
- Length of production.

Solutions

- Consider closing off area of building or entire building during shooting. Work at night when building is closed.
- Consider young library users to learn acting for the camera, rather than teach actors how to use the Library.
- Become flexible. It will require many takes to get a few usable scenes. A minimum of 10 times the length of the scene is a minimum to plan for.
- Keep the sentences short. Ours were too long for the talent to handle. Don't use library lingo. Remember who your primary audience is.
- Schedule extra breaks as needed.
- Use student staff.
- Shoot for 15-20 minutes.

Poster session 1 (DeLong): Part 4 - The Production

The Reactions, Other Uses and The Future

Student reactions to the finished production has been very positive. Freshman enjoy the tape and its light hearted look at the Library. Students came away feeling positive about the Library, knowing that they can always ask for help when they need it. Especially as they do the required library assignments for this course.

Other classes use the videotape as an introductory overview to the Library and Library Services. Advanced Library students see the tape and ask why sections of the Library were not covered. For example, do incoming students need to know how to order a book? Do these same students need to see how a book gets processed? Do we really want to show, in a short introduction to the Library, how to use 20 different types of microform readers and reader/printers? Students in media classes view the tape, write reviews of it, and then take the tape apart and show how these future directors would change this scene or that.

The future holds another production being planned for the summer of 1997. Our Library is changing, our periodical holdings will be on-line, more databases will be available. More technology will occur. We plan on showing students how to use their new University Library.

Poster session 1 (DeLong): Part 5 - The Reactions, Other Uses, and the Future

SCRIPT IDEAS
DRAFT #1, DECEMBER 8, 1994

Opening shot: aerial views of campus, zooming into front of Meyer Library. Music in background. Graphic overlays of : **Introducing Meyer Library**. Other Opening credits as needed.

Dolly through front doors and pan lobby area. Stop at Circulation. Ask someone about checking out a book. Show them the SMSU ID of Boomer Bear and state: Don't leave home without it! (Maybe have Boomer be a recurring figure, appearing every time we mention ID's.)

Go to busy Reference Desk. Explain building maps, scheduling CD-ROMS, answering questions, etc. Take guide to an On-line terminal. Explain what is found on there. Use other screens (computer generated for clarity). Explain thesaurus for data bases (*LCSH* and others). Show indexes, using *Readers' Guide* as an example. Show location of Reference Collection. Explain how to find Periodical Articles, keeping it simple as it will be hard to change from Periodical Holdings File to On-Line Catalog. Show locations of current and bound periodicals. Briefly explain about photocopiers. Throughout video, stress that help can always be found at a nearby service point.

Transition to Government Documents. Transition with slides of people helping people use the Library. Overlay these photos as a collection of loose snapshots placed on top of each other, possibly no more than 15-20 seconds. It might be nice to have a picture of Dr. Meyer included in here somewhere.

At Government Documents desk, have some people working quietly in the background as narrators begin speaking, then disappear. Explain what a Government Document is, and how to locate one, various formats available. Insert Voter Registration here and mention availability of Federal and Missouri tax forms.

Short Transition to Maps. Same scenario, use slides of Maps area. In Maps, have people start working in the background and leave

Poster session 1 (DeLong): Part 6 - Script Ideas

— EDWARD J. DELONG —

camera range. Explain what the Map Collection is and all the other goodies to be found there.

Explain all that is found on the Third Floor, including the General Collection, Special Collections, and the Library Administration. Perhaps use slides with a voice over. These pictures could serve double duty, such as showing books being shelved, people helping people, students studying, etc.

Transition to First Floor, showing slides of people using the First Floor areas, especially Curriculum Lab, A, and studying in Pit.

On First Floor, explain about reserves and non-print materials and Assistive Technology Lab. Go to Microforms. Explain what can be found here. Ask for help in loading the equipment or in finding materials. Tell students to get change here. Report any service problems to any desk area. Explain Mac Lab and Typing Rooms procedure (disk, paper, and Boomer's ID again).

Transition to wrapping up: slides of Music Library and Greenwood. Tell students about LIS 101 course for more detailed information. Conclude with reminder about ID and asking for help when needed.

Closing credits, as needed. Fade to Black.

Poster session 1 (DeLong): Part 6 - Script Ideas (continued)

EXTERIOR-MEYER LIBRARY-DAY
2 SHOT-MALE/FEMALE

FEMALE
The Meyer Library is the main library on campus. In addition, the library is a Government Document Depository.

MALE
Inside are more than 500,000 books as well as other library materials such as magazines, newspapers, and audio visual equipment.

EFX GRFX - OVERVIEW MAP of Library
Location

FEMALE
The library is located on the Southwest side of the campus near the football stadium. It's easy to find....almost everyone knows where the large fountains are....the library is right next door ---

MALE
Anyone have 8 a.m. or evening classes?....., the library opens early and closes late to enable busy students to utilize its resources. The library is open year round, even during breaks for the convenience of the students and staff.

GRFX-PROCESSED SHOT (if possible)
Exterior of Meyer Library. The sky changes from day to night and lights appear on in the library. HOURS are SUPERED over GRFX.

GRFX - SECOND FLOOR OVERVIEW

FEMALE
You'll enter the library on the second floor. An overview of the second floor shows the location of current periodicals and the circulation and reference areas.

INTERIOR-MEYER LIBRARY LOBBY
FEMALE addresses the CAMERA. In the Background is Circulation Desk activity.

The Circulation Desk - where you'll check out books and materials from the library is immediately on your left as you enter the building.

INTERIOR-LIBRARY CIRCULATION DESK
BOOMER the BEAR is attempting to "check out" materials.

FEMALE
(con't)
Be sure to always have your SMSU ID with you. No matter how well known you may be, an SMSU ID is required to check out materials from the library.

The FEMALE ENTERS above shot. BOOMER reinforces her instructions by showing his/her I.D. He/she gives the FEMALE a friendly hug as they part.

Poster session 1 (DeLong): Part 6 - Script Ideas (continued)

— EDWARD J. DeLONG —

Non-Traditional Students Need MORE

Brenda F. Green, M.L.S.
Instructor, Head, Instructional Services
Health Sciences Library
University of Tennessee, Memphis

At the University of Tennessee, Memphis, the library provides instructional services to many students in the colleges of Allied Health Sciences, Social Work, and other colleges.

Many of these students can be considered non-traditional students because they are returning to school after being absent for a period of time, have little or no prior research experience or have never conducted research in an academic health sciences library. They need additional assistance initiating and completing research assignments. Simply giving a demonstration of a database or providing instructions on using a printed index is usually insufficient.

Considerable time should be given to preparing lectures for these learners.

Today's non-traditional students require MORE!

Management techniques for sorting through the wealth of information sources.

Organizational skills needed to outline the research process.

Realistic guidelines for selecting a topic, and

Experience actually working through the process.

These four areas should be thoroughly discussed with appropriate learning experiences prior to beginning instruction in using print and/or online sources of information.

Poster session 2 (Green): Part 1 - Non-Traditional Students Need MORE

EVALUATING LIBRARY INSTRUCTION FOR GRADUATE EDUCATION STUDENTS BY ASSESSING STUDENT OUTCOMES & FACULTY ATTITUDES

Assessing student outcomes has become the focal point on many university campuses throughout the United States. Concomitant with this concern has been the desire on the part of university administrators to make faculty much more accountable regarding this process. These initiatives have become paramount as a result of limited financial resources available in higher education.

Likewise, new and emerging technologies have modified the roles of academic librarians and access to information that is provided to graduate students. Because these roles have been altered, diverse attitudes have also surfaced concerning the most effective way of improving and evaluating library instruction. Library administrators have sought to achieve a balance between the utilization of traditional and electronic resources in library instruction, while enhancing the public service philosophy of their respective libraries.

If student outcomes are to be accurately determined, the library administration and faculty must be supportive of evaluating library instruction programs on a continuous basis. By evaluating library instruction and assessing student outcomes in graduate education students, student achievement levels are more than likely to rise. These outcomes can be enhanced additionally if faculty expectations about library instruction are also discussed. If this support or dialogue is lacking, both student intellectual development and library instruction will be adversely affected.

Poster session 3 (Edwards): Part 1 - Evaluating Library Instruction for Graduate Education Students

REASONS FOR ASSESSMENT

To **reflect** the educational mission of the
university

To **build community** within and outside of
the university environment

To **inform** the university community of
instructional improvement

To **enhance** collegiality

To **demonstrate** achievement by both students
and faculty alike

To **manifest** the library and university's
commitment to student and faculty
intellectual development

To **reexamine** existing evaluation instruments
to accommodate future **reengineering**

HOW TO ASSESS

Standardized testing

Individual assessment

Questionnaires

Surveys

Interviews

Poster session 3 (Edwards): Part 2 - Reasons for Assessment and How to Assess

Identify areas within the College of Education where assessment will encounter the least resistance. These areas probably have faculty who want to participate.

Develop orientation sessions that will introduce faculty to assessment initiatives.

Clarify your vision! Make sure that students, and especially faculty, understand the goals and objectives of the program.

Conduct follow-up sessions to discuss goals and objectives, as well as to encourage continued faculty and administrative participation and support.

Create a program that will be the focus of continued interaction between faculty and students throughout the assessment process.

ASSESSMENT - RECOMMENDATIONS

Isolating other areas on campus will only prohibit the successful implementation of an assessment program. Avoid it!

Involving all affected areas to ensure cooperation and assistance is essential. Don't rely on just the administration for support.

Unrealizable goals and objectives may prove to be disastrous. Be practical in what you initially try to accomplish.

Ongoing! Assessment is an ongoing process requiring constant reengineering. It needs more than just individual involvement.

Poster session 3 (Edwards): Part 3 - Assessment Objectives and Assessment Recommendations

ASSESSMENT DESIGN - QUESTIONS TO CONSIDER

What knowledge (cognitive) and skills (application) should students have acquired through library instruction?

What performance level(s) should be achieved? What standard(s) is/are acceptable?

What kind of computer technology, print material, or manipulatives are necessary to enhance the learning environment?

How can faculty and students use these resources to achieve their goals and objectives? What other options are available to motivate students?

How will student achievement be determined? A test? Course-related assignment? Presentation?

What type of instrument will be used to accurately measure different levels of achievement?

What are you going to do next? What can be done to eliminate any deficiencies that may have surfaced? How can both library instruction and outcomes be improved?

Poster session 3 (Edwards): Part 4 - Assessment Design - Questions to Consider

Utilize Existing Information

Library Literature
LOEX Clearinghouse
Internet/WWW
Other librarians

Seek Financial and Personnel Support

University administration
Faculty
Library-wide
External grants

Experiment

Use other model programs
Collaborate with faculty
Learn from previous attempts/models

Be Proactive

Know your intent
Be persistent
Reexamine often
Use results for curriculum planning

Poster session 3 (Edwards): Part 5 - How to Implement Assessment Programs - Guidelines

LIBRARIAN ON THE LAM:
SOLVING THE MYSTERY OF INNOVATIVE LIBRARY INSTRUCTION
POSTER SESSION -- LOEX CONFERENCE 1996

Rational (Why We Did It)

"Librarian on the Lam" is a multi-part project designed to introduce students to subject specific sources, research strategies, and citation methods. Although originally designed for a freshmen composition course focused on ethics in science, it can be modified for any subject. Students played the roles of detectives solving a fictional murder mystery witnessed by an unnamed librarian at our campus. Fearing a media frenzy, the librarian fled the country, but not before her conscience moved her to leave a list of clues which the astute investigator could locate in library sources. By completing the project, students learned to use a variety of sources, on paper, computer and video; access sources which they would use in subsequent assignments throughout the course; understand MLA citation format (the hows and whys); collect, interpret, and synthesize data in order to create original work; create a coherent narrative using all the clues, but with individual flair; and appropriately cite all of their sources in their narrative.

Generating student enthusiasm for library skills is much harder than simply presenting students with demonstrations and tours. We wanted students to find out for themselves how exciting and entertaining library work can be. For that, we had to genuinely motivate them. Lively and creative scavenger hunts can include lists of challenging questions, cartoons, quotations and allusions to give students hands-on experience in doing research, but they fail to engage the student in creativity. While our project was certainly creative in design, ultimately it inspired students to think creatively about the information that they gathered. They mystery generated a curiosity which grabbed their attention and motivated them to complete the assignment. They wanted to know the solution to the mystery, and to find it they had to locate all the clues. They also needed all the clues in order to write the paper that followed.

The project also generated enthusiasm by making clue to students the importance of information literacy. In our investigation, information was not important for its own sake. Students had to interpret and combine their facts to build their investigative report. Our investigation developed as a required part of a college class, but it was much integral to the course work. The sources our students accessed proved to be foundational building blocks for each of their subsequent assignments. We stressed that the project had been carefully designed to provide them with exposure to the specific sources they would need to use to succeed in the class.

Students, librarians and the professor alike assessed this library unit as a overall positive experience. The fun nature of the assignment built relaxed relationships between students and professor and, more importantly, students and librarians. Because accuracy was never compromised students remained respectful, but because of the intensive and creative nature of the assignment, students felt more comfortable approaching librarians with questions throughout the rest of the term. They also gained enough knowledge about using the library to better articulate their questions and problems. In addition, the investigation gave students a leg up on all subsequent research work. They never began a paper with a completely blank page because they always had a list of sources they could access to start a new project.

Poster session 4 (Kenward): Part 1 - Librarian on the Lam - Rational

Designing the Unit
(How We Put It Together)

The first step in designing any educational project is to determine its goals. Both the librarians and the professor shared similar goals regarding students' abilities to access information. So we decided to collaborate on the design of a project which would meet our combined needs. We identified five goals we hoped our library project would meet:

1). To excite students about using the library.
2). To help students gain specific abilities using both electronic and paper sources.
3). To guide students in locating specific electronic and paper items in the library for the course.
4). To instruct students about plagiarism and appropriate citation usage.
5). To have students write a narrative of their own as preparation for discussing narrative literature in the course.

We determined that we would need one full week of class time, or approximately 3.5 hours, to provide the MLA citation instruction and to introduce students to the assignment we designed. We would expect students to complete the assignment on their own. The professor and the librarians then worked together to determine exactly which types of sources and which specific items student should access during the project. We brainstormed two lists: one of all the possible types of sources in the library, and one of all the specific items in the library which connected to the thematic content of the course. We also included often-used reference sources. Next, we prioritized each list. At this point, the two prioritized lists had to be intersected.

Having determined where we wanted students to go during their investigation, we had to write the scenario for the mystery and the clues which would lead students to the solution. This was, without a doubt, the most labor-intensive and time-consuming part of the project; it was also the most fun. To start this process, we made a third list of the sorts of clues one would need to solve a mystery. This included obvious things like murder weapon, motive, names and occupations of people involved, and locations. Next we examined all the sources for information which could fit the types of clues we needed. For instance, we scanned several books and magazine articles looking for some mention of a potential murder weapon. We then carefully documented each clue, so that we could create a master bibliography which students would ultimately have to recreate.

Once we had all the sources and clues identified, we write the actual assignment. We had to give students enough information so that they could find the correct sources and clues without guiding them too much. Each question, therefore, required several steps from the students. First, they had to determine what type of source they sought and how to access it in our college library. In most cases, they could not answer the question merely by locating the cataloging information on the computer; they had to get their hands on the source. This also required students to use tables of contents, indexes, copyright information, etc. Next they had to discover the clue to the murder. Finally, they had to record the MLA citation for the source they had used.

As the next step in our preparation of the murder mystery, we had two guinea pigs complete it. They helped us identify potentially confusing weaknesses in our clues and refine the project. After this test, the professor designed the paper assignment which would result from the project, and wrote it into the murder scenario.

Having finished the murder mystery, we worked together to decide how to present the unit as a whole to the class. We began by having the professor explain the entire unit to the class. This helped the students appreciate how the various elements of the unit fit together and how the unit itself could aid their success in the course and throughout college. During the first class period, the librarians taught the MLA citation procedures. We held class in the library and put actual sources into the students' hands for them to puzzle through. At this stage, they not only learned how to cite a source, but what types of information a source could provide to them. For instance, as they learned how to cite information from an almanac, we discussed what kind of information they could find in it. This took approximately 90 minutes.

Poster session 4 (Kenward): Part 2 - Designing the Unit

— KIMBERLY KENWARD —

For the remaining 15 minutes in the first class period, we introduced students to the murder mystery, reading through the assignment together. We clarified all questions, and encouraged students to try to work on it before the next class so that during that time, we could work on difficulties. We warned them to keep careful record of the sources they used as they went, so that they could complete the bibliography required. During the next class, students had all 105 minutes to work on the assignment, alone or in pairs. The assignment, with murder mystery completed, narrated, and accompanied by a full bibliography, was due on the third class period, one week from the start date.

Results

Following the assignment, we administered an evaluation form. Students assessed the mystery unit as one of the most helpful library instructions they had ever experienced. They felt that the most useful aspect of the unit was learning to use a variety of sources. Many students claimed the success of the unit hinged on the fact that it was enjoyable as well as informative.

The following pages contain the assignment itself and the evaluation sheet used.

Poster session 4 (Kenward): Part 2 (continued) and Part 3 - Results

College Writing II
Davenport College

Librarian on the Lam

You, a detective sergeant on the Ottawa County Sheriff's staff, have never faced a case more baffling than this! A man's body was discovered, last night, in the walkway leading to a fashionable condominium complex on Holland's north side. He had been stabbed, but you and your staff could not find any weapon. The man was dressed in a tuxedo, but so far, you have not been able to identify him. His wallet was missing.

This morning you got a strange phone call from a woman claiming to be a librarian at Davenport College. She witnessed the murder, she claimed, while waiting in her car for her husband to drop off papers for his business partner who lives in that condo complex. She wants the truth to come out, but she refuses to subject herself to any sort of courtroom ordeal. Thus she has fled the country by ship.

To help locate the truth, she has left you a sheet with eleven clues about the circumstances of the murder. Your assignment; discover the information you need from her clues. Then you must reconstruct the crime in a narrative 2-3 pages long. Your narrative must have a bibliography containing the eleven works you used to recover your information.

Remember this could be a huge opportunity for you. The media is scrambling for breakthroughs and the public is calling for an arrest. Other investigators hope they can write the most convincing crime narrative and receive credit for the arrest. So be on your toes! Handle this right and your career could skyrocket!

Like a real investigator, you may elect to work alone, or with one partner in recovering the clues. However, each person must write his or her own crime narrative with bibliography. Your narrative will be judged on how well it recognizes and synthesizes the clues, and on its accurate report of sources.

Good luck, detective sergeant!

Poster session 4 (Kenward): Part 4 - College Writing Assignment

Dear Ottawa County Sheriff,

Yes, I say the murder, but I can't bear to undergo the public scrutiny that the O.J. Simpson witnesses had endured. So I will leave you these clues and flee the country. I hope you catch the killer and see him convicted. But please! Don't try to find me!

I was sitting in my car minding my own business about 10:15pm last night. My husband was dropping off some important papers for his business partner who lives in the Dock Harbor Condominiums on the north side of town.

1. What made me look out my car window in that direction? A review in the <u>New York Times</u> of Kenneth Branagh's <u>Frankenstein</u> discusses Boris Karloff's depiction of the monster in 1931. What Karloff did after accidentally killing the little girl is the same thing that made me look out the window.

2. <u>Opposing Viewpoints</u> is a series of books on controversial issues. Find the one focusing on genetics. The editor's last name is the murder victim's first name.

3. In a slang dictionary which defines "Frankenstein," the first word of the next entry gives the victim's last name.

4. The November 1993 issue of <u>Current Biography</u> tells you the pseudonym under which Michael Crichton wrote eight novels. That is also the killer's name.

5. Two hours before the murder, I saw the victim loudly discussing the ethics of his job with someone whose face I couldn't see. You will find a clue about this profession (and a possible motive for murder?) in the title of volume nine of a video series.

6. The subtitle of a book about <u>Frankenstein</u> gives you a clue as to where the victim was immediately before he was murdered.

7. The victim had been nominated for a prestigious medical prize which was won by Dr. Phillip A. Sharp in 1993.

8. A particular type of knife was used to kill the man. My clue as to what kind of knife he used is in a quote from Herrick's <u>Hesperides, Argument of His Book</u>.

9. After the murder, the killer walked away from the scene humming a tune. It was a famous song written the same year that Shelley's <u>Frankenstein</u> was published, according to the <u>Timetables of History</u>.

10. Then the killer hid the knife in a car which he later parked in the Meijer lot on 16th Street. It is the same type of car that Michael Crichton drives (as stated in a 1990 <u>People Weekly</u> article).

11. A short version of Mary Shelley's biography will offer several possible situations which could be motives. Pick one.

On to your narrative! I hope you catch him!

Sincerely,

Marion L. Hill
Librarian Emeritus

Poster session 4 (Kenward): Part 4 - College Writing Assignment (continued)

Murder Mystery/Library Research Unit
Evaluation Unit

1. What was the most important thing you learned about using the library today? Please describe in detail.

2. Please rate the value of the following. (Write one of the numbers on each of the blank lines)

1 = very valuable   2 = valuable   3 = somewhat valuable   4 = not valuable

____Using the CD-ROM indexes
____Using the on-line card catalog
____Using reference sources
____Working in a small group
____Working with the librarians
____MLA citation workshop
____Class discussion

3. What is your overall opinion of the Murder Mystery Library exercise (including MLA citation workshop, the library exercise, and the writing of the short story)? Please describe in detail.

4. Before coming to COM122, have you ever had formal instruction on how to use the Davenport library? If so, briefly describe where.

5. How would you improve the library research unit?

Thank you for helping us to improve our services!

Poster session 4 (Kenward): Part 5 - Evaluation Unit

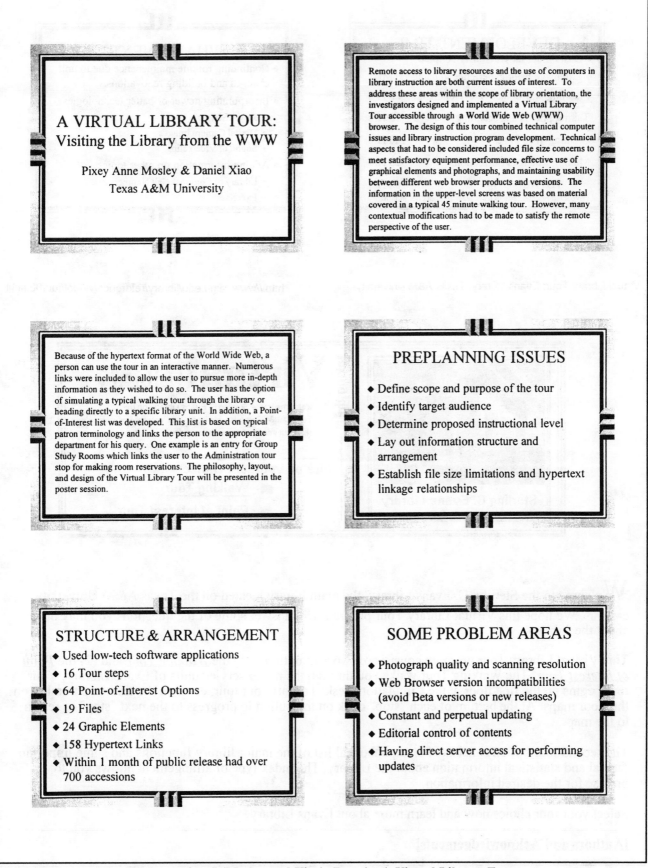

A VIRTUAL LIBRARY TOUR:
Visiting the Library from the WWW

Pixey Anne Mosley & Daniel Xiao
Texas A&M University

Remote access to library resources and the use of computers in library instruction are both current issues of interest. To address these areas within the scope of library orientation, the investigators designed and implemented a Virtual Library Tour accessible through a World Wide Web (WWW) browser. The design of this tour combined technical computer issues and library instruction program development. Technical aspects that had to be considered included file size concerns to meet satisfactory equipment performance, effective use of graphical elements and photographs, and maintaining usability between different web browser products and versions. The information in the upper-level screens was based on material covered in a typical 45 minute walking tour. However, many contextual modifications had to be made to satisfy the remote perspective of the user.

Because of the hypertext format of the World Wide Web, a person can use the tour in an interactive manner. Numerous links were included to allow the user to pursue more in-depth information as they wished to do so. The user has the option of simulating a typical walking tour through the library or heading directly to a specific library unit. In addition, a Point-of-Interest list was developed. This list is based on typical patron terminology and links the person to the appropriate department for his query. One example is an entry for Group Study Rooms which links the user to the Administration tour stop for making room reservations. The philosophy, layout, and design of the Virtual Library Tour will be presented in the poster session.

PREPLANNING ISSUES

- Define scope and purpose of the tour
- Identify target audience
- Determine proposed instructional level
- Lay out information structure and arrangement
- Establish file size limitations and hypertext linkage relationships

STRUCTURE & ARRANGEMENT

- Used low-tech software applications
- 16 Tour steps
- 64 Point-of-Interest Options
- 19 Files
- 24 Graphic Elements
- 158 Hypertext Links
- Within 1 month of public release had over 700 accessions

SOME PROBLEM AREAS

- Photograph quality and scanning resolution
- Web Browser version incompatibilities (avoid Beta versions or new releases)
- Constant and perpetual updating
- Editorial control of contents
- Having direct server access for performing updates

Poster session 5 (Mosley and Xiao): Part 1 - A Virtual Library Tour

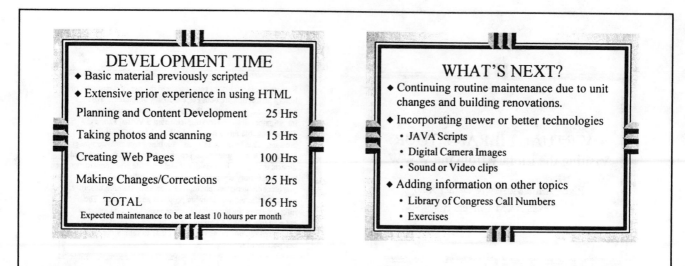

DEVELOPMENT TIME
- ◆ Basic material previously scripted
- ◆ Extensive prior experience in using HTML

Planning and Content Development	25 Hrs
Taking photos and scanning	15 Hrs
Creating Web Pages	100 Hrs
Making Changes/Corrections	25 Hrs
TOTAL	165 Hrs

Expected maintenance to be at least 10 hours per month

WHAT'S NEXT?
- ◆ Continuing routine maintenance due to unit changes and building renovations.
- ◆ Incorporating newer or better technologies
  - JAVA Scripts
  - Digital Camera Images
  - Sound or Video clips
- ◆ Adding information on other topics
  - Library of Congress Call Numbers
  - Exercises

Virtual Library Tour: Evans Library, Texas A&M University

http://www.tamu.edu/library/reference/virtual/tour00.html

Sterling C. Evans Library

taking the **Virtual** Library ■ Tour

Welcome to the Sterling C. Evans Library on the Texas A&M Campus. We hope that you will find this tour informative and educational.

Click on your tour choice:
- ■ **Walking Tour**
- ■ **Point of Interest Tour**

W elcome to the Sterling C. Evans Library, the main library located on the Texas A&M University campus. We hope this Virtual Library Tour program will answer some of the questions you may have about the Library.

This Virtual Library Tour program consists of two tour options: (1) the _Walking Tour_ and (2) the _Point of Interest Tour_. The Walking Tour walks you through the major service units of Evans Library. Your tour begins on the first floor at the Circulation Desk. To start your tour, click on the tour stop number on the floor maps. At the bottom of each "stop" click on the button to progress to the next "stop" or return to the map.

The second tour option consists of an alphabetical list of the major library functions and some important factual and statistical information about the Library. The index type of arrangement allows you to browse for the desired information.

Select your tour choice now and learn more about Evans Library.

[Authors and Acknowledgements]

Poster session 5 (Mosley and Xiao): Part 1 - A Virtual Library Tour (continued)

— PIXEY ANNE MOSLEY AND DANIEL XIAO —

Lori Ricigliano
University of Puget Sound

Background

Freshman Orientation is often an overwhelming and bewildering experience to students entering college. The schedule of events offers a dizzying array of choices, ranging from academic advising appointments to housing assignments and receptions. Although library tours are not usually scheduled as part of campus orientation at the University of Puget Sound, the library wanted to offer an opportunity for new students to learn about its services and facilities. With enrollment reaching 650 freshmen, we faced a daunting challenge.

We determined that our primary goal for the program was to provide a positive, welcoming, first experience with the campus library. We also wanted students to become acquainted with the physical layout of the building and make them aware of the range and variety of information resources available. Various approaches were considered and a self-guided, interactive tour seemed an effective solution. Librarians, staff, and students were invited to an idea sharing session where a number of activities were suggested. The mystery tour was chosen for several reasons: a mystery has wide appeal; it can easily be adapted as an introduction to the library; and, it has the potential for making orientation a fun experience.

The Plan

Once the idea of a mystery tour had been adopted, we searched the literature for programs in place. We discovered the American Library Association's 1995 National Reading Program, *Solve Mysteries--READ*. Its guide included a murder mystery game called "Righteous Revenge[1]," which provided a basis for the program. In our adaptation of the game, students play the role of detectives charged with investigating the mysterious death of a fictitious professor whose body was found in the library basement. By way of introduction, students are given some basic facts about the case along with a list of possible suspects and a map of the library. They retrace the professor's steps and are led to various locations during the investigation. The last location has clues which are part of a puzzle students piece together to find out how the professor died. They involve searching the online catalog, going to the book stacks in the general collection, asking for reserve material, and getting a videotape at the media desk. Students who successfully "solve" the mystery are awarded a copier card worth five copies. The tour takes about half an hour to 45 minutes.

---

[1] American Library Association. "Righteous Revenge," In *Solve Mysteries--READ Program Guide*. (Chicago: ALA, 1994), n.p.

Publicity

Most publicity was scheduled a week before the event. Flyers were posted throughout campus, inserted into freshmen packets, and were available in the library for students to pick up. A memo was also sent to faculty in the English Department to announce the event in the Freshman Writing Seminar classes.

Response

Before students claimed their prize, they were asked to record their comments in a Detective Log Book. The responses were overwhelmingly positive. Students thought it was fun to roam around the building and search for clues. A few faculty took the tour and liked it so well that they gave it as an extra credit assignment during the first week of class. Subsequently, the library has submitted a proposal to the Freshman Orientation Committee requesting that the mystery tour become a formal event during Orientation Week. The committee greeted the proposal with enthusiasm and plans to include the tour as a scheduled activity.

Why the Mystery Tour Works

    *It allows complete flexibility in timing. Students may take the tour whenever the library is open.

    *Students are actively engaged in library orientation.

    *The tour may be done by groups or individuals.

    *It is inexpensive to produce. Prizes may be donated.

    *It provides a positive learning experience for novice library users.

    *It doesn't require ongoing staff commitments like the traditional staff guided tours.

Ricigliano is Associate Director, Collins Memorial Library, University of Puget Sound.

Library Mystery Tour Handout

Welcome to Collins Library! This self-guided mystery tour is designed to introduce you to key locations and service areas within the building. It will take about half an hour to 45 minutes to complete. Read the scenario below and follow the directions. Each location has a clue identified with a Sherlock Holmes logo that will lead you to the next step which must be done in numerical order. Use the "Collins Library Guide" and map (attached) to find the locations. If at any point during the tour you are not sure you are in the right place, just ask the library staff for help.

Scenario

You are a detective for Campus Security investigating the death of Professor Harris Tweed. The Professor's body was found crushed in the Compact Shelving area. As detective, you will retrace his steps on his last day and determine whether or not there was foul play. You will meet the following cast of characters along the way.

Harris Tweed - tenured professor, gadfly, faculty prima donna, and natty dresser. He enjoys intimidating his colleagues and treating students like used furniture.

Ivory Tower - writing instructor and little known author. She and Tweed co-authored the book *The Fatal Art of Mystery Writing*. Tweed sent the manuscript to the publisher without Tower's name on it. Now the book is very successful and Tower is angry because her chance for fame and fortune has been stolen. She has threatened to sue Tweed.

Sally Sage - reference librarian. She harbors a great deal of resentment towards Tweed because he treats her like his personal slave.

Paige Turner - library assistant. She is upset with Tweed because he takes library books to his office without checking them out and then refuses to return them.

Chris Kleen - library custodian. Chris sees a lot during the course of a day and likes to hang out and talk with library patrons. Tweed has hassled him about keeping the office clean, and once or twice Chris mouthed off to Tweed.

Joe Cool - first year student. Joe was in Tweed's writing class. He worked hard but Tweed criticized absolutely everything he wrote. Tweed accused him of plagerism on his final research paper and gave him a failing grade.

Bertha Bigwig - dean of the university. Tweed has been a thorn in her side both professionally and personally ever since he was hired. He constantly challenges her authority and they often have shouting matches during faculty meetings.

Mac Muscle - football coach. He is involved in an on-going feud with Tweed over academics and college sports. They constantly fight over student time.

Directions

On the day of his death, Professor Tweed was first seen at the reference desk. Proceed to the **reference desk** to begin your investigation and locate your first clue.

Poster session 6 (Ricigliano): Part 2 - Library Mystery Tour Handout

Library Mystery Tour Clues

The following clues were used in the Library Mystery Tour to lead students to key locations and service areas within the building. They were prominently displayed on colored paper with a Sherlock Holmes logo.

Clue #1

Librarian Sally Sage had just started her shift at the reference desk when Professor Tweed rushed up to ask for help with a research project. In a condescending voice, he explained that he was writing his next best seller, a murder mystery entitled *All Fired Up*. He wanted statistics on arson rates. He was doubtful that Sally could help him, but he thought he would ask any way. Struggling to keep her cool, Sally told him about a book called *Uniform Crime Reports for the United States*, located in the **Reference stacks**. The call number is **HV6787 .A3**. Go to this area to continue your investigation.

Clue #2

While browsing *Uniform Crime Reports for the United States*, Tweed sees Professor Ivory Tower marching towards him. Tower is really upset. She just found out that the book she co-authored with Tweed has hit number one on the bestsellers list and it is going into a second printing. She corners Tweed and demands that Tweed include her as joint author for the second printing or she'll sue for authorship fraud. Tweed stubbornly refuses. Leaving the Reference stacks, Tower shouts "You'll never live this down!" Unruffled, Tweed continues with his arson research and decides to copy some statistics. He heads for the nearest **copy machine** which is located near the reference desk. Go to this area to continue your investigation.

Clue #3

Tweed copies the arson statistics without incident and returns to the Reference desk. He tells Sally the copy machine in reference is broken and demands that she fix it right away. He goes into a tirade about how he wasted valuable research time. Sally listens patiently and then and asks if there is anything else he needs. Tweed wants to browse earlier years of *Uniform crime reports for the United States*. Sally tells him that *Uniform crime reports* is a government publication and that the older editions can be found in the government documents stacks. As Tweed walks away, Sally mutters that she hopes Tweed gets his just desserts some day. Go to the **government documents** stacks and look for the documents number J 1.14/7: to continue your investigation.

Clue #4

Having found the information he needed, Tweed heads for the Reference Workstations to find some magazine articles about arson. Along the way, he runs into Bertha Bigwig who is coming out of meeting in room 134. Bigwig pulls him aside and says she would like him

Poster session 6 (Ricigliano): Part 3 - Library Mystery Tour Clues to come to her office to discuss a serious matter. Tweed says he doesn't have time--he is conducting important research for his next book. Bigwig demands "Come to my office immediately or you'll lose your job--one way or another!" Tweed shrugs her off and goes to **reference workstation #4**. Proceed to this area to continue your investigation.

Clue #5

During the course of his research, Tweed discovers an interesting article called "Setting a Sooty Trap for Arsonists" in *Science News*. Since it is fairly recent, he figures it will be shelved with the current issues in **Display Periodicals**. Go to this area to continue your investigation.

Clue #6

Tweed notices that issues from the last six months are shelved in the Display Periodicals. His article is dated 1992 so he heads downstairs to find *Science News* in the **Bound Periodicals**. Go to this area to continue your investigation.

Clue #7

The volume of *Science News* that Tweed needs is missing from the shelf. Disgusted, he goes back upstairs to ask the staff at the Circulation Desk about it. But before he does, he sees student Joe Cool studying at a nearby table. Tweed is surprised to see Joe; he thought Joe dropped out after he failed the writing class. Joe gives Tweed a dirty look and says "You'd better watch your back, Tweed. I'm going to get you!" Go to the **Circulation Desk** to continue your investigation.

Clue #8

Paige Turner sees Tweed approaching the Circulation Desk. Tweed looks mad enough to spit. Paige takes a deep breath and says in her sweetest voice "May I help you?" Tweed goes into a tirade about how the 1992 volume of *Science News* is missing and he can never find anything he wants in the library. Paige searches SIMON and discovers that the 1992 issue of *Science News* is also on microfiche and suggests he look there. Tweed leaves and Paige mutters that the university would be better off without him. Continue your investigation by going to the **microfiche** cabinet where *Science News* would be found.

Clue #9

It is in the microform area that you, the detective, run into Custodian Chris Kleen, who is sweeping the floor. Chris hands you a crumbled piece of paper that he found while cleaning up the crime scene. There are three titles scribbled in Professor Tweed's handwriting: *Hot on the Trail of a Cold Mystery*, *Solving a Mystery Without any Clues*, and *The Mystery is in the Writing*. Do a title search in SIMON, the online catalog, for

Poster session 6 (Ricigliano): Part 3 - Library Mystery Tour Clues (continued)

each of these items. Write down the call numbers and go to the locations where you will find the remaining clues. Once you've pieced these clues together, you'll be led to a source that solves the mystery.

Note: The clues are *Fortune* (found in a book on the 4th floor), volume 52 (found in a book on reserve at the circulation desk), and 1955 (found in a video on reserve at the media desk).

Students go to the location where the 1955 volume of *Fortune* is shelved and find the following note:

Professor Harris Tweed was knocked unconscious by a blow to the head from a huge volume falling from the top shelf. Unknowingly, a library patron rolled compact shelf over Tweed's body and he died.

Congratulations! You have just completed the mystery tour while learning about the library. Go back to the Circulation desk and sign in the detective log book. To collect a prize, tell the Circulation staff that you finished the mystery tour and "Fortune" caught up with Professor Tweed.

Poster session 6 (Ricigliano): Part 3 - Library Mystery Tour Clues (continued)

BIBLIOGRAPHY

LIBRARY INSTRUCTION AND INFORMATION LITERACY—1995

Hannelore B. Rader

The following is an annotated list of materials dealing with information literacy including instruction in the use of information resources, research, and computer skills related to retrieving, using, and evaluating information. This review, the twenty-second to be published in *Reference Services Review*, includes items in English published in 1995. After 21 years, the title of this review of the literature has been changed from "Library Orientation and Instruction" to **"Library Instruction and Information Literacy,"** to indicate the growing trend of moving to information skills instruction.

A few items are not annotated because the compiler could not obtain copies of them for this review.

The list includes publications on user instruction in all types of libraries and for all levels of users, from beginning levels to the most advanced. The items are arranged by type of library and are in alphabetical order by author (or by title if there is no author) within those categories.

Overall, as shown in the example below, the number of publications related to user education and information literacy increased by *46 percent* from 1994 to 1995. This is the longest bibliography since the series began in 1973.

These figures are approximate and are based on the published information that was available to the reviewer; however, since the availability of this

Rader is director, University Library, Cleveland State University, Cleveland, Ohio.

information does not vary greatly from year to year, these figures should be reliable.

Publications dealing with user instruction in academic libraries continue to be the largest number; they increased by 53 percent. The number of publications about user instruction in public libraries increased although they remain the smallest number in the group; school library publications increased by 36 percent; special library publications increased by 50 percent; publications for all levels increased only 8 percent.

User education publications in libraries continue to deal with teaching users how to access, retrieve, and organize information, including online searching, online system use, and bibliographic computer applications. An increasing percentage deal with evaluative research of user education.

It is noteworthy that in 1995 articles dealing with instruction in the use of electronic information and the World Wide Web increased substantially as did articles dealing with information literacy, resource-based and active learning, and integrating information literacy into the curriculum both in the schools and in higher education. In fact, for the first time there are publications treating the topic of information literacy and higher education accreditation. The continual growth of electronic information has made all libraries more aware of the need for assistance and instruction and even public libraries are beginning to institute various types of user instruction modules.

It must be noted that librarians are beginning to mount information skills instruction on the World Wide Web and to address instructional needs of remote users.

Type of Library	# of 1994 Publications	# of 1995 Publications	% Change
Academic	131	197	+50%
Public	03	05	+66%
School	28	38	+36%
Special	12	18	+50%
All Types	12	13	+ 8%
TOTAL	186	271	+46%

Academic Libraries

Abdulezer, Susan. *The HyperSign Project.* ERIC Document, 1995. ED 380 927.

Describes activities and results of the HyperSign Immersion Project developed at the Public School for the Deaf in New York to help them develop and improve basic literacy and math skills.

Adalian, Paul T., Jr. "Cal Poly's Multi-Media Approach to Research." *College and Research Libraries News* 56 (January 1995): 10-16.

The library is using the *Retriever* program, a colorful user interface, which provides library users with a complete learning environment to identify and locate point sources and access to local and remote online databases.

Adalian, Paul T., and Ilene F. Rockman. "Issues in Implementing and Teaching the Lexis/Nexis Services in an Undergraduate Library." *Reference Librarian* 48 (1995): 99-113.

Addresses the teaching of the legal materials database Lexis/Nexis to undergraduates at California Polytechnic University.

Afifi, Marianne. "The Leavey Library at USC: Planning for Bibliographic Instruction in a High Tech Environment." *Catholic Library World* 65 (January/March 1995): 19-20.

Discusses the planning for library instruction in a technological environment at the University of Southern California.

Ajibero, Matthew I. "User Expectations from Nigerian University Libraries Services in the 21st Century." *Public and Access Services Quarterly* 1 (1995): 33-49.

Describes present services offered by university libraries in Nigeria including the need for library instruction.

Alberico, Ralph. "Serving College Students in an Era of Recombinant Information." *Wilson Library Bulletin* 69 (March 1995): 29-32.

Reports on how academic libraries are improving services in response to students and within the electronic environment by incorporating electronic resources into the curriculum.

Alexander, Linda. "LME 101: A Required Course in Basic Library Skills." *Research Strategies* 13 (Fall 1995): 245-249.

Describes Western Kentucky University's basic library skills course including the syllabus and grading policy.

Allan, David W., and Lisa A. Baures. "BI Instructional Design: Applying Modes of Consciousness Theory." In *The Impact of Technology on Library Instruction.* Ed. by Linda Shirato, 77-84. Ann Arbor, MI: Pierian Press, 1995.

Discusses an instructional session developed to accommodate nonverbal learning styles.

Allen, Eileen. "Active Learning and Teaching: Improving Post Secondary Library Instruction." *Reference Librarian* 51-52 (1995): 89-103.

Several active teaching examples in library instruction as well as the importance of student involvement in the learning process are discussed.

AmRhein, Richard. "Internet Resources on the Internet." *College and Research Libraries News* 56 (December 1995): 760-763.

Describes how users can be introduced to music resources available on the Internet.

Anderson, Judy. "Have Users Changed Their Style? A Survey of CD-ROM vs. OPAC Product Usage." *RQ* 34 (Spring 1995): 362-368.

Reports a survey of online search techniques of 50 undergraduates and graduate students at Arizona State University's Hayden Library.

Arp, Lori. "Library Literacy: Reflecting on Reflecting: Views on Teaching and Internet." *RQ* 34 (Summer 1995): 453-457.

Discusses rapid changes in electronic information and implication for training and education as related to the changing role of the instruction librarian.

Arp, Lori, et al. "Library Literacy: Teaching Behind the Screens: Practical Advice for a Practical World." *RQ* 35 (Winter 1995): 179-186.

Addresses screen designs within the library instruction environment and for better access to electronic information whether on the online catalog, CD-ROM network, local area networks, the World Wide Web, or any other system.

Bailey, Lynnette, and Martin Jenkins. "Evolution of a Workbook as Part of an Information Skills Programme." *Library Review* 44 (1995): 13-20.

Describes use of a workbook to teach information skills at the Cheltenham and Gloucester College of Higher Education in Great Britain and how internal and external changes have caused workbook revisions.

Baker, Robert K. "Working with Our Teaching Faculty." *College and Research Libraries* 56 (September 1995): 377-379.

Discusses the importance of librarians to become involved with faculty in the academic area, especially in regards to teaching students information skills.

Becker, Karen. "Luddites in Library Instruction: Back to Basics." In *Proceedings of the ACRL 7th National Conference*. Ed. by Richard AmRhein, 289-294. Chicago: Association of College and Research Libraries, 1995.

Describes a rethinking of basic library instruction for freshmen at Northern Illinois University.

Benson, Larry D. "Scholarly Research and Reference Service in the Automated Environment." *Reference Librarian* 48 (1995): 57-69.

Discusses the challenges and opportunities facing social sciences librarians who work with researchers in a rapidly changing technological environment.

Beiser, Karl. "You Could Look It Up." *Database* 18 (June/July 1995): 94-97.

Reviews the *Oxford Education Dictionary* in CD-ROM format.

Biggs, Mary. "Librarians as Educators: Assessing Our Self-Image." *Public Access Quarterly* 1 (1995): 41-50.

Talks about how problems with librarians' self-image and professional identification are partly responsible for the limited effectiveness of instruction programs and for the lack of a central position in the information society.

Blackwell, Cheryl. "Remote Access OPAC Searching." In *The Impact of Technology on Library Instruction*. Ed. by Linda Shirato, 159-164. Ann Arbor, MI: Pierian Press, 1995.

Discusses in detail how to teach students remote searching of electronic resources based on experiences at Albion College in Michigan.

Blandy, Susan G. "Keeping Library Instruction Alive." *Reference Librarian* 51-52 (1995): 425-447.

Discusses the importance of constantly reaffirming the goals of library instruction and collaborating with faculty. Includes examples of assignments.

Blandy, Susan G., and Patricia O. Libutti. "As the Cursor Blinks: Electronic Scholarship and Undergraduates in the Library." *Library Trends* 44 (Fall 1995): 279-305.

Presents a model to teach students research and critical thinking skills based on librarians' unique training and experience.

Bober, Christopher, et al. "Evaluating Library Instruction in Academic Libraries: A Critical Review of the Literature, 1980-1993." *Reference Librarian* 51-52 (1995): 53-71.

Discusses the reasons for evaluation, how much is evaluated, which aspects are evaluated, and which methodologies are used.

Bodi, Sonia. "Scholarship or Propaganda: How Can Librarians Help Undergraduates Tell the Difference." *Journal of Academic Librarianship* 21 (January 1995): 21-25.

Compares characteristics of propaganda and scholarship, and lists indicators that can enable librarians to help students tell the difference between genuine scholarship and that which passes as scholarship.

Boisse, Joseph, and Carla Stoffle. "Conference Summary." In *Upside of Downsizing*. Ed. by Cheryl LaGuardia, 239-243. New York: Neal-Schuman, 1995.

Provides 20 thoughts and ideas from the conference participants regarding user instruction and downsizing.

Bowley, Barbara J., and Lynn W. Meng. "Information Literacy for ESL Students: Retooling Instructional Models to Accommodate Diversity." In *Proceedings of the ACRL 7th National Conference*. Ed. by Richard AmRhein, 403-407. Chicago: Association of College and Research Libraries, 1995.

Describes the development of a teaching model for ESL (English as a second language) students to teach these students information skills.

Brown, Janet D., et al. "Enabling Options: An Undergraduate Library Instruction Proposal." *Research Strategies* 13 (Summer 1995): 144-152.

Discusses a proposal at Wichita State University library for a basic library skills competency test for undergraduates to be followed by a multi-optional program designed to enable every student to pass the test. Includes examination of political hurdles to gain acceptance for the proposal.

Bruffee, Kenneth A. "Sharing Our Toys: Cooperative Learning Versus Collaborative Learning." *Change* 27 (January/February 1995): 12-18.

Provides a discussion on cooperative and collaborative learning within the university environment, the differences, the advantages and disadvantages, and implications for learning outcomes.

Burrows, Toby. "Educating for the Internet in an Academic Library: The Scholars' Centre at the University of Western Australia." *Education of Information* 13 (1995): 229-242.

Discusses Internet instruction for staff and graduate students in the arts and social sciences within an integrated, client-centered framework.

Burton, Melody. "The Knee-Bone Is Connected to the Thigh Bone: Postmodernism, Critical Pedagogy, and Logic in the CD-ROM Workshop." *Reference Librarian* 51-52 (1995): 131-141.

Considers CD-ROM instruction for research in an interdisciplinary environment and identifies key components of postmodernism.

Callahan, Daren. "Two Thumbs Up! Library Applications for Video Technology." *Information Technology and Libraries* 14 (September 1995): 173-176.

Discusses use of videos to explain collections at Southern Illinois University and explains how to make videos for many other subjects.

Carter, Tom. "The Human Touch in Bibliographic Instruction." *Catholic Library World* 65 (January-March 1995): 14-16.

Article examines the effects of technology on academic library reference services and bibliographic instruction.

Cassel, Rachel. "Selection Criteria for Internet Resources." *College and Research Libraries News* 56 (February 1995): 92-93.

Discusses the importance of evaluation and quality control in providing users with access to Internet resources.

Chappell, Virginia, et al. "Beyond Information Retrieval: Transforming Research Assignments into Genuine Inquiry." *Journal of Teaching Writing* 13 (1995): 209-224.

Describes a collaborative workshop between faculty and librarians to teach students evaluation of information sources.

Clark, Irene L. "Information Literacy and Writing Centers." *Computers and Composition* 12 (1995): 203-209.

Discusses how to make information literacy a goal for writing centers and how these centers can help students gain research and critical thinking skills.

Coder, Ann, and Margie Smith. "Overcoming Mazes and Minotaurs: Achieving User Independence in the Academic Library Labyrinth." In *Upside of Downsizing.* Ed. by Cheryl LaGuardia, 39-49. New York: Neal-Schuman, 1995.

Advocates clarifying and simplifying information in libraries, locating it where most needed, and using better sign systems.

Cohen, Charlotte. "Faculty Liaison: A Cooperative Venture in Bibliographic Instruction." *Reference Librarian* 51-52 (1995): 161-169.

Describes a case study between librarians and faculty in business to prepare students for information seeking in the business world.

Connolly, Bruce. "Presentation Hardware: A Review Roundup of Color LCD Panels and Projectors." *Online* 19 (May/June 1995): 12-22.

Cook, Kim N., et al. "Cooperative Learning in Bibliographic Instruction." *Research Strategies* 13 (Winter 1995): 17-25.

Discusses cooperative learning as an alternative to lecturing. Gives evaluation criteria and advantages of cooperative learning.

Coombs, Merolyn, and Janice Houghton. "Information Skills for New Entry Tertiary Students: Perceptions and Practice." *Australian Academic and Research Libraries* 26 (December 1995): 260-270.

Describes a study at the University of Technology in Sydney regarding students' first encounters with information skills.

Cooper, Tasha, and Jane Burchfield. "Information Literacy for College and University Staff." *Research Strategies* 13 (Spring 1995): 94-106.

Explores the advantages of and difficulties in offering information literacy programs to college and university staff by integrating sessions into workplace situations.

Cordell, Rosanne M. "Enhancing Library Instruction of At-Risk Students with Multimedia Presentations." *Indiana Libraries* 14 (1995): 37-45.

Describes the use of multimedia in library instruction to help at-risk students at Indiana University in South Bend.

DeDecker, Sherry, and Lynn Westbrook. "Public Service Strategies for Minimizing Library Anxiety." In *Upside of Downsizing*. Ed. by Cheryl LaGuardia, 51-66. New York: Neal-Schuman, 1995.

Discusses rethinking public services to make them more user-oriented using better physical layout, more staff training, improved outreach, and teaching programs for technology.

Deekle, Peter V. "Books, Reading, and Undergraduate Education." *Library Trends* 44 (Fall 1995): 264-269.

Discusses the role of books and reading in undergraduate education and the importance of developing critical reading skills and self-directed learning.

Diamond, Tom, and Joan E. McGee. "Bibliographic Instruction for Business Writing Students: Implementation of a Conceptual Framework." *RQ* 34 (Spring 1995): 340-360.

Reviews bibliographic instruction for business writing students at Louisiana State University and how it was restructured to ensure better learning outcomes.

DiMartino, Diane, et al. "CD-ROM Search Techniques of Novice End-Users: Is the English-as-a-Second-Language Student at a Disadvantage?" *College and Research Libraries* 56 (January 1995): 49-60.

This study compares the CD-ROM search techniques of 42 undergraduate native speakers of English with those of 34 undergraduates speaking English as a second language.

Dixon, Lan, et al. "Building Library Skills: Computer Assisted Skills for Undergraduates." *Research Strategies* 13 (Fall 1995): 196-208.

Describes the use of computer-assisted instruction as a replacement for basic library instruction for 3,000 students.

Doty, Paul. "How Index-Learning Turns No Student Pale: An Essay on Rhetoric and Bibliographic Instruction." *Reference Librarian* 51-52 (1995): 121-129.

Presents an exercise to encourage people to use ERIC as arguments in rhetoric sense.

Downing, Karen. "Peer Information Counselors: Experienced Students Assist Librarians in Extending Bibliographic Instruction Program." In *Upside of Downsizing*. Ed. by Cheryl LaGuardia, 67-75. New York: Neal-Schuman, 1995.

Discusses the use of student peer counseling program at the University of Michigan to help students gain information skills.

Duda, Andrea L. "Burrowing into BI: The Care and Feeding of a Library Gopher." In *Upside of Downsizing*. Ed. by Cheryl LaGuardia, 77-87. New York: Neal-Schuman, 1995.

Explains how an Internet gopher at the University of Minnesota was utilized to provide students with library instruction tutorials online to stretch human resources and address remote users.

Duff, Alistair S., et al. "Is Intellectual Property Theft? BI's Hidden Ideology... and Two Reactions." *Research Strategies* 13 (Summer 1995): 132-143.

Presents several controversial ideas regarding bibliographic instruction and intellectual property rights and copyright laws raised by Alistair Duff followed by reactions from William Miller and Sidney Berger defending bibliographic instruction.

Duling, Sandra, and Patrick Max. "Teaching the Teachers in an Electronic Environment." In *The Impact of Technology on Library Instruction*. Ed. by Linda Shirato, 103-112. Ann Arbor, MI: Pierian Press, 1995.

Describes how to prepare librarians to teach in an electronic environment using resource-based learning techniques.

DuMont, Mary, and Barbara F. Schloman. "The Evolution and Reaffirmation of a Library Orientation Program in an Academic Research Library." *Reference Services Review* 23:1 (Spring 1995): 85-92.

Relates the evolution of a library orientation program from a lecture/tour format to an audio tape tour.

Dunn, Rita, and Barbara Waggoner. "Comparing Three Innovative Instructional Systems." *Emergency Librarian* 23 (September/October 1995): 9-15.

Describes different learning styles, neuro-linguistic programming and suggestopoedia (environmental and cultural applications for learners).

Dyckman, Lise M. "Beyond 'First You Push This Button, Then...': A Process-Oriented Approach to Teaching Searching Skills." *Reference Librarian* 51-52 (1995): 249-265.

Describes a program at New York University where librarians developed a syllabus that teaches common techniques and strategies of computer-based research.

Eckman, Richard H., and Richard E. Quandt. "Scholarly Communication, Academic Libraries and Technology." *Change* 27 (January/February 1995): 34-44.

Edwards, Susan, and Mairead Browne. "Quality in Information Services: Do Users and Librarians Differ in Their Expectations?" *Library and Information Science Research* 17 (Spring 1995): 163-182.
    Describes a project designed to develop a user-based approach to measuring library services provided for them.

Engeldinger, Eugene A., et al. "Library Instruction in the Carthage College Heritage Studies Program." In *The Impact of Technology on Library Instruction*. Ed. by Linda Shirato, 165-180. Ann Arbor, MI: Pierian Press, 1995.
    Describes an integrated approach to information skills instruction within a basic core curriculum (Heritage Studies), a cooperative venture between faculty and librarians.

Engle, Michael O. "Forty Five Years After Lamont: The University Undergraduate Library in the 1990s." *Library Trends* 44 (Fall 1995): 368-386.
    Discusses the evolution of the undergraduate library and the effect of the information revolution and the virtual library on its future.

Ercegova, Zorana. "Information Access Instruction (IAI): Design Principles." *College and Research Libraries* 56 (May 1995): 249-264.
    Proposes four design principles: the user, active learning, conceptual model of teaching, and modularity, as a conceptual framework of an information access instruction.

Evans, Lorraine, and Peggy Keeran. "Beneath the Tip of the Iceberg: Expanding Students' Information Horizon." *Research Strategies* 13 (Fall 1995): 235-244.
    Presents a summary of a survey at the University of Denver to assess students' reactions to the new DIALOG library instruction program to develop lifelong independent learners.

Farber, Evan. "Bibliographic Instruction Briefly." In *Information for a New Age. Redefining the Librarian*. Ed. by American Library Association Library Instruction Roundtable, 23-34. Englewood, CO: Libraries Unlimited, 1995.

Provides a history and rationale for bibliographic instruction and gives some thoughts about the future.

Farber, Evan. "Plus Ca Change..." *Library Trends* 44 (Fall 1995): 430-438.
    Re-examines library instruction in terms of electronic information and how that will affect instruction programs in the future.

Farber, Evan, and Sara Penhale. "Using Poster Sessions in Introductory Science Courses: An Example at Earlham." *Research Strategies* 13 (Winter 1995): 55-59.
    Describes an introductory geology course assignment where students work collaboratively in groups preparing for a poster session. Includes the handout used to guide students through the assignments.

Feinman, Valerie J. "The Core Curriculum at Adelphi and an Approach to Library Instruction." In *The Impact of Technology on Library Instruction*. Ed. by Linda Shirato, 113-122. Ann Arbor, MI: Pierian Press, 1995.
    Describes the evolution from a workbook to a self-guided tour and test for freshmen as part of a bibliographic instruction program throughout the curriculum at Adelphi University.

Fenske, Rachel F., and Susan E. Clark. "Incorporating Library Instruction in a General Education Program for College Freshmen." *Reference Services Review* 23:3 (Fall 1995): 69-74.
    Discusses planning, implementing, evaluating, and revising library instruction in a general education course for freshmen at the University of the Pacific.

Fidzani, Babakisi T. "User Education in Academic Libraries; a Study of Trends and Development in Southern Africa." *Booklet 7: 61st IFLA General Conference Proceedings, August 20-25, 1995*. Istanbul, Turkey: International Federation of Library Associations, 136-142.
    Examines user education programs in academic libraries in Southern Africa. Focuses on the planning, organization, and implementation of the programs and highlights problems and barriers.

Fjallbrant, Nancy. "EDUCATE—a Networked User Education Project in Europe." *Booklet 7: 61st IFLA General Conference Proceedings*. Istanbul, Turkey: International Federation of Library Associations, 130-135.
    Describes the EDUCATE (End-User Courses in Information Access) through the three-year communication technology project for end-user training in information access, involving six members of the

European Union. Its aim is to produce a new type of model for a self-paced user education course in the selection and use of information tools within physics and electrical/electronic engineering.

Frank, Donald G. "Toward Innovative Instructional Options for the 1990's: Collaboration in the Science/Technology Libraries of Harvard University." In *Upside of Downsizing*. Ed. by Cheryl LaGuardia, 89-106. New York: Neal-Schuman, 1995.

Discusses various academic and political realities in large, decentralized institutions and how to incorporate information literacy instruction through collaboration.

Frank, Polly P., and Lee-Allison Levene. "Everyone in the Pool: Staying Afloat with a Good BI Team." In *Upside of Downsizing*. Ed. by Cheryl LaGuardia, 107-125. New York: Neal-Schuman, 1995.

Proposes a model at Mankato University to build and expand the bibliographic instruction team and involve a variety of staff as well as the campus community.

Geffert, Bryn. "Beginning with MARC: Providing a Foundation for Electronic Searching." *Research Strategies* 13 (Winter 1995): 26-33.

Suggests reasons why many students have problems using catalogs; they need instruction in record structure. Advocates the teaching of MARC record formats. Presents a sample module used at St. Olaf College in Minnesota.

Gibson, Craig. "Critical Thinking: Implications for Instruction." *RQ* 35 (Fall 1995): 27-35.

Provides a concise overview of the critical thinking movement in education and implications for library instruction.

Glogoff, Stuart. "Library Instruction in the Electronic Library: The University of Arizona's Electronic Library Education Centers." *Reference Services Review* 23:2 (Summer 1995): 7-12, 39.

Discusses electronic library education centers at the University of Arizona to improve library instruction in the use of electronic resources. Includes Internet resources for planning and redesigning electronic classrooms.

Gonzalez, Edward L.F., and Helen J. Seaton. "Internet Sources for Nursing and Allied Health." *Database* 18 (June/July 1995).

Gowler, Steve. "The Habit of Seeking: Liberal Education and the Library at Berea College." *Library Trends* 44 (Fall 1995): 387-399.

Gives an overview of Berea College's integrated library instruction programs as part of the emphasis of liberal studies.

Grassian, Esther, and Joan Kaplowitz. "Teaching Future Librarians to Teach." In *Upside of Downsizing*. Ed. by Cheryl LaGuardia, 127-135. New York: Neal-Schuman, 1995.

Describes a course in UCLA's Library and Information Science School that prepares graduate students on how to become good bibliographic instruction librarians.

Graubart, Marilyn. "Orientation Sessions in Israeli Academic Libraries." *Research Strategies* 13 (Summer 1995): 165-175.

Gives an overview of differences and similarities between U.S. and Israeli academic libraries and a brief overview of orientation programs offered by each of seven Israeli libraries visited.

Greenfield, Louise, et al. "A Model for Teaching the Internet: Preparation and Practice." *Computers in Libraries* (March 1996): 22-25.

Presents a model instructional session on joining electronic discussion groups on the Internet. Gives learning outcomes and teaching design using hands-on sessions.

"Guidelines for Instruction Programs in Academic Libraries: Draft." *College and Research Libraries* 56 (December 1995): 767-769.

Summarizes the latest draft of the Association of College and Research Libraries' guidelines for library instruction programs.

Gupta, Usha, et al. "SuperService: Reshaping Information Services for Graduate Students." *Research Strategies* 13 (Fall 1995): 209-218.

Describes a new service at the University of Arkansas for graduate students to provide them with information access and training.

Gurn, Robert M. "Measuring Information Providers on the Internet." *Computers in Libraries* 15 (January 1995): 42.

Briefly talks about evaluating content on the Internet.

Hanson, Michele G. "BI and Collaborative Learning: A Partnership in Library Literacy." In *Upside of*

Downsizing. Ed. by Cheryl LaGuardia, 135-146. New York: Neal-Schuman, 1995.

Discusses the benefits of collaborative learning in teaching library and information skills.

Hanson, Michele G. "Joining the Conversation: Collaborative Learning and Bibliographic Instruction." *Reference Librarian* 51-52 (1995): 147-159.

Discusses the importance of collaborative learning and teaching to improve library instruction outcomes.

Hardesty, Larry. "Faculty Culture and Bibliographic Instruction: An Exploratory Analysis." *Library Trends* 44 (Fall 1995): 339-367.

Examines faculty culture and how it impedes bibliographic instruction. Discusses the need for librarians to continue their outreach efforts if they want to become part of the educational process.

Harvell, Tony. "Teaching the Use of the Internet in Traditional Library Instruction Program." In *Upside of Downsizing*. Ed. by Cheryl LaGuardia, 147-154. New York: Neal-Schuman, 1995.

Describes how instruction librarians at the University San Diego incorporated the use of the Internet into their library instruction program.

Helms, Cynthia M. "Reaching Out to the International Students Through Bibliographic Instruction." *Reference Librarian* 51-52 (1995): 295-307.

Highlights a bibliographic instruction program for international students at Andrews University.

Holland, Maurita P., and Christina K. Powell. "A Longitudinal Survey of the Information Seeking and Use Habits of Some Engineers." *College and Research Libraries* 56 (January 1995): 7-15.

Concludes that many engineers have access to the tools needed for electronic information retrieval and they are interested in learning how to use them.

Howze, Philip S., and Dana E. Smith. "Library Instruction as Independent Study: The Summer Enrichment Program Experiment at Iowa State University." *Reference Services Review* 23:4 (Winter 1995): 75-82.

Describes a program at Iowa State University with students of color to assess an independent study bibliographic instruction packet and the use of culturally oriented materials.

Hubbard, Taylor E. "Bibliographic Instruction and Postmodern Pedagogy." *Library Trends* 44 (Fall 1995): 439-452.

Discusses how postmodernism can assist in making information studies an integrated part of the academic curriculum.

Hults, Patricia. "Noodling Down the Internet: Or, One Foot in the Fast Lane, the Other Stuck in the Trenches." *Reference Librarian* 51-52 (1995): 235-240.

Discusses staff issues, structure of the Internet, and preparing users for the Internet by applying bibliographic instruction methods.

Isbell, Dennis, and Dorothy Broaddus. "Teaching Writing and Research as Inseparable: A Faculty-Librarian Teaching Team." *Reference Services Review* 23:4 (Winter 1995): 51-62.

Describes a faculty/librarian team-teaching approach to writing and research at Arizona State University West.

Jackman, Lana W., and Patricia Payne. "Information Literacy: For the Privileged Only?" In *Upside of Downsizing*. Ed. by Cheryl LaGuardia, 155-164. New York: Neal-Schuman, 1995.

Describes a cooperative approach among the library and other departments to teach information literacy in an urban setting at the University of Massachusetts-Boston.

Jacobsen, Kristen. "Time to Put the Internet into Perspective." *College and Research Libraries News* 56 (March 1995): 144-147.

Jacobson, Trudi E., and Beth L. Mark. "Teaching in the Information Age: Active Learning Techniques to Empower Students." *Reference Librarian* 51-52 (1995): 105-120.

Considers student apprehension when encountering new information technologies and proposes a variety of active learning exercises within the framework of questions.

Jacobson, Trudi, and David A. Tyckoson. "Bringing in the Reserves: Generating Confident and Skillful New Instructors." In *Upside of Downsizing*. Ed. by Cheryl LaGuardia, 165-170. New York: Neal-Schuman, 1995.

Discusses how at the University of Albany, SUNY, librarians have begun a program to improve the teaching skills of staff members from various areas around the library, so they can successfully participate in the instruction program.

Jensen, Ann, and Julie Sih. "Using E-Mail and the Internet to Teach Users at Their Desktops." *Online* 19 (September/October 1995): 82-88.

Describes how librarians are teaching users at the University of California, San Diego, remotely through electronic tutorials on the use of INSPEC, an engineering database.

Kabel, Carol, et al. "The Electronic Library: Library Skills for Off-Campus Students, Program and Evaluation." In *The Impact of Technology on Library Instruction*. Ed. by Linda Shirato, 127-134. Ann Arbor, MI: Pierian Press, 1995.

Discusses how librarians at National-Louis University in Illinois work with their many distance students to help them gain information and lifelong learning skills in the electronic environment.

Kaufman, Diane. "Building Preservation Awareness." *College and Research Libraries News* 56 (November 1955): 707-708.

Discusses Virginia Tech's approach to user education including preservation and care of library materials.

Kesselman, Martin. "The IFLA User Education Round Table and IFLA '94 Havana, Cuba." *Research Strategies* 13 (Winter 1995): 51-54.

Provides brief history of the IFLA User Education Round Table, and discusses current and future projects of the Round Table.

Kilman, Leigh A. "BI and the Twenty First Century: An Opinion." In *Information for a New Age. Redefining the Librarian*. Ed. by American Library Association Library Instruction Roundtable, 171-183. Englewood, CO: Libraries Unlimited, 1995.

Provides ideas for the future of the bibliographic instruction librarian.

Klatt, Edward, et al. *Windows to the World: Utah Library Network Internet Training Manual*. Eric Reproduction Service, 1995. ED 381 174.

This guide reviews the basic principles of Internet exploration for the novice user. It describes various functions using screen displays.

Klavano, Ann M., and Eleanor R. Kulleseid. "Bibliographic Instruction: Renewal and Transformation in One Academic Library." *Reference Librarian* 51-52 (1995): 359-383.

Examines the impact of institutional evaluation on the library's bibliographic instruction program and its evolution into an information literacy program.

Kohut, Dave, and Joel Sternberg. "Using the Internet to Study the Internet: An Active Learning Component." *Research Strategies* 13 (Summer 1995): 176-181.

Describes an Internet component in an undergraduate course on mass communication in which students receive hands-on instruction so they can use the Internet to research emerging technology.

Kohl, David F. "As Time Goes By...Revisiting Fundamentals." *Library Trends* 44 (Fall 1995): 423-429.

Reviews the importance of library instruction in planning future library services within the changing environment of higher education.

Krikos, Linda. "BI Challenges in Women's Studies: The Gateway Answer." *Research Strategies* 13 (Spring 1995): 69-79.

Describes how the Gateway to Information at Ohio State University Library was used to facilitate students' research in the area of women's studies and how it also changed the focus on bibliographic instruction.

Kupersmith, John. "Teaching, Learning, and Technostress." In the *Upside of Downsizing*. Ed. by Cheryl LaGuardia, 71-181. New York: Neal-Schuman, 1995.

Suggests that teaching about electronic information systems may help librarians overcome technostress through appropriate staff development.

"The Library Becomes a Teaching Instrument." In *Academic Libraries as High-Tech Gateways. A Guide to Design and Space Decisions*. Ed. by Richard J. Bazillion and Connie Braun, 129-149. Chicago: American Library Association, 1995.

Provides guidelines for librarians to identify design features to make their libraries into teaching instruments.

List, Carla. "Branching Out: A Required Library Research Course Targets Disciplines and Programs." *Reference Librarian* 51-52 (1995): 385-398.

Describes why and how five subject focus areas for a library research course were developed at the State University of New York, Plattsburgh.

Loomis, Abigail. "Building Coalitions for Information Literacy." In *Information for a New Age. Redefining the Librarian*. Ed. by American Library Association Library Instruction Roundtable, 123-134. Englewood, CO: Libraries Unlimited, 1995.

Discusses the importance of outreach to build coalitions on campus and with the community to help students achieve information literacy on all levels.

Mabry, Celia H. "Using Cooperative Learning Principles in BI." *Research Strategies* 13 (Summer 1995): 182-185.

Describes how cooperative learning techniques can be incorporated into user instruction to involve students in shaping class discussions.

MacAdam, Barbara. "Sustaining the Culture of the Book: The Role of Enrichment Reading and Critical Thinking in the Undergraduate Curriculum." *Library Trends* 44 (Fall 1995): 237-263.

Discusses the role of language and of books in undergraduate education and user instruction in relation to helping students develop reasoning and analytic skills.

Mardikian, Jackie, and Martin Kesselman. "Beyond the Desk: Enhanced Reference Staffing for the Electronic Library." *Reference Services Review* 23:1 (Spring 1995): 21-28.

Provides rationale in rethinking reference services and instruction in an electronic environment and when dealing with remote patrons.

Mark, Beth L., and Trudi E. Jacobson. "Teaching Anxious Students Skills for the Electronic Library." *College Teaching* 43 (Winter 1995): 28-31.

Describes the use of active learning techniques to help students overcome library and computer anxiety.

Martin, Lynne M. "Breaking Out of the Basement: A Survey of Catalogers Who Teach in State University of New York (SYNY) Libraries." *Reference Librarian* 51-51 (1995): 209-230.

Reports on a survey of 124 librarians at SUNY regarding their participation in bibliographic instruction. Conclusions challenge public and technical librarians to become more involved in teaching information skills.

Martin, Lynne M., and Trudi E. Jacobson. "Reflections on Maturity: Introduction, Library Instruction Revisited: Bibliographic Instruction Comes of Age." *Reference Librarian* 51-52 (1995): 5-13.

Provides an overview of two related concepts dealing with user instruction and their development in the past decade.

Martin, Rosetta P. "Integrating Library Computer Skills into a Credit Course at Trident Technical College." In *Proceeding of the ACRL 7th National Conference.* Ed. by Richard AmRhein, 107-115. Chicago, IL: Association of College and Research Libraries, 1995.

Examines how to enlarge library instruction models in credit courses and focuses on how to integrate a library computer skills component into such courses.

Master, Nancy. "Taking the Mystery out of the Library: User Education at UNLV's Dickinson Library." *Reference Librarian* 48 (1995): 115-129.

Describes user instruction and end-user searching for students at the University of Las Vegas.

Matenje, Flossie A. "Library Orientation at the University of Malawi." *Information Development* 11 (March 1995): 42-45.

Describes the library orientation program for freshmen at Chancellor College in the University of Malawi in Africa.

Matthews, Roberta S., et al. "Building Bridges Between Cooperative and Collaborative Learning." *Change* 26 (July/August 1995): 34-40.

Provides a comparison between cooperative and collaborative learning and a comprehensive bibliography.

McNeal, Ann P., and Michelle Murrain. "Tips on Writing a Library Research Paper." *College Teaching* 43 (Winter 1995): 15-16.

Provides suggestions for college students to prepare for writing a library research paper.

Mech, Terence F., and Charles I. Brooks. "Library Anxiety Among College Students: An Exploratory Study." In *Proceeding of the ACRL 7th National Conference.* Ed. by Richard AmRhein, 173-179. Chicago: Association of College and Research Libraries, 1995.

Summarizes a study to examine library anxiety among students. It was found that freshmen reported significantly higher levels of library anxiety and lower confidence in their ability to use the library than seniors.

Meltzer, Ellen, et al. "Undergraduate in Focus: Can Student Input Lead to New Directions in Undergraduate Library Services?" *Library Trends* 44 (Fall 1995): 400-415.

Discusses focus groups and their use in planning and improving library services including user instruction at the University of California.

Miller, Donna L., and Michael C. Zeigler. "Striking It Rich with the Internet: An Interactive Workshop for Teaching Faculty the Internet." In *The Impact of Technology on Library Instruction.* Ed. by Linda Shirato, 85-102. Ann Arbor, MI: Pierian Press, 1995.

Describes the planning and implementation of a day-long workshop on the Internet for faculty and staff at Lebanon Valley College in Pennsylvania.

Miller, Marcia. "Self Paced Tours in the Electronic Library." *Research Strategies* 13 (Fall 1995): 219-234.

Discusses students' preference for self-paced tours and whether or not this is a good alternative.

Moeckel, Nancy, and Jenny Presnell. "Recognizing, Understanding, and Responding: A Program Model of Library Instruction Services for International Students." *Reference Librarian* 51-52 (1995): 309-325.

Presents a model for library instruction for international students adaptable to any size institution. Includes promotion, instruction, staff development, and a review of the literature.

Morner, Claudia J. "Measuring the Library Research Skills of Education Doctoral Students." In *Proceedings of the ACRL 7th National Conference.* Ed. by Richard AmRhein, 381-391. Chicago: Association of College and Research Libraries, 1995.

The paper focuses on the development of a reliable and valid test of library research skills for doctoral students in education and the results of an administration of this instrument to a sample of students.

Murdoch, Jeanne. "Re-Engineering Bibliographic Instruction: The Real Task of Information Literacy." *Bulletin of the American Society for Information Science* 21 (February/March 1995): 26-27.

Describes the teaching of end-user searching.

Nahl, Diane. "Guidelines for Creating User-Centered Instruction for Novice End-Users." In *The Impact of Technology on Library Instruction.* Ed. by Linda Shirato, 9-19. Ann Arbor, MI: Pierian Press, 1995.

Summarizes users' search behavior in the area of online searching and its implication for viable point-of-use instruction in the electronic environment.

Natowitz, Allen. "International Students in U.S. Academic Libraries: Recent Concerns and Trends." *Research Strategies* 13 (Winter 1995): 4-16.

Examines writings on international students' use of American academic libraries. Issues and concerns are identified and some solutions are proposed. Lists implications for staff development and bibliographic instruction programs.

Nowakowski, Fran, and Elizabeth Frick. "Are Faculty Attitudes Towards Information Literacy Affected by Their Use of Electronic Databases? A Survey." In *Proceedings of the ACRL 7th National Conference.* Ed. by Richard AmRhein, 117-124. Chicago: Association of College and Research Libraries, 1995.

Summarizes a survey of faculty at Dalhousie University in Canada to explore instructors' expectations of students' library knowledge, attitudes towards librarians' roles, and priorities regarding teaching and information literacy, and the instructor's use of the library.

Oberman, Cerise. "Avoiding the Cereal Syndrome; or, Critical Thinking in the Electronic Environment." In *Information for a New Age. Redefining the Librarian.* Ed. by American Library Association Library Instruction Roundtable, 107-119. Englewood, CO: Libraries Unlimited, 1995.

Discusses the important role librarians must play in preparing students in the area of critical thinking and information skills. Advocates the use of an active learning model to accomplish this.

Oberman, Cerise. "Unmasking Technology: A Prelude to Teaching." *Research Strategies* 13 (Winter 1995): 34-39.

States that bibliographic instruction librarians need a more balanced view of technology to present electronic resources in an appropriate context.

Oka, Christine K., et al. "Diversity and Diversifying in a Downsized Library." In *Upside of Downsizing.* Ed. by Cheryl LaGuardia, 183-190. New York: Neal-Schuman, 1995.

Describes diversity efforts at the University of California, Santa Barbara, where downsizing was used as an opportunity to diversify the staff and library services.

Orme, Bill. "A Library Instruction Course Via the Community Learning Network." In *The Impact of Technology on Library Instruction.* Ed. by Linda Shirato, 123-125. Ann Arbor, MI: Pierian Press, 1995.

Describes the community learning network at Indiana University-Purdue University where a course on "information resources and student research" was developed for distance education.

Osborne, Nancy S., and Cecilia Poon. "Serving Diverse Library Populations Through the Specialized Instructional Services Concept." *Reference Librarian* 51-51 (1995): 285-294.

Describes specialized instructional services at the State University of New York College at Oswego as a unique cultural diversity library initiative.

Pasicznyuk, Robert W. "Application Development for User Instruction: Constructing an Interactive Kiosk." *Colorado Libraries* 21 (Summer 1995): 44-45.

Describes the automated reference desk at the University of Colorado in relation to computer-assisted and user instruction.

Pask, Judith M., and Carl E. Snow. "Undergraduate Instruction and the Internet." *Library Trends* 44 (Fall 1995): 306-317.

Describes how specific Internet resources can be integrated into undergraduate teaching and learning and gives some specific problems.

Pastine, Maureen D. "Integrating Library Use Skills into the General Education Curriculum, an Additional Commentary." *Reference Librarian* 51-52 (1995): 15-24.

Gives an overview and introduction to user education and its integration into the curriculum.

Pederson, Ann. "Teaching Over an Interactive Video Network." In *The Impact of Technology on Library Instruction*. Ed. by Linda Shirato, 187-191. Ann Arbor, MI: Pierian Press, 1995.

Explains North Dakota's statewide distance-learning network using interactive video technology and its application to library instruction.

Perry, Clifford. "Travelers on the Internet." *Online* 19 (March/April 1995): 29-34.

Discusses how people actually use the Internet.

Piette, Mary I. "Library Instruction: Principles, Theories, Connections, and Challenges." *Reference Librarian* 51-52 (1995): 77-88.

Discusses principles of learning and instructional theories in relation to the challenges and problems of user instruction.

Powell, James. "Spinning the World-Wide Web: An HTML Primer." *Database* 18 (February/March 1995): 54-59.

Provides a good introduction to using HTML language for the World Wide Web.

Quint, Barbara. "On Beyond Bill Comma Buffalo: Maximum Value, Minimum Resources, and 'Good-Enoughness'." In *Upside of Downsizing*. Ed. by Cheryl LaGuardia, 25-37. New York: Neal-Schuman, 1995.

Discusses the future of bibliographic instruction and calls it document instruction. In the future such instruction must be closely related to user needs and include Internet training.

Rader, Hannelore B. "Information Literacy and the Undergraduate Curriculum." *Library Trends* 44 (Fall 1995): 270-278.

For many years librarians have struggled to integrate library instruction and information literacy into the undergraduate curriculum. Although there have been some successes the struggle continues, especially

in this age of information, technology, and curricular reforms. Provides a case study at Cleveland State University.

Ragains, Patrick. "Four Variations on Drueke's Active Learning Paradigm." *Research Strategies* 13 (Winter 1995): 40-50.

Describes a lesson structured for one-time instructional sessions based on an active learning technique called a "jigsaw method" at the Montana State University. An evaluation of the technique is included.

Ragains, Patrick. "The Legislative/Regulatory Process and BI: A Course-Integrated Unit." *Research Strategies* 13 (Spring 1995): 116-122.

Describes a two-part library instruction unit developed for a community nutrition course at Montana State University using an active learning technique known as the jigsaw method.

Ragains, Patrick. "Promoting U.S. Census Data in an Academic Environment: Opportunities and Challenges." *Journal of Government Information* 22 (July-August 1995): 321-335.

Discusses efforts at Montana State University library to promote use of census data and how instructional sessions are used to facilitate that.

Rettig, James. "The Convergence of the Twain or Titanic Collision? BI and Reference in the 1990's Sea of Change." *Reference Services Review* 23:1 (Spring 1995): 7-20.

Suggests that in the future bibliographic instruction and reference services become a single service.

Ridgeway, Trish. "Too Many Databases and Systems...Too Little Time...How Do You Teach?" In *The Impact of Technology on Library Instruction*. Ed. by Linda Shirato, 181-185. Ann Arbor, MI: Pierian Press, 1995.

Describes how to teach students to search databases and other systems in a constricted time frame.

Rielly, Loretta J., and Garry A. Browning. "Point-of-Use Instruction: The Evolving Role of Stacks Support Staff and Student Assistants in an Academic Library." *Reference Librarian* 51-52 (1995): 195-208.

Describes how stack personnel at Oregon State University have become adjuncts to the library instruction program through training students how to locate materials in the library.

Rodda, Arlene. "The Information Revolution and the Battle between Content and Format." *Computers in Libraries* 15 (February 1995): 40-41.

Many users have become more concerned with format than content when using information resources.

Roeker, Fred. "Successful Research Using the Gateway of Information: Meeting the Challenge of User Independence." In *Upside of Downsizing*. Ed. by Cheryl LaGuardia, 191-202. New York: Neal-Schuman, 1995.

Describes Ohio State University Library's attempt to automate their large library instruction program by using one-stop computer workstations to teach students search strategy for research.

Russell-Bogle, Marilyn, and Deborah Petersen-Perlman. "Managing a Three-Ring Circus: A Case Study of Collaborative Teaching and Learning." In *Upside of Downsizing*. Ed. by Cheryl LaGuardia, 203-215. New York: Neal-Schuman, 1995.

Presents a case study at the University of Minnesota, Duluth, where a librarian and a faculty collaborate to teach students in communication critical thinking and problem solving skills.

Ryan, Steve, and Dean Leith. "Training with the Web: Internet Training in an Academic Library Environment." *Australian Library Journal* 44 (February 1995): 22-26.

Describes the first phase of an Internet overview training program for academic staff at the University of Sydney, in Australia. Uses World Wide Web browsers as an aid in training.

Ryans, Cynthia C., et al. "Assessing an Academic Library Liaison Programme." *Library Review* 44 (1995): 14-23.

Explains academic library liaison programs and how they work and provides a case study from Kent State University in Ohio.

Sager, Harvey. "Implications for Bibliographic Instruction." In *The Impact of Emerging Technologies on Reference Service and Bibliographic Instruction*. Ed. by Gary M. Pitkin, 49-62. Westport, CT: Greenwood Press, 1995.

Reviews bibliographic instruction from the 1960s to the present and technology's influence on how librarians teach users information skills.

Salony, Mary F. "The History of Bibliographic Instruction: Changing Trends from Books to the Electronic World." *Reference Librarian* 51-52 (1995): 31-51.

Provides a detailed overview of the history of bibliographic instruction in academic libraries.

Sauer, Janice A. "Conversation 101: Process, Development and Collaboration." In *Information for a New Age. Redefining the Librarian*. Ed. by American Library Association Library Instruction Roundtable, 135-151. Englewood, CO: Libraries Unlimited, 1995.

Argues that librarians will have a larger, more important role in the future as teachers of information skills in a collaborative learning environment.

Scales, B. Jane, and Mary M. Gilles. "Lexis-Nexis in an Academic Reference Environment: User Policies and Instruction Methods." *Reference Services Review* 23:3 (Fall 1995): 85-90, 96.

Describes a self-instruction program within a workstation to help users learn the use of Lexis-Nexis at Washington State University.

Shaw, Deborah. "Bibliographic Database Searching by Graduate Students in Language and Literature: Search Strategies, System Interfaces, and Relevance Judgements." *Library and Information Science Research* 17 (1995): 327-425.

Summarizes a study of graduate students in language and literature studies searching CD-ROM databases in relationship to their search strategies and value judgments.

Sheridan, Jean. *Writing Across the Curriculum and the Academic Library: A Guide for Librarians, Instructors, and Writing Program Directors*. New York: Greenwood Press, 1995.

Provides guidelines and information on cooperation between faculty and librarians in relation to the curriculum and user instruction for college and university students.

Simmons-Welburn, Janice. "Alternative Models for Instruction in the Academic Library: Another View of the Upside of Downsizing." In *Upside of Downsizing*. Ed. by Cheryl LaGuardia, 15-23. New York: Neal-Schuman, 1995.

Proposes several different approaches to bibliographic instruction utilizing electronic classrooms, computer-assisted instruction at the point of need, and teaching remote users over electronic networks.

Smith, J. Christina, and Andrea Weinschenk. "I'm Coping as Fast as I Can: Instructing the Instructor at Boston University." In *Upside of Downsizing*. Ed. by Cheryl LaGuardia, 217-228. New York: Neal-Schuman, 1995.

Discusses how Boston University librarians trained instructors of introductory courses to teach students library and research skills to relieve librarians' workloads.

Snyder, Lise. "The Human Touch: It's Future in a World of Bibliographic Instruction Technology." *Catholic Library World* 65 (January-March 1995): 17-18.

Discusses the librarian's role as human, value-added interface in the technological library environment and user instruction.

Stoffle, Carla. "The Upside of Downsizing: Using the Economic Crisis to Restructure and Revitalize Academic Libraries." In *Upside of Downsizing*. Ed. by Cheryl LaGuardia, 1-15. New York: Neal-Schuman, 1995.

Outlines the current academic environment and how it affects libraries, especially, in the area of funding. Discusses library services in terms of user needs for training and library instruction.

Suresh, Raghini S., et al. "The Library-Faculty Connection. Starting a Liaison Programme in an Academic Setting." *Library Review* 44 (1995): 7-13.

Defines liaison programs in academic libraries and discusses their importance in building collaboration with faculty in collection building and user instruction.

Sutton, Ellen D., et al. "Bibliographic Instruction in Psychology: A Review of the Literature." *Reference Services Review* 23:3 (Fall 1995): 13-22.

Presents information sources for librarians providing library instruction in psychology.

Tenopir, Carol. "Impacts of Electronic References on Instruction and Reference." In *The Impact of Technology on Library Instruction*. Ed. by Linda Shirato, 1-8. Ann Arbor, MI: Pierian Press, 1995.

Summarizes a survey of academic research libraries to assess the effect of electronic resources on librarians. Among the findings emerged a stronger teaching role of librarians, a rethinking of how instruction and reference may be done, and the fact that users will continue to need guidance and assistance in academic libraries.

Tenopir, Carol. "Online Databases." *Library Journal* 120 (April 1995): 39-40.

Compares current and past results from two surveys to determine how electronic reference services affect staff, patron expectations, and user instruction.

Thompson, Gary B., and Billie Reinhart. "The Concept of Equity: Applications for Electronic Reference and Information Literacy." In *Proceedings of the ACRL 7th National Conference*. Ed. by Richard AmRhein, 295-299. Chicago: Association of College and Research Libraries, 1995.

Explains the concept of equity in relation to reference service and information literacy and provides suggestions for the future.

Tiefel, Virginia. "Education for the Academic Library User in the Year 2000." In *Information for a New Age. Redefining the Librarian*. Ed. by American Library Association Library Instruction Roundtable, 57-77. Englewood, CO: Libraries Unlimited, 1995.

Discusses current and future goals for library instruction in the academic environment within a growing technological environment.

Tiefel, Virginia. "Library User Education: Examining Its Past, Projecting Its Future." *Library Trends* 44 (Fall 1995): 318-338.

Examines the role of library instruction in the present and future of academic libraries by looking at its history and current status.

Turner, Diane J., and Marilyn E. Grotzky. "They Teach Too: A Role for Paraprofessionals in Library Instruction." *Reference Librarian* 51-52 (1995): 181-193.

Describes the library instruction program at Auraria Library in Colorado where one-third of the instruction is handled by paraprofessionals.

Tyson, John C. "The Impact of Emerging Technologies on Library Clientele." In *The Impact of Emerging Technologies on Reference Service and Bibliographic Instruction*. Ed. by Gary M. Pitkin, 63-73. Westport, CT: Greenwood Press, 1995.

Discusses the academic library's role in computer and information literacy for students.

Ury, Connie J., and Terry L. King. "Reinforcement of Library Orientation Instruction for Freshman Seminar Students." *Research Strategies* 13 (Summer 1995): 153-164.

Describes a study at Northwest Missouri State University to determine which of two methods of teaching library orientation produces better retention.

Walsh, Mary Jane. "Graphic Design for Library Publications." In *The Impact of Technology on Library Instruction*. Ed. by Linda Shirato, 141-158. Ann Arbor, MI: Pierian Press, 1995.

Provides guidelines for planning, designing, and preparing appealing library publications.

Weissinger, Nancy J., and John P.L. Edwards. "Online Resources for Internet Trainers." *College and Research Libraries News* 56 (September 1995): 535-539, 572.

Lists course materials, guides, and tutorials both in print and online to help librarians teach the use of the Internet.

Wells, Jennifer. "The Influence of Library Usage on Undergraduate Academic Success." *Australian Academic and Research Libraries* 26 (June 1995): 121-128.

Describes a study of undergraduates at the University of Western Sydney to assess the influence of library usage on academic success. Positive correlation was found between academic achievement and the use of a number of different library resources and services.

West, Sharon M., and Diane Ruess. "The Electronic Library: Teaching Students at a Distance." In *The Impact of Technology on Library Instruction*. Ed. by Linda Shirato, 135-140. Ann Arbor, MI: Pierian Press, 1995.

Describes the distance-education library instruction program at the University of Alaska, Fairbanks, by combining the online systems in the library with the telecommunication system.

White, Fred D. *Information Management and Composing: Reassessing Our Research Paper Protocols*. ERIC Reproduction Service, 1995. ED 384 897.

Discusses how to teach students the effective writing of research papers, especially the use of information in support of an original thesis.

White, Robert L., and Lee David Jaffe. "Rewiring a Working Library of Teaching an Old Dog New Tricks." *Online* 19 (January 1995): 62-68.

Whitehead, Anita, and Maxine M. Long. "Providing Off-Campus Bibliographic Instruction: When Off-Campus Means Someone Else's Campus." *Reference Librarian* 51-52 (1995): 171-180.

Focuses on the experiences of Genesee Community College in New York, where distance-education students receive bibliographic instruction in a library of another campus.

Whitson, William L. "Differentiated Services: A Reference Model." *Journal of Academic Librarianship* 21 (March 1995): 103-110.

Examines a variety of traditional reference services including library instruction, and suggests that service should be built on user needs and staff skills.

Whyte, Susan B. "Spanning the Distance: Using Computer Conferencing as Part of a Team-Taught Research/Writing Class." *Reference Librarian* 51-52 (1995): 267-279.

Describes a team-taught research and writing class for adult students who are geographically dispersed within the state of Oregon using computer conferencing.

Willis, Elizabeth I., and Diane J. Turner. "Streamlining Library Instruction: The Auraria Experience." *Research Strategies* 13 (Spring 1995): 107-115.

Describes how librarians at the Auraria Libraries in Colorado have rethought their traditional classroom-based instruction program for lower level undergraduates and changed to a self-directed program.

Wilson, Lizabeth A. "Library Literacy: Building the User-Centered Library." *RQ* 34 (Spring 1995): 297-302.

Describes user-centered services at the University of Washington and the implications for services.

Wilson, Lizabeth A., et al. "Cooperative Learning: A Guided Discovery Workshop." In *The Impact of Technology on Library Instruction*. Ed. by Linda Shirato, 21-75. Ann Arbor, MI: Pierian Press, 1995.

Provides an overview of cooperative learning, its rationale and research base, as well as an introduction to various techniques and implementation issues.

Wilson, Vicky. "Information Literacy and Remote External Students: Exploring the Possibilities Offered by New Communications Technologies." *Australian Academic and Research Libraries* 25 (December 1994): 247-252.

Wilson, Vicky. "Learning to Learn: The Acquisition of Information Literacy by Isolated Students of Edith Cowan University." *Education for Library and Information Services: Australia* (May 1995): 19-.

Examines adult learning theory and the concepts of information literacy. Reports responses to a study to examine level of satisfaction with present information literacy skills teaching at Edith Cowan University.

Withers, Carol. "Teaching Scratch Paper." *College and Research Libraries News* 56 (March 1995): 160, 183.

Provides an example of minimalist library instruction.

Wittkopf, Barbara. "Current Trends in User Education in the United States." *Booklet 7: 61st IFLA General Conference Proceedings, August 20-25, 1995*. Istanbul, Turkey: International Federation of Library Associations, 119-129.

Provides a detailed overview of user education in the United States in relation to simple retrieval methods for students of periodical articles at New Mexico State University.

Wittkopf, Barbara. "Is Your Library a Learning Organization?" *Research Strategies* 13 (Winter 1995): 2-3.

Discusses the learning organization in terms of Peter Senge's book *The Fifth Discipline*, which advocates the value of individual and collective continuous learning.

Worley, Joan H. "KAPOW: The Impact of CD-ROMs on Bibliographic Instruction." In *Upside of Downsizing*. Ed. by Cheryl LaGuardia, 229-237. New York: Neal-Schuman, 1995.

Advocates flexibility on the part of librarians when dealing with library instruction in the area of technology and new information formats to ensure that students continue to learn what is needed.

Young, JoAnne. "Faculty Collaboration and Academic Librarians." *Catholic Library World* 66 (September 1955): 16-21.

Discusses the results of a survey of faculty and administrators at four academic institutions to determine how librarians are perceived by their colleagues in academia.

Young, Virginia E., and Linda G. Ackerson. "Evaluation of Student Research Paper Bibliographies: Refining Evaluation Criteria." *Research Strategies* 13 (Spring 1995): 80-93.

Reports a five-semester study at the University of Alabama comparing two bibliographic instruction programs by using the Kohl and Wilson criteria measuring each method's effect on student term paper bibliographies.

Public Libraries

Dupuis, Alice A. "Bibliographic Instruction at the Miami-Dade Public Library." *Florida Libraries* 38 (March 1995): 45.

Describes a user instruction program at the Miami-Dade Public Library in Florida.

Dupuis, Alice A. "Education Express: Workshops in the Public Library." *Florida Libraries* 38 (November/December 1995): 141.

Provides information on a public library user instruction program at the Miami-Dade Public Library.

Halverstadt, Julie. "Catering to Students. A Public Library Serves Alternative Schools." *School Library Journal* 41 (July 1995): 16-18.

Discusses library skills instruction for students taught at home.

Jackson, Susan. "Information Literacy and the Public Libraries: A Community-Based Approach." In *Information for a New Age. Redefining the Librarian*. Ed. by American Library Association Library Instruction Roundtable, 35-45. Englewood, CO: Libraries Unlimited, 1995.

Discusses the importance of information literacy for public libraries in relationship to lifelong learning, active citizenship, and informed decision making and how the community can become involved in teaching these skills.

McClure, Charles R. "Public Access to the Information Superhighway through the Nation's Libraries." *Public Libraries* 34 (March 1995): 80-84.

A call to action for public librarians to become involved in introducing the public to Internet resources and ensure that citizens receive information literacy training to utilize this important resource.

School Libraries

Aaron, Shirley L. "Bridges, Windows and Frameworks: A Twenty-First Century School Library Media Education Curriculum." *School Library Media Annual* 13 (1995): 24-30.

Discusses future education for school librarians in view of the school restructuring, global perspectives, individual learning styles, and information literacy.

Abdulezer, Susan. *The HyperSign Project*. Eric Reproduction Service, 1995. ED 380 927.

Describes ongoing activities and results of the HyperSign Immersion Project developed at the Public School for the Deaf in New York to help students improve literacy and math skills in a self-directed way.

American Association of School Librarians. "Information Literacy: A Position Paper on Information Problem Solving." *Emergency Librarian* 23 (November/December 1995): 20-23.

This position paper provides guidelines for teachers and librarians to incorporate information and problem-solving skills throughout the curriculum while restructuring learning.

Barron, Daniel D. "Constructivism: New Ways to Love Them to Learn." *School Library Media Activities Monthly* 12 (February 1995): 48-50.

Discusses information literacy and transferrable library skills as the result of active learning and curriculum-integrated library instruction.

Callison, Daniel. "Expanding the Evaluation Role in the Critical Thinking Curriculum." In *Information for a New Age. Redefining the Librarian*, 153-169. Englewood, CO: Libraries Unlimited, 1995.

Assesses the expanding role of information literacy in the education environment for all levels. Discusses the expanding role of librarians and the school media center within the curriculum.

Callison, Daniel. "Restructuring Pre-Service Education." *School Library Media Annual* 13 (1995): 100-112.

Lists steps to improve pre-service education for teachers and school library media specialists by including library and information-literacy skills instruction.

Dame, Melvina A. "Teaching Library Skills and Content to Linguistically Diverse Students: The Role of Advance Organizers and Visual Resources." *Multi-Cultural Review* 4 (December 1995): 40-44.

Discusses how to link library skills with existing knowledge students have of ESL (English as a Second Language). Suggests the use of multi-sensory aids to help students learn new concepts through association with prior knowledge.

Duncko, Theresa, et al. "Into the Curriculum." *School Library Media Activities Monthly* 12 (September 1995): 14-30.

Presents six library activity guides for reading, science, and social studies.

Eaton, Gale, and Cheryl McCarthy. "The Art of the Possible: Integrating Information Skills and Literature into the Curriculum." *Emergency Librarian* 23 (September-October 1995): 24-29.

Describes how a teacher-librarian at an elementary school in Rhode Island applied the challenges of information power to realize the educational outcomes for the students.

Eisenberg, Michael B. "The Six Habits of Highly Effective Students; Using the Big Six to Link Parents, Students and Homework." *School Library Journal* 41 (August 1995): 22-25.

Outlines several steps for parents to help their children with homework and discusses how to prepare students for assignments during information literacy instruction.

Garland, Kathleen. "The Information Search Process: A Study of Elements Associated with Meaningful Research Tasks." *School Libraries Worldwide* 1 (January 1995): 41-53.

Describes a study at a Michigan high school that investigated elements that contributed to a meaningful library research project.

Gillen, Rose. "Celebrating Our Animal Friends." An Across-the-Curriculum Unit for Middle Level Students." *School Library Media Activities Monthly* 12 (December 1995): 15-18.

Provides library media skill objectives, curriculum objectives, required resources, activities, and evaluation for junior high school students.

Hancock, Vicki E. "Information Literacy, Brain-Based Learning, and the Technological Revolution: Implications for Education." *School Library Media Activities Monthly* 12 (September 1995): 31-34.

Presents 12 principles for learning to serve as guidelines for instructional programs and methods including information literacy skills instruction.

Hycock, Ken. "Research in Teacher-Librarianship and the Institutionalization of Change." *School Library Media Quarterly* 23 (Summer 1995): 227-233.

Discusses the importance of involving school library media specialists in the teaching/learning process to further the development of student competence.

Henri, James, and Lyn Hay. "Teacher-Librarians Must Be Principally Minded." *School Libraries in Canada* 15 (Fall 1995): 20-21.

Discusses the importance of principals understanding the value of information literacy and their support of it in terms of teacher-librarian relationships.

Hodges, V. Pauline. "Teaching Writing to At-Risk Students in a Rural High School." *Rural Educator* 16 (Winter 1994-95): 28-31.

Describes strategies for improving writing skills of rural at-risk high school students including writing stories for kindergarten students.

"Into the Curriculum." *School Library Media Activities Monthly* 11 (January/February 1995): 15-30.

Provides six fully developed library media activities designed for art, reading, science, and social studies. (Other issues of this journal include similar curriculum guides for library and information skills.)

Kuhlthau, Carol C. "The Instructional Role of the Library Media Specialist in the Information Age School." In *Information for a New Age. Redefining the Librarian*. Ed. by American Library Association Library Instruction Roundtable, 47-55. Englewood, CO: Libraries Unlimited, 1995.

Discusses three current trends in schools, the move toward information literacy for all students, the move to skills instruction, and the integration of the school media center into the curriculum.

Kuhne, Brigitte. "The Library—the Brain of the School?" *Scandinavian Public Library Quarterly* 28 (1995): 11-19.

Summarizes a study at Malmo Institute of Education in Sweden about user instruction for elementary and high school students.

McInturff, Johanna R. *Creating a Public Domain Software Library to Increase Computer Access of Elementary Students with Learning Disabilities*. ERIC Reproduction Center, 1995. ED 385 179.

Provides information on a practicum that addressed the lack of access to computer-aided instruction by elementary-level students with learning disabilities.

Moore, Penny. "Information Problem Solving: A Wider View of Library Skills." *Contemporary Educational Psychology* 20 (January 1995): 1-31.

This study examined the cognitive and metacognitive demands of information retrieval and use for an elementary school research assignment.

Neal, Nancy L. *Research and Publication on the World Wide Web: A Fifth Grade Class' Experience*. ERIC Reproduction Center, 1995. ED 384 345.

Teachers are discovering valuable applications of the Web within their classrooms. Explores use of the Web as a research and publication tool in a fifth-grade class project on the formation of the United States.

O'Brien, Eileen, et al. *Libraries/Media Centers in Schools: Are There Sufficient Resources?* ERIC Reproduction Service, 1995. ED 385 293.

Discusses the role of the library/media center in school reform.

Pitts, Judy M. "Mental Models of Information: The 1993-94 AASL/Highsmith Research Award Study." *School Library Media Quarterly* 23 (1995): 177-184.

Discusses how library instruction must be based on how students learn.

Sanders, Evelin. *Library Research Assignments: Photocopyable Worksheets Across the Curriculum for High Schools*. Jefferson, NC: McFarland, 1995.

Provides problems and exercises to teach library skills to high school students.

Simpson, Carol M. *Internet for Library Media Specialists*. ERIC Reproduction Service, 1995. ED 381 165.

Introduces library media specialists to the Internet and gives specific uses of the Internet in school libraries.

Stripling, Barbara K. "Learning-Centered Libraries: Implications from Research." *School Library Media Quarterly* 23 (1995): 163-170.

Discusses implication of Judy M. Pitts' research on student learning and how it can assist teachers and librarians in teaching information skills to students.

Tallman, Julie I. "Connecting Writing and Research through the I-Search Paper: A Teaching Partnership between the Library Program and Classroom." *Emergency Librarian* 23 (September/October 1995): 20-23.

Describes the library instruction experiences at Stearns High School in Millinocket, Maine, where librarians and teachers work within the curriculum to provide students with library skills.

Tallman, Julie I. "Curriculum Consultation: Strengthening Activity through Multiple-Content Area Units." *School Library Media Quarterly* 24 (Fall 1995): 27-33.

Analyzes an earlier study regarding librarians' relationship with teachers and involvement in the curriculum in regards to library skills teaching.

Taylor, Nansi. "Find the Lady...Once and Future Skills." *School Librarian* 43 (February 1995): 11-13.

Describes a program for 12- to 13-year-olds in Great Britain to teach them library skills through questions and answers.

Teaching Information Retrieval and Evaluation Skills to Education Students and Practitioners. A Casebook of Applications. Ed. by Patricia O. Libutti and Bonnie Gratch. Chicago: American Library Association, 1995.

This casebook intends to assist education librarians with teaching information literacy concepts and processes through many examples of teaching learning situations in K-12 situations. Includes examples for teaching graduate students and practitioners information literacy.

Todd, Ross J. "Integrated Information Skills Instruction: Does It Make a Difference?" *School Library Media Quarterly* 23 (Winter 1995): 133-138.

Documents ongoing research in Sydney, Australia, into impact of information-literacy programs on student learning. Defines information skills and the competencies to be achieved.

Todd, Ross J. "What Research Will Be Required to Lead and Support the Future Information Professional?" *School Library Media Annual* 13 (1995): 39-44.

Examines research in relation to preparing future information professionals in the context of school education, multimedia, new technologies, individual learning styles, and information literacy.

Troutner, Joanne. "Internet Resources." *Emergency Librarian* 23 (November-December 1995): 43-44.

Discusses policies for the use of the Internet in school libraries.

Tuttle, Harry G. "From Productivity to Collaboration. Part I: School Networks Deliver Innovative Education." *MultiMedia Schools* 2 (March/April 1995): 31-35.

Examines the use of various networks in schools for productivity and student activities.

Van Deusen, Jean D. "Prerequisites to Flexible Planning." *Emergency Librarian* 23 (September/October 1995): 16-19.

Discusses flexible planning with teachers and school librarians to bring library skills into the curriculum.

Wesson, Caren L., et al. *Serving Special Needs Students in the School Library Media Center. Greenwood Professional Guides in School Librarianship.* ERIC Reproduction Service, 1995. ED 385 999.

These papers consider how the school library media specialist serves special needs students and classroom teachers in multiple roles as teacher, information specialist, and instructional consultant.

White, Jackie. "Information Literacy in School Libraries." *Kentucky Libraries* 59 (Summer 1995): 16-17.

Advocates that library media specialists promote information literacy throughout the school community and provides guidelines for Kentucky.

Special Libraries

Adams, Mignon S. "Library Instruction in Special Libraries: Present and Future." *Information for a New Age. Redefining the Librarian*, 79-87. Englewood, CO: Libraries Unlimited, 1995.

Discusses current and future trends in special libraries related to information training, especially in the virtual environment and regarding remote users.

Brandt, Kerryn A., and Jayne M. Campbell. "Bibliographic Instruction Plus: A Short Course in Scientific Communication for Graduate Students in the Basic Sciences." *Medical Reference Services Quarterly* 14 (Winter 1995): 77-85.

Describes a short intensive course for medical students at Johns Hopkins University in Baltimore, which teaches students Medline and beyond.

Canning, Cheryl S. "Using Focus Groups to Evaluate Library Services in a Problem-Based Learning Curriculum." *Medical Reference Services Quarterly* 14 (Fall 1995): 75-81.

Describes how focus groups were used at the University of Missouri, Columbia School of Medicine library to evaluate the bibliographic training programs and library services as related to the curriculum.

Courtois, Martin P., et al. "Cool Tools for Searching the Web: A Performance Evaluation." *Online* 19 (November/December 1995): 14-32.

Discusses the best search engines on the World Wide Web.

Duff, Alistair S. "Using Medical Dictionaries to Teach the Critical Evaluation of Information Sources." *Nurse Education Today* 15 (April 1995): 121-124.

A course-integrated library instruction session was developed to help students gain skills in evaluating biomedical information sources.

Francis, Barbara W., and Clarissa C. Fisher. "Multilevel Library Instruction for Emerging Nursing Roles." *Bulletin of the Medical Library Association* 83 (October 1993): 492-498.

Describes a program presented at the Medical Library Association conference on providing future nurses with information skills.

Fraysse, Susan, and Dale Luchsinger. "Technical Institute Libraries: Georgia's Best-Kept Secret!" *Georgia Librarian* 32 (Spring 1995): 4-8.

Profiles eight successful library/media/information technology programs at technical institutes in Georgia. Includes information on library instruction.

Harris, Sylvia. "Into the 21st Century Now: The Architecture Librarian as Mediator." *Art Libraries Journal* 20 (1995): 18-20.

Discusses the important role architecture librarians play in preparing architects and architecture students for research and information use.

Hughes, Glenda J., et al. "Cartobibliographic Instruction: Another Path in the Library Instruction Program." *Reference Librarian* 51-52 (1995): 399-414.

Encourages the inclusion of cartobibliographic instruction as part of library instruction programs in view of the abundance of such materials across the curriculum.

Layton, Beth, and Karla L. Hahn. "The Librarian as a Partner in Nursing Education." *Bulletin of the Medical Library Association* 83 (October 1995): 499-502.

Summarizes a program delivered at the 1994 Medical Library Association conference involved with providing nursing students with bibliographic instruction.

McGowan, Julie J. "The Role of Health Sciences Librarians in the Teaching and Retention of the Knowledge, Skills, and Attitudes of Lifelong Learning." *Bulletin of the Medical Library Association* 83 (April 1995): 184-189.

Summarizes research that found no different perceptions of lifelong learning between graduates of problem-based learning curricula and traditional curricula. Suggests new ways to assess teaching and retention of knowledge, skills, and lifelong learning skills and the important role librarians should play.

Ng, Wendy E. "Students' Legal Research Skills: They Only Have Themselves to Blame." *Canadian Law Libraries* 20 (Winter 1995): 205-208.

Discusses low competency in legal research due to insufficient training in law schools. Talks about research training in law firms as compared to that in law schools.

Nicholls, Paul. "CD-ROM and Multi-Media Trends: The Year in Review." *Computers in Libraries* 15 (November/December 1995): 56-60.

Discusses how the Internet supplements Lexis/Nexis and may in the future influence online services.

Schwartz, Diane G. "How Physicians and Biomedical Scientists in India Learn Information-Seeking Skills." *Bulletin of the Medical Library Association* 83 (July 1995): 360-362.

Describes a program given at the 1993 Medical Library Association conference regarding bibliographic instruction for medical students.

Staheli, Kory D. "Motivating Law Students to Develop Competent Legal Research Skills: Combating the Negative Findings of the Howland and Lewis Survey." *Legal Reference Services Quarterly* 14 (1994): 195-203.

Addresses methods that law librarians can use to eliminate negative attitudes on the part of law students toward legal research.

Strife, Mary L. "Special Libraries and Instruction: One-on-One Public Relations." *Reference Librarian* 51-52 (1995): 415-419.

Discusses how to use the library and information skills instruction in marketing the special library.

Tooey, Mary J. "Planning an Internet Curriculum." *Medical Reference Services Quarterly* 14 (Summer 1995): 85-89.

Describes a cooperative effort between the health sciences librarians and the Information Services Division staff at the University of Maryland, Baltimore, to develop an Internet curriculum for students.

Warling, Brian N., and Christopher S. Stave. "The Health Sciences Librarian as Internet Navigator and Interpreter." *Bulletin of the Medical Library Association* 83 (October 1995): 395-401.

Shows how health sciences librarians can play an increasingly important role in shaping the information policies and practices within their institutions due to the electronic information environment.

All Levels

American Library Association. "Information Literacy." In *Information for a New Age: Redefining the Librarian*. Ed. by American Library Association Library Instruction Roundtable, 89-105. Englewood, CO: Libraries Unlimited, 1995.

This is a reprint of the American Library Association Presidential Committee on Information Literacy Final Report, issued in 1989.

Barclay, Donald. *Teaching Electronic Information Literacy. A How-To-Do-It Manual*. New York: Neal-Schuman, 1995.

This guide will help librarians and others teach users to access and use electronic information. Includes helpful guidance to introduce, guide, and instruct people in the use of the Internet and related electronic information resources so that they can become full participants in the information society.

Billings, Harold. "The Tomorrow Librarians." *Wilson Library Bulletin* 69 (January 1995): 34-37.

Discusses the future of librarians, libraries, and library schools in the age of electronic information. Comments on the role of the librarian in instruction.

Doran, Kirk. "The Internot: Helping Library Patrons Understand What the Internet Is Not (Yet)." *Computers in Libraries* 15 (June 1995): 22, 24, 26.

Discusses the Internet and the need for librarians to teach patrons how to use it effectively.

Doyle, Christina S. "ERIC Digest: Information Literacy in an Information Society." *Emergency Librarian* 22 (March/April 1995): 30-32.

This bibliography features references to bibliographic instruction, critical thinking, and information literacy publications.

"Electronic Information Sources: Guidelines for Training Sessions." *RQ* 35 (Winter 1995): 187-192.

These guidelines are intended to aid trainers in preparing to teach sessions and to assist those attending in evaluating such sessions.

Ensor, Pat L. "Library Instruction in the Digital Age: Least Likely to Succeed?" *Technicalities* 15 (July 1995): 10-12.

Gives some thoughts on evaluating library instruction in the electronic age.

Ford, Barbara J. "Information Literacy as a Barrier." *IFLA Journal* 21 (February 1995): 99-101.

Discusses the need for and definition of information literacy in the Information Age around the world and how the lack of information skills will constitute a barrier to personal and national empowerment and development.

Galler, Anne M. "Strategies to Educate Librarians to Introduce New Technologies to Users, Especially Disadvantaged Ones." *61st IFLA General Conference Proceedings, August 20-25, 1995.* Istanbul, Turkey: International Federation of Library Associations, 1995.

Suggests strategies for librarians to train themselves and to introduce users to specific technologies such as online searching and the Internet.

Gorman, Michael. "The Domino Effect, or Why Literacy Depends on All Libraries." *School Library Journal* 41 (April 1995): 27-29.

Discusses the relationship between declining literacy levels and a lack of library skills in view of California's Proposition 13 and proposes a program of cooperation between libraries and schools.

Rader, Hannelore B. "Library Orientation and Instruction-1994." *Reference Services Review* 23:4 (Winter 1995): 83-96.

Provides a comprehensive, annual review of the library instruction and information literature in English for all types of libraries.

Shonrock, Diana D. *Evaluating Library Instruction. Sample Questions, Forms and Strategies for Practical Use.* Chicago: American Library Association, Research Committee, Library Instruction Round Table, 1995.

This is a simple guide to developing, conducting, and tabulating a library services survey or evaluation and programs relating to user instruction. Includes 14 sections of sample questions for various settings, appendixes with sample forms, glossary, and a bibliography.

Tennant, Roy. "The Virtual Library Foundation: Staff Training and Support." *Information Technology and Libraries* 14 (March 1995): 46-49.

Considers the need for staff training in virtual libraries; highlights instruction and training, self-paced instruction, electronic discussions, and other types of online learning and teaching.

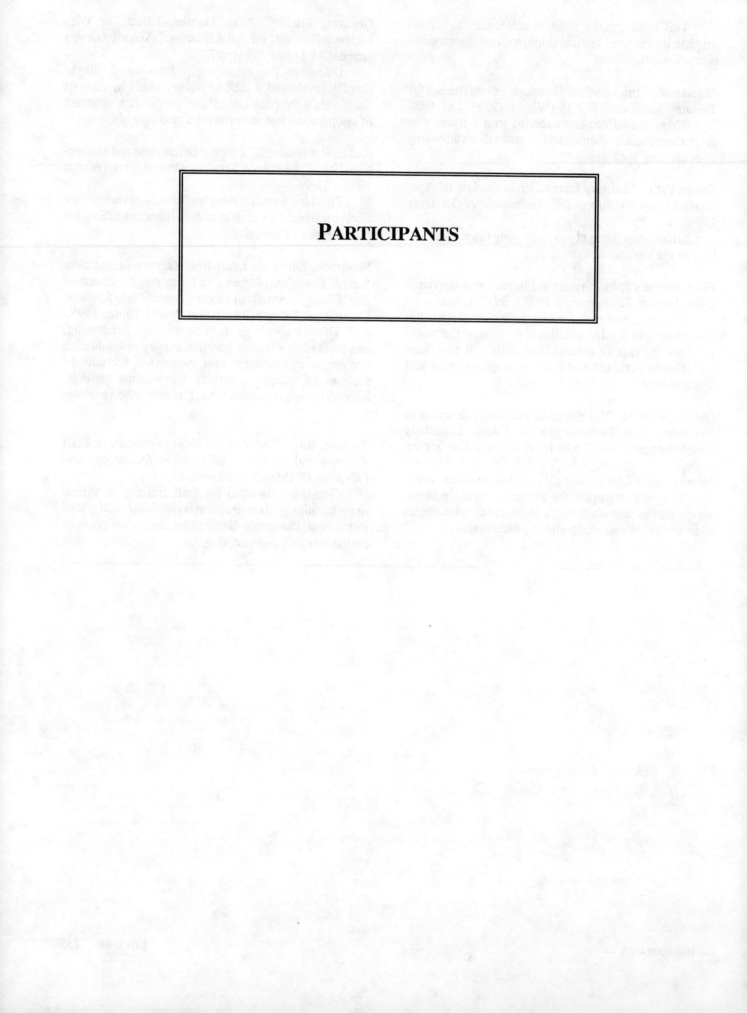

PARTICIPANTS

Sallie J. Alger
James White Library
Andrews University
Berrien Springs, MI 49104
alger@andrews.edu

Judith Arnold
Waldo Library
Western Michigan University
Kalamazoo, MI 49008
judith.arnold@wmich.edu

Donna Bachmann
University of Puget
        Sound Library
Tacoma, WA 98416

Joe Badics
Eastern Michigan University
        Library
Ypsilanti, MI 48197

Anne Barker
Pius XII Library
St. Louis University
St. Louis, MO 63108-3302
barker@sluvca.slu.edu

Mary Barton
Livingston Lord Library
Moorhead State University
Moorhead, MN 56563
bartonm@mhd1.moorhead.
        msus.edu

Abbie Basile
Folsom Library
Rensselaer Polytechnic Institute
Troy, NY 12180
basila@rpi.edu

Georgia Baugh
Pius XII Library
Saint Louis University
St. Louis, MO 63108
baugha@sluvca.slu.edu

Goodie Bhullar
Ellis Library
University of Missouri
Columbia, MO 65201
ellisgb@mizzoul.
        missouri.edu

Cheryl Blackwell
Albion College Library
Albion, MI 49224
cblackwell@alph.albion.edu

Sarah Blakeslee
Meriam Library
CSU Chico
Chico, CA 95929-0295
sarah_blakeslee@margate.
        csuchico.edu

Jane T. Bradford
duPont-Ball Library
Stetson University
DeLand, FL 32720
bradford@mbox.stetson.edu

Ann Breitenwischer
Libraries
Ferris State University
Big Rapids, MI 49307
breitenw@libol.ferris.edu

Judith Brow
Delta College Library
University Center, MI 48710
judith_brow@delta.edu

Barbara Burg
Widener Library
Harvard University
Cambridge, MA 02138
bburg@fas.harvard.edu

Suzanne Byron
UNT Libraries
University of North Texas
Denton, TX 76203
sbyron@library.unt.edu

Patti Caravello
UCLA University
Research Library
Los Angeles, CA 90095
ecz5psc@mvs.aoc.ucla.edu

Linda Carder
Kent Library
Southeast Missouri State
        University
Cape Girardeau, MO 63701
c351lib@semovm.semo.edu

Elizabeth Carroll
Library
American University
Washington, DC 20016
carroll@american.edu

Betsey Carter
Daniel Library
The Citadel
Charleston, SC 29409
cartere@citadel.edu

Holly Chambers
Crumb Library
SUNY-Potsdam
Potsdam, NY 13676
chamberhe@potsdam.edu

Lena Chang
Library
Holy Names College
Oakland, CA 94619
chang@academmail.hnc.edu

Madeleine Charney
Ely Library
Westfield State College
Westfield, MA 01086
m_charney@foma.wsc.mass.edu

Danielle Clarke
Beehgly Library
Ohio Wesleyan University
Delaware, OH 43015
mdclarke@ccowu.edu

Derek Dixon
Library
John Carroll University
University Hts., OH 44118
ddixon@jcvaxa.jcu.edu

Meg Frazier
Loop Campus Library
DePaul University
Chicago, IL 60604
mfrazier@wppost.depaul.edu

Nancy Clark Fogarty
Jackson Library
UNC-Greensboro
Greensboro, NC 27412
fogartyn@uncg.edu

Rosemarie Cooper
Richardson Library
DePaul University
Chicago, IL 60014
rcooper@wwpost.depaul.edu

Susan Cooperstein
Loyola/Notre Dame Library
Loyola College
Baltimore, MD 21212
cooperstein@loyola.edu

Rosanne Cordell
Schurz Library
IU-South Bend
South Bend, IN 46634
rcordell@indiana.edu

Julie Czisny
Payson Library
Pepperdine University
Malibu, CA 90263
jczisny@pepperdine.edu

Mary Cummings
Library
Shawnee State University
Portsmouth, OH 45662
mcummings@shawnee.edu

Joan D'Andrea
Library
St. John's University
Jamaica, NY 11439

Bill Deese
Payson Library
Pepperdine University
Malibu, CA 90263-4786

Brian DeHart
Loop Campus Library
DePaul University
Chicago, IL 60604
bdehart@wppost.depaul

Edward DeLong
Meyer Library
Southwest Missouri State
    University
Springfield, MO 65804
ejd449f@vma.smsu.edu

Linnea Dudley
Library
Marygrove College
Detroit, MI 48221-2599
marygrov@mlc.lib.mi.us

Ron Edwards
Jerome Library
Bowling Green State University
Bowling Green, OH
redward@bgnet.bgsu.edu

Sherry Evans
Fogelson Library
College of Santa Fe
1600 St. Michael's Drive
Santa Fe, NM 87501
sevans@fogelson.csf.edu

Sally Fagan
Library
Davenport College
Holland, MI 49423
sfagan@davenport.edu

Margaret Fain
Library
Coastal Carolina University
Conway, SC 29526
margaret@coastal.edu

Deborah Fink
University of Colorado Libraries
Boulder, CO 80389
deborah.fink@colorado.edu

Iva Freeman
Library
Kendall College
Evanston, IL 60201
freemani@nslsilus.org

Joanne Galanis
Library
St. Louis Community College
Florissant Valley
St. Louis, MO 63105
c1737054@umsl.vma.edu

Kay L. Garsnett
St. Florence Library
Our Lady of the Lake University
San Antonio, TX 78207-4689

Cheryl Ghosh
Langsam Library
University of Cincinnati
Cincinnati, OH 45221-0033
cheryl.ghosh@uc.edu

Debra Gilchrist
Library
Pierce College
Tacoma, WA
dgilchri@ctc.ctc.edu

Ronda Glikin
Eastern Michigan University
    Library
Ypsilanti, MI 48197
lib_glikin@online.emich.edu

Linda L. Glover
Harper College Library
Palatino, IL 60067
lglover@harper.cc.il.us

Gail Gradowski
Orradre Library
Santa Clara University
Santa Clara, CA 95053
ggradowski@scuacc.scu.edu

Marilyn Graubart
Miller Nichols Library
University of Missouri-Kansas
    City
Kansas City, MO 64110
graubarm@smtpgate.umkc.edu

Rachel Greeley
Library
University of Missouri
Columbia, MO 65201
mulgree@mizzou1.missouri.edu

Brenda Faye Green
Health Sciences Library
University of Tennessee-
    Memphis
Memphis, TN 38163
bfgreen@utmem.edu

Paul Gregorio
Shoen Library
Marylhurst College
Marylhurst, OR 97036

Barbara Greil
Hinkle Library
SUNY College of Technology
Alfred, NY 14802
greilbj@snyalfra.cc.alfred
    tech.edu

Elizabeth Gulacsy
Scholes Library
NY State College of Ceramics
Alfred, NY 14802
gulacsy@bigvax.alfred.edu

Becky Hagen O'Shaughnessy-
    Frey
Library
University of St. Thomas
St. Paul, MN 55105
rlhagen@stthomas.edu

Trudi Bellardo Hahn
UMPC Libraries
University of Maryland
College Park, MD 20742
th90@umail.umd.edu

Julie Hansen
Lovejoy Library
Southern Illinois
University at Edwardsville
Edwardsville, IL 62026
jhansen@siue.edu

Naomi Harrison
Olin Library
Rollins College
Winter Park, FL 32789

Cynthia Mae Helms
Library
Andrews University
Berrien Springs, MI 49104-1400
helms@andrews.edu

Patricia Herrling
Steenbock Library
University of Wisconsin
Madison, WI 53706
pherrling@doit.wisc.edu

Sharon Hewitt
Harford Community College
    Library
Bel Air, MD 21015
shewitt@mail.bcpl.lib.md.us

Beth Hillemann
DeWitt Wallace Library
Macalester College
St. Paul, MN 55105
hillemann@macalester.edu

Carole Hinshaw
University of Central Florida
    Library
Orlando, FL 32816-2666
chinshaw@pegasus.cc.ucf.edu

Gretchen McCord Hoffmann
Anderson Library
University of Houston
Houston, TX 77204-2091
gmhoffmann@uh.edu

Gerald Holmes
Langsam Library
University of Cincinnati
Cincinnati, OH 45221
gerald.holmes@uc.edu

Charlene Hovatter
Hillman Library
University of Pittsburgh
Pittsburgh, PA 15260
cehova@vms.cis.pitt.edu

Karen Hovde
Founders Library
Northern Illinois University
DeKalb, IL 60115

Sue Huff
Lewis Library
Loyola University
Chicago, IL 60601
shuff@luc.edu

Jon Hufford
Library
Texas Tech University
Lubbock, TX 79409
lijrh@ttacs.ttu.edu

Janet Hurlbert
Snowden Library
Lycoming College
Williamsport, NY 17701
hurlbjan@lycoming.edu

Sandra Hussey
Lauinger Library
Georgetown University
Washington, DC 20057
shussey@guvax.georgetown.edu

Patricia Iannuzzi
Florida International
University Library
Miami, FL 33199
iannuzzi@servms.fiu.edu

Lydia Jackson
Lovejoy Library
Southern Illinois
University-Edwardsville
Edwardsville, IL 62026
ljackso@siue.edu

Rebecca Jackson
Gelman Library
George Washington University
Washington, DC 20052
rjackson@gwuvm.gwu.edu

Jennean Kabat-Cyrul
Library
Delta College
University Center, MI 48710
jennean_mackay@delta.edu

Veronica Kenausis
Franklin & Marshall College
    Library
Lancaster, PA 17604-3003
v_kenausis@fandm.edu

Kim Kenward
Woodhouse Library
Aquinas College
Grand Rapids, MI 49506
woodlib@mlc.lib.mi.us

Marcia King-Blanford
Carlson Library
University of Toledo
Toledo, OH 43606
mkingbl@utnet.utoledo.edu

Tom Kirk
Lilly Library
Earlham College
Richmond, IN 47374
kirkto@earlham.edu

Elizabeth Kocevar-Weidinger
Frostburg State University
    Library
Frostburg, MD 21532
d2lbkoc@fra00.fsu.umd.edu

Cynthia Krolikowski
Purdy/Kresge Library
Wayne State University
Detroit, MI 48202
ckrolik@cms.cc.wayne.edu

Amy Krug
Truxal Library
Anne Arundel Community
    College
Arnold, MD 21012
zamk@aacci.aacc.cc.md.us

Michael Kruzich
Mardigian Library
University of Michigan-Dearborn
Dearborn, MI 48128-1491

Bess Lambert
McWherter Library
University of Memphis
Memphis, TN 38152
mrlambert@cc.memphis.edu

Deborah Lauseng
Public Health Library
University of Michigan
Ann Arbor, MI 48109
cqlbcl@umich.edu

Corinne Laverty
Library
Queen's University
Kingston, Ontario
Canada K7L 5C4
lavertyc@qucdn.queensu.ca

Sally Lawler
Purdy/Kresge Library
Wayne State University
Detroit, MI 48202
slawler@cms.cc.wayne.edu

Judy Lee
Rivera Library
UC Riverside
Riverside, CA 92517
leejudy@ucracl.ucr.edu

Wade Lee
Carlson Library
University of Toledo
Toledo, OH 43606-3399
wlee@utnet.utoledo.edu

Katy Lenn
Knight Library
University of Oregon
Eugene, OR 97403
klenn@orgon.uoregon.edu

Susan Levendosky
Bracken Library
Ball State University
Muncie, IN 47306
Chapel Hill, NC 27599
00levendos@bsuvc.bsu.edu

Richard Lezenby
Paley Library
Temple University
Philadelphia, PA 19122
rlfile@astro.ocis.temple.edu

Carla List
Feinberg Library
SUNY-Plattsburgh
Plattsburgh, NY 12901
listck@splava.cc.plattsburgh.edu

Julie Livingston
University Libraries
Ball State University
Muncie, IN 47306
01jalivingst@bsuvc.bsu.edu

Abigail Loomis
Memorial Library
University of Wisconsin
Madison, WI 53706
loomis@macc.wisc.edu

Pamela S. Luebke
Woodhouse Library
Aquinas College
Grand Rapids, MI 49506
woodlib@mlc.lib.mi.us

Karen McBride
William Rainey Harper College
    Library
Palatine, IL 60067
ksteltma@harper.cc.il.us

Margaret McCasland
University Library
Texas Tech University
Lubbock, TX 40002
limjm@ttacs.ttu.edu

Jo McClamroch
McDonald Library
Xavier University
Cincinnati, OH 45207-5011
mcclamro@xavier.xu.edu

Betty McCool
Flanagan Campus LRC
Community College of
    Rhode Island
Lincoln, RI 02865
bmccool@ccri.cc.ri.us

Gail MacKay
Indiana University-Kokomo
    Library
Kokomo, IN 46904-9003
gmackay@iukfs1.iuk.indiana.edu

Sharyl McMillian-Nelson
Nicholls Library
University of Kansas-
    Kansas City
Kansas City, MO 64110
mcmillis@smtpgate.umkc.edu

Gayle Poirier
Middleton Library
Louisiana State University
Baton Rouge, LA 70803
notgap@lsuvm.sncc.lsu.edu

Phillip Powell
Library
College of Charleston
Charleston, SC 29424
powellp@cofc.edu

Carl Pracht
Library
Southeast Missouri State
	University
Cape Girardeau, MO 63701
c862lib@semovm.semo.edu

Cris Prucha
Library
University of Wisconsin-
	Platteville
Platteville, WI 53818
prucha@mail.uwlex.edu

Jing Qui
Wise Library
West Virginia University
Morgantown, WV 26505
jqiu@wvnvm.wvnet.edu

Wency Rains
Cullom-Davis Library
Bradley University
Peoria, IL 61625
wrains@bradley.bradley.edu

Marea E. Rankin
Lupton Library
University of Tennessee
Chattanooga, TN 37403
mrankin@utcvm.utc.edu

Dan Ream
Library
Virginia Commonwealth
	University
Richmond, VA 23284-2033
dream@gems.vcu.edu

Carol Reed
Shapiro Science Library
University of Michigan
Ann Arbor, MI 48109
creed@umich.edu

Joan Reitz
Ruth Haas Library
Western Connecticut State
	University
Danbury, CT 06810
reitzj@wcsub.ctstateu.edu

Elizabeth Retzel
Eastern Michigan University
	Library
Ypsilanti, MI 48197
lib_retzel@online.emich.edu

Gretchen Revie
Burling Library
Grinnell College
Grinnell, IA 50112
revie@ac.grin.edu

Robin Riat
Libraries
University of Evansville
Evansville, IN 47722
rr3@evansville.edu

Lorraine Ricigliano
Collins Library
University of Puget Sound
Tacoma, WA 98416
ricigliano@ups.edu

Michael Romary
Kuhn Library
University of Maryland
	at Baltimore
Baltimore, MD 21214
romary@umbc8.umbc.edu

Carol Rusinek
Library
Indiana University-NW
Gary, IN 46408
crusin@ucsun1.iun.indiana.edu

Laurie Sabol
Tisch Library
Tufts University
Medford, MA 02155
lsabol@library.tufts.edu

Sue Samson
Mansfield Library
University of Montana
Missoula, MT 59812
ss@selevay.umt.edu

Linda St. Clair
Zimmerman Library
University of New Mexico
Albuquerque, NM 87131
lstclair@unm.edu

Megan Schenk
Rentschler Library
Miami University-
	Hamilton
Hamilton, OH 45011
schenkm@muohio.edu

Randall Schroeder
Englebrecht Library
Wartburg College
Waverly, IA 50677
schroeder@wartburg.edu

Susan D. Scott
Newark Campus Library
Ohio State University
Newark, OH 43055
sscitt@magnus.acs.ohio-state.edu

Zary M. Shafa
Library
University of Dallas
Irving, TX 75062
zshafa@acad.udallas.edu

Julia Shaw-Kokot
Health Sciences Library
UNC-Chapel Hill
Chapel Hill, NC 27599
jsk@med.unc.edu

Rena Sheffer
Medical Science Library
University of Arkansas
Little Rock, AR 72205
sheffer@liblan.uams.edu

Linda Shirato
Eastern Michigan University
    Library
Ypsilanti, MI 48197
lib_shirato@online.emich.edu

Hope Siasoco
Library
Delta College
University Center, MI 48710
hope_siasoco@delta.edu

Dena Siegel
Bracken Library
Ball State University
Muncie, IN 47306
00desiegel@bsuvc.bsu.edu

Arlie Sims
Library
DePaul University
Chicago, IL 60614-3210
asims@wppost.depaul.edu

Carol Smith
Library
Kalamazoo College
Kalamazoo, MI 49006
csmith@kzoo.edu

Tim Smith
Ohio University Library
Athens, OH 45701
tsmith1@ohiou.edu

Keith Stanger
Eastern Michigan University
    Library
Ypsilanti, MI 48197
lib_stanger@online.emich.edu

Beverly Stearns
Jerome Library
Bowling Green State
    University
Bowling Green, OH 43403
bstearn@bgnet.bgsu.edu

Clara Stewart
Kellogg Community College
LRC
Battle Creek, MI 49017
stewartc@mlc.lib.mi.us

Terry Taylor
Richardson Library
DePaul University
Chicago, IL 60614
ttaylor@wppost.depaul.edu

Heidi Armstrong Temple
University of Minnesota-
    Duluth Library
Duluth, MN 55812
htemple@d.umn.edu

Debbie Tenofsky
Cudahy Library
Loyola University
Chicago, IL 60626
dtenofs@luccpua.it.luc.edu

Charles Terbille
Carlson Library
University of Toledo
Toledo, OH 43606-3390
cterbil@uoft02.utoledo.edu

Miriam H. Thompson
Grand Rapids Community
    College Library
Grand Rapids, MI 49503
mthompso@post.grcc.ccmi.us

Sandra L. Tidwell
Harold B. Lee Library
Brigham Young University
Provo, UT 84602
sandy_tidwell@byu.edu

Ellen Tillett
Sandor Teszler Library
Wofford College
Spartanburg, SC 29303
tillettel@wofford.edu

Lily Torrez
University of Texas-Pan
    American Library
Edinburg, TX 78539-2999
LILY@Panam.edu

Wolfhard Touchard
James White Library
Andrews University
Berrien Springs, MI
    49104-6263
touchard@andrews.edu

Anne Tracy
Jerome Library
Bowling Green State
    University
Bowling Green, OH 43403
atracy@bgnet.bgsu.edu

Melissa D. Trevvett
DePaul University Library
Chicago, IL 60614
mtrevvet@wppost.depaul.edu

Winnie Tseng
Sinclair Community College
LRC
Dayton, OH 45402
wtseng@sinclair.edu

Sarah J. Vasse
LRC-Reference Department
Orange County CC
Middletown, NY 10940
vasses@aol.com

John Walker
Sinclair Community College
LRC
Dayton, OH 45402
jwalker@sinclair.edu

James E. Ward
Library
David Lipscomb University
Nashville, TN 37204
JWARD@dlu.edu

Ora M. Wagoner
Mesa Community
    College Library
Mesa, AZ 85202
wagoner@mc.maricopa.edu

Barbara E. Weeg
Rod Library
University of Northern Iowa
Cedar Falls, IA 50613
barbara.weeg@uni.edu

Emily Werrell
Steely Library
Northern Kentucky University
Highland Heights, KY 41099
werrell@nku.edu